MAKING STORIES, MAKING SELVES

HELEN HOOVEN SANTMYER PRIZE WINNERS

This Strange Society of Women
*Reading the Letters and Lives of
the Woman's Commonwealth*
Sally L. Kitch

Salvador's Children
A Song for Survival
Lea Marenn

Making Stories, Making Selves

FEMINIST REFLECTIONS ON THE HOLOCAUST

R. Ruth Linden

A Helen Hooven Santmyer Prize Winner

Ohio State University Press
COLUMBUS

The following are gratefully acknowledged for permission to use extended quotations from copyrighted works: From "Walter Benjamin, 1892–1940," in *Men in Dark Times* by Hannah Arendt. Copyright 1968 by Hannah Arendt. Reprinted by permission of Harcourt Brace Jovanovich, Inc. From *Illuminations* by Walter Benjamin. Copyright 1955 by Suhrkamp Verlag, Frankfurt a.M. English translation copyright 1968 by Harcourt Brace Jovanovich, Inc. Reprinted by permission of Harcourt Brace Jovanovich, Inc. From "Surviving Stories: Reflections on *Number Our Days*" by Barbara Myerhoff, in *Between Two Worlds: Ethnographic Essays on American Jewry*, ed. Jack Kugelmass. Copyright 1988 by Cornell University. Reprinted by permission of Cornell University Press. From *Hitler's Death Camps: The Sanity of Madness* by Konnilyn Feig. Copyright 1979 by Konnilyn G. Feig. Reprinted by permission of Holmes & Meier Publishers, Inc. From *The Tulips Are Red* by Leesha Rose. Copyright 1978 by Leesha Rose. Reprinted by permission of Leesha Rose. From life-history interview with Leesha Rose by Lani Silver (1981). Archives of the Holocaust Oral History Project. Reprinted by permission of Lani Silver and Leesha Rose. From *Woman and Nature* by Susan Griffin. Copyright 1978 by Susan Griffin. Reprinted by permission of HarperCollins Publishers.

Library of Congress Cataloging-in-Publication Data

Linden, R. Ruth, 1956–
    Making stories, making selves: feminist reflections on the Holocaust /
R. Ruth Linden.
        p.   cm. — (The Helen Hooven Santmyer prize in women's studies)
    Includes bibliographical references and index.
    ISBN 0–8142–0583–6 (alk. paper). — ISBN 0–8142–0584–4 (pbk. : alk.
paper)
        1. Holocaust survivors — United States — Interviews.   2. Women, Jewish —
United States — Interviews.   3. Jews — United States — Interviews.
4. Jews — United States — Cultural assimilation.   5. Holocaust, Jewish
(1939–1945) — Influence.   6. United States — Ethnic relations.   I. Title.
II. Series.
E184.J5L668   1992
940.53′18′0922 — dc20
[B]   92–20410
                                                                                  CIP

Text and jacket design by Donna Hartwick.
Type set in Bembo by Focus Graphics, St. Louis, MO.
Printed by Cushing-Malloy, Inc., Ann Arbor, MI.

9 8 7 6 5 4 3 2 1

To the memory of my father,
Edwin Robert Linden (1919–1969),
and to my mother,
Berna Berry Linden.

To Sharon Traweek, Maury Stein,
and Irv Zola,
beloved teachers and friends.

CONTENTS

PREFACE
"But Is It Sociology?"

I want to know nothing—less than I know.
Gail Mazur, "Next Door," in *Pose of Happiness*

Galut. Remnants. Fragments. Ruptures. The condition of Jews since the destruction of the First Temple, of European Jewry after the Holocaust. The postmodern condition. This morning, my friend, a poet, and I are talking about our struggle as writers. Our talk turns to my work, this book, and I tell my friend how I am plagued by a harsh, internal voice incessantly asking, "But is it sociology?"

I tell my friend how, in my personal life, among friends, I recognize that I have sometimes fudged autobiographical truths, settling for telling "less than I knew." Many times, I have taken shortcuts to short-circuit my own pain. The pain of self-recognition. But concerning my work, I explain to my friend, my standards are uncompromising. There is less room for ambiguity, for those well-concealed chambers where silences sometimes take refuge.

Later on, I recognize a certain hollowness—naiveté, in these words, for truth is rarely singular or absolute. There are only truths: relative, changing, emergent—as new light is shed on familiar circumstances. And silences, too, are a matter of degree.

I tell my friend I can ask no less of myself than I ask of my ethnographic subjects. I must be prepared to be at least as vulnerable and honest as I ask them to be. I must be willing to stand beside them, not to speak *for* them but to speak for myself and *with* them. This, I believe, is the first principle of a postpositivist research ethic.

Memories are tricky. They come and go according to their own rhythms and reasons, like waves on the ocean, revealing themselves in mysterious, unpatterned ways. Chronological storytelling—first this happened and next that happened, involves a high level of interpretation, for memories are never "pure"—raw or uninterpreted. Even as the vicissitudes of memories may elude us, we do well to respect them.

As I exercise my own memories, I find it difficult to establish whether specific thoughts and feelings I want to record originate in past or present moments. Did I really think or feel *that* way at Pesach in 1983 or at my sister's wedding during the same year? Or have I improvised an account in order to tell a good story? Did *this* memory occur alongside *that* remembered event? Or is it an artifact of the process of reconstruction?

Is the "problem" of memory's veracity really a problem? For as we fashion the stories of our lives, memories naturally blur with subsequent interpretations of remembered events. Fragments and ruptures braid themselves into a seamless, continuous whole. Memories, after all, are arranged synchronically. Buddhism teaches us that time is an illusion. In sociology, we call such illusions "social constructions."

Recall has its limits. "I don't know—or remember" is a valid and meaningful response, one that is often more honest than an unequivocal "yes." Certitude can be suspect. As Monique Wittig wrote in *Les Guérillères*: "You say you have lost all recollection of it, remember. . . . You say there are no words to describe this time, you say it does not exist. But remember. Make an effort to remember. Or failing that, invent."[1] Inventing, in any case, is the sine qua non of Homo narrans, humankind as storyteller.[2]

ACKNOWLEDGMENTS

I would like to express my deep gratitude to more than two hundred survivors and their families who allowed my colleagues and me to interview them at the 1983 American Gathering of Jewish Holocaust Survivors. I am especially indebted to Regine Winder Barshak, Susan E. Cernyak-Spatz, Helen Chalef, Gloria Hollander Lyon, and Leesha Rose, who read my work-in-progress, challenged my interpretive errors, and corrected my factual ones. These women—great storytellers—are my teachers in the deepest sense of the word. They have given me parts of myself I hadn't recognized before and helped me find my place in the stream of Jewish culture and history.

Lani Silver made it possible for me to begin working with Holocaust survivors. Together, we founded the Holocaust Media Project in San Francisco (renamed the Holocaust Oral History Project in 1984) and sowed the seeds for this book.

Many friends and colleagues, including my teachers and students, helped me bring this book to life. I have been vitalized by our conversations over the years and by their support and advice at every stage of my writing. Without them this book would not exist in its present form.

From the very beginning, Mary Canedy Burt believed in the importance of this project. For more than a decade her generous friendship has been a source of inspiration and sustenance. After I moved to Cambridge, Vera Ruth Obermeyer helped keep me connected to my home in San Francisco. Her unswerving optimism and faith have given me courage in my darkest moments. In 1986 Vera arranged for me to receive a grant from Learning Associates that allowed me to begin analyzing survivors' life stories. The Henry A. Murray Research Center at Radcliffe College administered the grant and welcomed me as a visiting scholar during 1986–87.

Acknowledgments

An earlier version of this book was written as my doctoral dissertation at Brandeis University. Three remarkable advisors with whom I worked closely guided my writing with wisdom and love. Sharon Traweek of the MIT Program in Anthropology and Archeology *and* the Program in Science, Technology, and Society (now in the anthropology department at Rice University) has been my mentor and friend. She taught me that knowledge is a conversation and that an ethnographer's own story belongs in the text. In the sociology department at Brandeis, Maurice R. Stein taught me that the life of the mind and the heart are one. His example first inspired my understanding that sociologists must overcome Western, academic conventions and confront global issues of survival, genocide, and omnicide. Irving K. Zola, also at Brandeis, taught me to listen to my own voice—voices, actually—and to dare to write a different kind of sociology. I was also fortunate to have an opportunity to study with Dorinne K. Kondo at Harvard (now at Pomona College), whose 1987 seminar on ethnographic writing catalyzed my interest in rhetorics of the human sciences.

Other friends in the sociology department at Brandeis read successive drafts of different chapters and eased the solitude of writing. For their thoughtful criticism, and for the warmth of their friendships during New England's harsh winters, I want to thank Iris Alpert, Ulrike Dettling, Gordon A. Fellman, Janet R. Kahn, Robbie Pfeufer Kahn, Tema Nason, the late Marianne A. (Tracy) Paget, Shulamit Reinharz, Lynn Schlesinger, and Morris S. Schwartz. I am especially grateful to Elena Stone, who has encouraged my writing in countless ways. It is also my pleasure to thank Stephen M. Scheinthal, Heather S. Zakson, and Ellen Ross, Brandeis students with whom I was privileged to work closely during the years 1985–87.

In 1990–91 I taught at Wesleyan University in Connecticut. Early on I had the good fortune to meet Ruth P. Ginzberg, who became a close friend and colleague. Our conversations about the Holocaust and Jewish identities reverberate throughout this book. The congeniality of the Science in Society Program, chaired by Joseph T. Rouse, helped to ease the pressures of my short-term appointment. I appreciate the hospitality and support the program offered me while I revised the manuscript.

At Wesleyan, Susan M. Ferris, Connie Mary Colangelo, and Jacqueline A. Didier provided expert administrative help. My workload was considerably lighter because of their efficiency and deftness. Elise Springer worked with me as my research assistant. Her cheerfulness, skillful editing, and patience with dozens of manuscript details are rare attributes in any scholar. I also want to thank several exceptionally talented students who inspired my work: Jennifer S. Birk and Jennifer P. Blaine, at Wesleyan; and Maria C. Fox, whom I met the previous year at William Smith College.

My mother, Berna Berry Linden, and my sister, Tracey Linden Adams, are unwitting participants in my research, for in telling my own life stories, I have told fragments of theirs as well. As in all families, our memories and interpretations of events may vary, yet I hope they recognize their immense part in my life and writing. My cousins Lola Curiel, Martin Gersh, and Bruce Livingston took the time to answer an endless barrage of questions about my father and my paternal grandparents and great-grandparents. Their family stories helped to fill in gaps that have haunted me for many years. Dorothy Brinckerhoff, Jill S. Fields, Kirsten Greer, Lauren Suhd, and Lynne Toerne kindly reviewed my account of the Thorn Collective and permitted me to include it in this book.

Celia Brickman, Marjorie L. DeVault, Carolyn Ellis, Rebecca D. King, Holly Korda, Linda Kuzmak, Rabbi Herbert Morris, Tillie Olsen, Laurel Richardson, Paula Salvio, Benson Snyder, Patricia J. Stamm, and Susan Leigh Star read the full manuscript at an early stage. Their encouraging words and incisive criticism have enriched my work immeasurably.

Celia Brickman prepared the glossary with precision and care. Tom Rawson, WordPerfect wizard, rescued me during many software snafus. When I returned to Brandeis in 1991, I received a generous faculty research grant that enabled me to complete work on the manuscript. Eberhard Frey kindly translated from German the Brecht quote that appears as the epigraph to Part 1. Charlotte Dihoff, my editor at the Ohio State University Press, guided me through the publishing maze with an uncommon, steady patience. I am indebted to her for her commitment to this book, and also to her assistant editor, Lynne M. Bonenberger. Their meticulous attention to an unending array of details has brought this work into your hands. Thanks also go to Barbara Folsom for her deft copyediting. Jaffa has been my devoted companion, lounging beside the keyboard or on my lap as I worked late into the night.

Doubtless, the book contains some misconceptions and factual errors, and for these I am wholly responsible.

Author's Notes

All non-English words are defined at their first appearance in the text. For simple reference, they are also listed in the glossary.

Throughout the book, I interchange Sephardi (Spanish and Portuguese) and Ashkenazi (Eastern European) pronunciations of Hebrew words. This practice reflects my own polyglot use of language—itself shaped by the process of Jewish assimilation.

Ethnographers conventionally make claims about actual persons, whether living or deceased. For this reason I have chosen not to alter or in any way mask the identities of persons mentioned or quoted in this book. Wherever possible, I sought and received permission to quote from (or reconstruct) all conversations with and references to living persons, including my informants, colleagues, friends, and family members. All unpublished materials, including manuscripts, letters, journals, and speeches, are quoted by permission of their authors.

In the spirit of open dialogue, I have encouraged my key informants to respond to my writing. They have often contested my interpretations, including the "facts" as I presented them. I have incorporated their comments and our disagreements into the text and/or revised my original statements as I have deemed appropriate.

MAKING STORIES, MAKING SELVES

Because post-modern ethnography privileges "discourse" over "text," it foregrounds dialogue as opposed to monologue, and emphasizes the cooperative and collaborative nature of the ethnographic situation in contrast to the ideology of the transcendental observer. In fact, it rejects the ideology of "observer-observed," there being nothing observed and no one who is observer. There is instead the mutual, dialogical production of a discourse, of a story of sorts.
Stephen A. Tyler, in *Writing Culture*

Every version of an "other," wherever found, is also the construction of a "self," and the making of ethnographic texts . . . has always involved a process of "self-fashioning."
James Clifford, in *Writing Culture*

If you want to explain some phenomenon . . . take a look at your own experience of what it is to have—or be—a mind.
Gregory Bateson and Mary Catherine Bateson,
Angels Fear

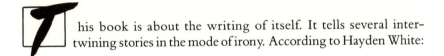

his book is about the writing of itself. It tells several intertwining stories in the mode of irony. According to Hayden White:

> providing the "meaning" of a story by identifying the *kind of story* that has been told is called explanation by emplotment. If, in the course of narrating his story, the historian provides it with the plot structure of a tragedy, he has "explained" it in one way; if he has structured it as a comedy, he has "explained" it in another way. Emplotment is the way by which a sequence of events fashioned into a story is gradually revealed to be a story of a particular kind.

Following literary theorist Northrop Frye, White explains that "stories cast in the Ironic mode . . . gain their effects precisely by frustrating normal expectations about the kinds of resolutions provided by stories cast in other modes (Romance, Comedy, or Tragedy, as the case may be)."[1] One story highlights my efforts to represent fieldwork I conducted with Jewish Holocaust survivors during 1983 and 1984. In this sense, the book is about Holocaust survivors.

But this statement is partial and might even be misleading, for the book also tells a story about my confrontations with meanings of the Holocaust in my own life and for my generation. I was born, after World War II had ended and the liberation of the concentration camps, into an assimilated Jewish-American family apparently unscathed by the destruction. Even so, the Holocaust has profoundly marked my life, in ways that have become clear to me in and through my research.

Writing this book has compelled me, repeatedly, to turn inward. Over and over again, I have examined the impress of the Holocaust on my Jewish consciousness. My self-reflections became an integral component of my research, inseparable from the book "about" Holocaust survivors I had initially planned to write. This process transformed my Jewish identity, and the book tells that story as well.

I had been working with Holocaust survivors and their narratives for several years when my work took an unexpected turn toward the issues James Clifford and George Marcus refer to as "the poetics and politics of ethnography."[2] What did it mean to regard ethnography as a literary genre? I wondered. I began exploring how authors position themselves in their texts, and how power and domination are embedded in interpretations of cultural "others." No longer could I take for granted what Marcus calls "deskwork"[3] in contrast with fieldwork. Nor could I ignore how I would (or would not, as convention has it) inscribe myself in my own writing. How I would represent survivors' life stories became the central problem of my study.

Gradually, in small, disjointed increments, I recognized that my research was rooted in a tangled web of taken-for-granted assumptions and practices. I discovered that my primary rhetorical strategy for writing about Holocaust survivors—"allowing" respondents to speak about their lives in their own words—was problematic indeed. This seemingly innocent narrative practice served to obscure both subjectivity and agency: whose voice, point of view, and interpretation I was representing at any given moment—mine or theirs. It blurred the fact that meanings, by their very nature, are indeterminate, situated, and emergent—negotiated between partners in discourse.

Working with Holocaust survivors and their texts has shattered most of my beliefs about how knowledge is constructed and represented in the human sciences. Thus, a third story emplotted in this book explores my shifting assumptions about how lives and experiences are "textualized," as Paul Ricoeur would say.[4] These issues are the subject of intense debate in the social sciences and in cultural studies.

Let me begin by calling your attention to the book's narrative structure. Ethnography is a literary genre, like the epic novel, sonnet, political speech, and biography, to name several examples. Any work claiming membership within a particular genre necessarily evokes a set of expectations in readers regarding its structure, style, and resolution, as well as its content.

Embedded in traditional ethnography is a host of assumptions about how data and "reality" and data and texts are linked, about how data is (or ought to be) produced in relationships between researchers and respondents, and about how to construct correct explanations or interpretations. These can be summarized as follows:

1. Field data (audiotaped interviews, fieldnotes, questionnaire responses, and so on) are "raw," that is, uninterpreted versions of "reality," until they are "worked over" during coding, analysis, and finally, writing.
2. "Writing up the data"—representing one's findings (the so-called "facts")—is a mechanical, unmediated process. Ethnographic texts are transparent mirrors that provide precise (or precise *enough*) reflections of field settings.
3. Rigorously applied research methods, including systematic recording of fieldnotes, ensure that an ethnographer will maintain the detached, disinterested role of participant-observer. Methods are designed to protect boundaries between the self and "others." In order to produce valid and reliable findings, firm boundaries are considered desirable, even necessary.
4. The goal of ethnography is to construct definitive interpretations and explanations of cultural "others," and other cultures or social worlds. Ambiguities, uncertainties, and contradictions have no place in social science discourses.

Since the Second World War, numerous sociologists have criticized methodological positivism within the discipline.[5] To some extent, during the past two decades, relativist approaches, such as hermeneutics and phenomenology, have become integrated into the mainstream of sociology. Yet the radical challenges posed by works in these interpretive traditions have yet to be realized. I believe this is because narrative concerns—distinct from issues of methodology—have rarely been recognized as such.

Clifford Geertz has suggested that, in anthropology, demands of writing have generally been confused with matters of data collection. This has meant that problems inherent in ethnographic writing have been obscured.[6] Within sociology as well, it seems that methodological and discursive concerns have been blurred.

The narrative structure of this book deliberately breaks with ethnography's positivist literary practices. Following recent trends in some quarters of anthropology and sociology, my writing is experimental.[7] As such, it violates many time-honored conventions in an effort to expose them by their absence. This is an ethnomethodological breaching experiment of sorts, intended to reveal the means of textual production, and to remind readers that data lend themselves to multiple representations and interpretations.

In fact, experimental ethnography has become a canon (countercanon) in its own right, with its own high priests and dogmas. However, virtually all of its principle players are white, male anthropologists. Yet the new ethnography and some feminist critical approaches pose similar challenges to positivism by unmasking modern, Western structures of knowledge and discourse, and hegemonic modes of representation. Both seek to reveal the political foundations of knowledge, to shatter lines of authority in texts, and to create libertory narrative forms.[8]

As a reader of this study, and as a producer and consumer of ethnography, you play a vital part in this experiment. It is your encounters with this and other texts, your expectations—satisfied, frustrated, or refigured—which help to define acceptable and appropriate representations, and which ultimately shape ethnography as a literary genre.

Making Stories, Making Selves unfolds around three core chapters, written during the early years of my research: "Bearing Witness: Reflections on Interviewing Jewish Holocaust Survivors" (Chapter 6); "The Phenomenology of Surviving: Toward a Sociology of the Holocaust" (Chapter 8); and "'In the Name of the House of Orange': A Life History of Leesha Rose during the Holocaust" (Chapter 10). Each chapter represents a different phase in my study of Holocaust survivors.

I wrote "Bearing Witness" with Lani Silver, with whom I founded the Holocaust Media Project in 1983. With the assistance of a team of interviewers, we had collected two hundred life histories at the American Gathering of Jewish Holocaust Survivors. "Bearing Witness" was my first attempt to write about the interviews.

When I returned home from the Gathering, I experienced a prolonged state akin to culture shock. In my mind and heart, it seemed I was still "in the field." Eventually, I came to understand why I felt this way: indeed, I had never left the field because *I* was the field. This was a liminal time when my social boundaries—the membrane between me and the rest of the world—were fragile and fluid. My mind—my whole being, actually—was saturated by the Holocaust stories I had listened to and was struggling to absorb.

Nearly two years later, I wrote "The Phenomenology of Surviving." In this piece, I explored strategies that Jewish women used to survive in the death camps. It had become clear to me that survival in the camps was fundamentally a social process. I wanted to understand what circumstances enabled survival: its vicissitudes, precariousness, and uncertainties; the interplay of luck, determination, and careful calculation; the interdependence of human beings upon one another for life itself.

In the following year, I wrote "'In the Name of the House of Orange.'" This study fused my interests in narratives, women's lives, and Jewish resistance during the Holocaust. Working closely with personal documents—a life history transcript and published memoir—gave me an opportunity to focus on understanding the life of just one other person, an extremely rich kind of ethnography.

In order to expose the constraints on my early writing about Holocaust survivors, I wrote companion chapters reflecting on each of the three core chapters. These metachapters examine the strategies I used to inscribe my authoritative, if usually silent, presence. They problematize concerns I prematurely foreclosed or altogether ignored the first time around: how claims on truth and reality, and points of view, voices, and interpretations are established and maintained. "Reflections on 'Bearing Witness'" (Chapter 7), "Reflections on 'The Phenomenology of Surviving'" (Chapter 9), and "Reflections on 'In the Name of the House of Orange'" (Chapter 11) explore a wide range of textual, ethical, and epistemological issues.

To the greatest possible extent, I have inscribed my evolving research process in this book, rather than simply presenting you with discrete "findings" or artifacts of the study. As a matter of course, ethnographers construct idealized and oversimplified representations of their research process, deleting problems in which they lost interest, hunches that failed to pan out, errors, and so on.[9] It is generally assumed that misunderstandings and discarded interpretations do not matter, provided that they are discovered and corrected before the manuscript goes to press. I disagree, for it seems to me that outtakes can be as interesting and revealing as the final cut of the research.

Making Stories, Making Selves is deliberately structured to represent my research as emergent, subject over time to reformulations and reinterpretations. My aim is to provide a reasonably complete picture of how I have worked with my data thus far. This is a move against the fragmenting conventions of ethnography and textual positivism.

So we begin at the beginning — rather, *a* beginning. I ask that you read these chapters in the light of what follows them. In Paul Rabinow's words (after Paul Ricoeur), this book "is meant to be a whole, in which the meaning of each chapter depends on what comes after it."[10]

Both sacred and secular sources have inspired my experimentation with a montage-like form for *Making Stories, Making Selves*. The first source is the *Talmud*, the body of traditional Jewish laws and commentaries, which commands, "Turn it and turn it again, for everything is in it" (Avot 5:22). The second source is Van Maanen's primer on writing ethnography, *Tales of the Field*, which uses a text/commentary approach. I share Van Maanen's appraisal of this narrative practice:

> My excuse for using my own writing for lengthy genre illustrations is not because I am unduly impressed (or distressed) with its literary quality, but because I think that writing ethnography is an isolated and highly personal business and that those who discuss it in print are certain to discover that their best examples must be their own. Writers are the privileged readers of their own texts and are, within limits, the only ones who can speak with some advantage and special authority on their own intentions and textual assumptions.[11]

Walter Benjamin, a Frankfurt School cultural and literary critic, is my third source of inspiration.[12] His greatest literary aspiration was to fashion a work entirely out of quotations — a text akin to a mosaic, patchwork quilt, or surrealistic montage.[13] For Benjamin, claims made in a single, authoritative voice falsified history. Modern narratives told from a seamless point of view betrayed phenomena as they appeared in reality. The power of quotations, he wrote, is "not the strength to preserve but to cleanse, to tear out of context, to destroy."[14] I hope this book honors Benjamin's unfinished project and his vision of the storyteller.

What did fieldwork mean to you? How did it affect you? Or have you not yet experienced it?
Do you believe that you could write about your field experiences without telling us something
about your childhood, or your adolescence, or your precarious steps into your twenties?
Manda Cesara, *Reflections of a Woman Anthropologist*

Ethnographers' self-censorship ("editing" and "discretion") and disciplinary censorship ("the poetics and politics of ethnography")[15] have distorted our understanding of fieldwork. The rhetoric of positivism has prevented the development of discourses on two key concerns: the process of interpretation (whence we discover meaning in our data, thereby coming to understandings of "others," and other cultures and social worlds); and the impact of our research on our own lives (understandings of ourselves, the cultures and social worlds of which we are members, and the times in which we live).

All too often, the dialectical relationship between an ethnographer's life and the research she conducts remains implicit and unarticulated—or worse yet—actively suppressed. Thus, we also need to consider how our lives, prior to and apart from our research, continuously shape our epistemological positions, the problems we explore and do not explore, the sites in which we choose to work, and so on.

Sociologist Shulamit Reinharz and anthropologist Manda Cesara have probed the intimate connections between experience and interpretation. Reinharz's approach, "experiential analysis," fuses

> intensive self-consciousness, critical awareness of the method used, and exploration of the substantive issues. The findings of such an approach would be presented in three categories: description of and discoveries about the self, the method, and the substantive questions. My goals for any search for knowledge (research) become tripartite: insights into *the person, the problem*, and *the method*. Since each is a component of the study, each should be a component of the product. Each reflexive study is an occasion for personal growth, potential illumination of existent or new methods, and presentation of new conceptual frameworks, information, theories, or correlations.
>
> The final task of an ideal study would be to interrelate the three components: For example, how do the substantive findings relate to the investigator and the conditions of investigation? With this kind of information we could explore the relation between a particular account and a particular researcher, so that the relationship between the sociologist's and the subject's perceptions could be understood.[16]

Cesara is less schematic than Reinharz. For her, the impress of research on an ethnographer's life is what makes interpretations possible in the first place. She understands experience and interpretation as an inseparable unity. "According to Sartre," writes Cesara,

> culture (or the [cultural] environment) can act on the subject only to the exact extent that he comprehends it; that is, transforms it into a situation.

7

From the perspective of a fieldworker I might convert Sartre's . . . statement into the following: to the extent that Lenda culture acted on me, as subject, to that exact extent did I comprehend it and transform it into my situation. Had the Lenda left me unaffected, I could not have claimed that I understood them. In other words, all researchers who have studied a foreign culture and claim that they understand it, should have been affected by it somehow. Most researchers claim such an understanding, yet virtually all of them shy away from telling how it affected them. It is like claiming that a coin has only one side.[17]

My "tales of the field"[18] are a tight braid of Holocaust survivors' stories. Unwinding the knot, in the course of writing this book, has been tantamount to a process of intellectual and spiritual death and rebirth. Survivors' narratives permeate my life. Their stories have become my own. They have given me parts of myself and my culture.

Victor Turner observed that rebirth (necessarily preceded by death) is indeed a fitting metaphor for fieldwork. In the foreword to Barbara Myerhoff's classic study, *Number Our Days*, he recounted the words of M. N. Srinivas, an Indian anthropologist and a Brahmin—hence "twice-born."

Srinivas . . . urged anthropologists . . . to seek to be "thrice-born." The first birth is our natal origin in a particular culture. The second is our move from this familiar to a far place to do fieldwork there. In a way this could be described as a familiarization of the exotic, finding that when we understand the rules and vocabulary of another culture, what had seemed bizarre at first becomes in time part of the daily round.

The third birth occurs when we have become comfortable within the other culture—and found the clue to grasping many like it—and turn our gaze again toward our native land. We find that the familiar has become exoticized; we see it with new eyes. The commonplace has become the marvelous. What we took for granted now has power to stir our scientific imaginations. Few anthropologists have gone the full distance. Most of us feel that our professional duty is done when we have "processed" our fieldwork in other cultures in book or article form. Yet our discipline's long-term program has always included the movement of return, the purified look at ourselves. "Thrice-born" anthropologists are perhaps in the best position to become the "reflex-ivity" of a culture.[19]

No boundaries cordon off my research—"the field"—from the rest of my life. Momentary flashes of insight into questions I've pondered for years resound in the deep reaches of my being. The ineffability of the

Holocaust often leaves me mute, trembling with confusion and sadness. So much has already been said by survivors, scholars, and survivor-scholars who have devoted decades of their lives to studying the Nazi era. So much remains unspeakable, for now and forever.

I am heartened by Manda Cesara's assertion that "all researchers who have studied a foreign culture and claim that they understand it, should have been affected by it somehow."[20] Fieldwork confessions abound,[21] yet reflexive accounts of how other cultures and cultural "others" act on fieldworkers are rare. Such accounts would make a vital contribution to the human sciences, not only by fostering researchers' personal growth, as Shulamit Reinharz suggests, but, more importantly, because ethnographic understanding and reflexivity are of a piece—conjunct. Heeding my own call, the third strand of *Making Stories, Making Selves* considers how my work with Holocaust survivors has acted on me. Thus, my reflexive inquiry into the construction and reconstruction of memories, identities, and stories is interwoven with survivors' narratives. Anthropologists refer to such juxtapositions of self and "other" as cultural critique.[22]

Marcus and Fischer explain that cultural critiques are fashioned through defamiliarization. "Disruption of common sense, doing the unexpected, placing familiar subjects in unfamiliar, or even shocking, contexts are the aims of this strategy to make the reader conscious of difference" (p. 137). They describe two related modes of cultural critique in anthropology. The first technique, defamiliarization by epistemological critique, aims to expose Western ideologies and practices—ways of thinking about the world. Examples culled from the margins of Europe and America are used to demonstrate how Western institutions, values, and knowledge and classification systems are constructed. The second technique, defamiliarization by cross-cultural juxtaposition, is more empirical and dramatic, hence less subtle, than epistemological critique. Cross-cultural juxtaposition

> is a matching of ethnography abroad with ethnography at home. The idea is to use the substantive facts about another culture as a probe into the specific facts about a subject of criticism at home. This is the classic technique of defamiliarization pioneered by Margaret Mead, and it is the most frequently employed means of demonstrating cultural relativism. (P. 138)

Making Stories, Making Selves fuses these two modes of cultural critique, creating a third, hybrid approach. On the one hand, epistemological concerns lie at the heart of this study, and I explore them subtly and ironically, like a Zen archer aiming for the bull's-eye from an off-centered position.[23] On the other hand, my reflexive inquiry into the construction and reconstruction of my own identities and memories is a variation on the theme of "ethnography at home," as Marcus and Fischer would say.

In survivors' narratives, I discovered the problematic nature of identities and memories. These are the so-called substantive facts about another culture, and I use them to probe fragments of my own life story. In my autobiographical inquiry into the process of making stories and making selves, I am both subject and recorder, "self" and "other." Writing and revising was an authentic, phenomenological exercise, requiring continuous tacking back and forth between two dialectical moments—"self" (a storyteller) and "other" (a listener, interpreter, questioner).

My method adapts phenomenological and hermeneutical approaches that emphasize critical self-reflection and reflexivity.[24] Reflexivity refers to the process of a self becoming conscious of the nature of consciousness. Barbara Myerhoff and Deena Metzger described how reflexivity can emerge from reflection. I see myself, shape myself,

> acquire self-knowledge by beholding [my]self at a little distance, differentiated from the phenomenological experience of being. Nearly always, serving thus as subject and object, observer and audience, self and other at the same time, the self becomes conscious of the nature of this knowledge, and seeing itself being itself, develops consciousness about the nature of consciousness.[25]

Life histories are the joint production of two subjects, a listener-interpreter-questioner and a storyteller. (At other moments, of course, storytellers may listen to, interpret, and ask questions of their own stories.) I seek to be fully present in my research, to explore and expose myself at least as thoroughly as I explore and expose my respondents and their texts. Thus, I position myself alongside the survivors with whom I've worked. By writing myself into the text autobiographically, I aim to keep the self/other dialectic in constant motion—first, exploring survivors' memories; next, reflexively probing my own; then, returning to the "other"—turning the various inscriptions by a sort of intellectual perpetual motion into explications of one another.[26]

This strategy is designed to expose how ethnographers fashion (and manipulate) ourselves and others in our texts. I construct the text, and the text, in turn, constructs me. Indeed, in the course of writing this book, my own life stories have been profoundly transformed.

I want to mention the sequence of chapters in this book. The linearity of a text imposes its own causal order, and thus sequence shapes meaning. The order I have chosen reinforces my emphasis on the dialectic between self-fashioning and storytelling. This book could have been arranged in several different ways, each of which would have produced its own distinctive interpretations.

Part I includes five chapters. The first chapter draws on Walter Benjamin and Hannah Arendt's understandings of the significance of stories in the modern era. In contrast with stories, I juxtapose what Arendt referred to as "sheer happenings"—fragments of experiences that refuse narrative forms—which literally cannot be talked about. "Sheer happenings" are woven into Holocaust survivors' stories, as well as my own, as silences.

The next four chapters are a sequence of autobiographical sketches. Chapter 2 begins with the generations in my family that emigrated from Eastern Europe to America. From family memories and documents, I reconstruct the process of assimilation in my great-grandparents' and grandparents' lives. Chapter 3 explores Jewish assimilation in my natal family. Chapter 4 examines how I constructed a feminist identity during college in my first women's group. In the early 1980s, as the women's movement segmented, my feminist identity shattered. Against a backdrop of loss and fragmentation, Chapter 5, the last essay in this set, describes my gradual turn toward Jewish culture.

Part II consists of six chapters—three paired studies of Holocaust survivors. Chapter 6, coauthored with Lani Silver, describes our experiences conducting interviews at the American Gathering of Jewish Holocaust Survivors. Chapter 8 is about Jewish women surviving in the death camps. Chapter 10 is a life history of Leesha Rose, a nurse who joined the Dutch resistance. Chapters 7, 9, and 11 each reflects on the immediately preceding chapter.

In the Epilogue, I use the strategy of cultural critique to defamiliarize the Holocaust. To close the book, I reframe the Holocaust as a crisis of ecology whose consequences challenge binary oppositions at the heart of Western cultures.

I

TO BE AN ASSIMILATED JEW IN THE LATE TWENTIETH CENTURY

In the following I shall note where I myself have learned, at least as far as I remember. And I shall write it down, not only so that others might gain from it, but also so that I myself can get an overview. One learns yet once again when one finds out what one has learned.
Bertolt Brecht, "Wo ich gelernt habe"
(Where I have learned), in *Gesammelte Werke*

1

REFLECTIONS ON
"SHEER HAPPENINGS"

alter Benjamin's greatest literary aspiration was to fashion a work entirely out of quotations, which he called the *Passagenarbeit* or *Passagen-Werk*, the Arcades "project."[1] According to historian Martin Jay, this project "expressed a quasi-religious desire to become the transparent mouthpiece of a higher reality."[2] Benjamin envisaged a mosaic, akin to a surrealistic montage, that would stand completely on its own, without accompanying text.[3] Hannah Arendt tells us that, for him, the force of surrealism was its "attempt to capture the portrait of history in the most insignificant representations of reality, its scraps, as it were." The power of quotations, he wrote, is "not the strength to preserve but to cleanse, to tear out of context, to destroy."[4]

Benjamin's work can be viewed as an extended meditation on plain objects. Arendt notes that he was not concerned with "theories or 'ideas' which did not immediately assume the most precise outward shape imaginable." Instead, what he cared about were "directly, actually demonstrable concrete facts, . . . single events and occurrences whose 'significance' is manifest."[5] Jay tells us that Benjamin dismissed philosophical jargon as burdensome, "the chatter of pimps." At the center of his work is what Arendt refers to as "the wonder of appearance." "What seems paradoxical about everything that is justly called beautiful is the fact that it appears," wrote Benjamin.[6]

Benjamin found wonder in life being lived (especially in the streets and cafés of the Paris he loved), and he took great delight in collecting. He wrote of the "inner need to own a library,"[7] and his description of being reunited with his cherished book collection is affectionate, even tender.

> What I am really concerned with is giving you some insight into the relationship of a book collector to his possessions, into collecting rather than a collection. If I do this by elaborating on the various ways of acquiring books, this is something entirely arbitrary. This or any other

procedure is merely a dam against the spring tide of memories which surges toward any collector as he contemplates his possessions. Every passion borders on the chaotic, but the collector's passion borders on the chaos of memories.[8]

For Benjamin, both storytelling and book collecting nourished the pleasures of remembering. He described the heart of storytelling as the "exchange [of] experiences . . . mouth to mouth." He considered the emergence of the modern novel "the earliest symptom of a process whose end is the decline of storytelling."[9]

The story is an oral-aural form, in contrast with the novel, which emerged alongside and depends upon the technology of printing. "A man listening to a story is in the company of the storyteller; even a man reading one shares this companionship. The reader of the novel [like the novelist], however, is isolated, more so than any other reader." Benjamin viewed the storyteller as "the figure in which the righteous man encounters himself." For him, the storyteller was part alchemist and part *bricoleur* ("tinkerer"). Storytelling, like collecting, is a composite or makeshift form using leftover, discarded materials: "The storyteller takes what he tells from experience—his own or that reported by others. And he in turn makes it the experience of those who are listening to his tale."[10]

Yet the story has no author in the conventional sense of the term. Indeed, anyone who listens to and remembers a tale, discovering their own experiences in the teller's words, can claim it as their own. So, too, Benjamin's work, composed entirely out of quotations, would be "authorless."

> *Memory* creates the chain of tradition which passes a happening on from generation to generation. . . . It starts the web which all stories together form in the end.[11]

Benjamin's ideal text stemmed from his desire to weave a different sort of web from the ruins of modern literature. His vision, however, was not nostalgic.[12] This web would have nothing of the spiderweb's elegant symmetry. Rather, it would consist of "fragments [torn] out of their context and arrange[d] . . . afresh in such a way that they illustrated one another and were able to prove their *raison d'être* in a free-floating state."[13] Benjamin's method would "plumb the depths of language and thought . . . by drilling rather than excavating" "so as not to ruin everything with explanations that seek to provide a causal or systematic connection."[14]

For Benjamin to quote is to name, and naming rather than speaking, the word rather than the sentence, brings truth to light. . . . [He] regarded truth as an exclusively acoustical phenomenon: "Not Plato but Adam," who gave things their names, was to him the "father of philosophy." Hence tradition was the form in which these name-giving words were transmitted; it too was an essentially acoustical phenomenon. [15]

Perhaps the story comes closest to Benjamin's ideal project, though he imagined his method as "forcing . . . insights . . . [with] inelegant pedantry." [16] Indeed, more than any other genre, the story juxtaposes unattributable quotations gathered from disparate times and places — fragments whose exact source is long forgotten but whose origins are memories.

Hannah Arendt has quoted the great storyteller Isak Dinesen as saying, "All sorrows can be borne if you put them into a story or tell a story about them." Elaborating on Dinesen, Arendt added, "The story reveals the meaning of what otherwise would remain an unbearable sequence of sheer happenings." [17] Precisely what Arendt meant by "sheer happenings" is my concern in the second part of this chapter and throughout this book.

What shall we make of Arendt's "sheer happenings"? — those unassimilable fragments of experience that refuse to be woven into a neat tale, the unspeakable, what literally cannot be talked about? Or long forgotten events leaving no memory traces? Or simply those vaguely remembered incidents, like individual snapshots fallen from the yellowed pages of a childhood scrapbook, sorted into no particular order? Or a dream interrupted by a ringing telephone? We would recognize neither the snapshots nor the dream as narratives with conventional beginnings and endings, for the scrapbook, nap, and telephone call are themselves external to the "texts" — the photos and dream. How, then, can the dreamer describe the dream without referring to these narrative props (the ringing telephone that tore the dreamer from sleep; the nap on a lazy, hot afternoon), thereby sacrificing the remembered fragments for the sake of narrative continuity?

The problem is this: if we want to understand the dream, it must be constituted as a narrative, "forced" into a story. (In the language of psychoanalysis, this would be the "latent content.") In order to construct an adequate interpretation, certain commonplace anchors must be present, such as time, place, and identifiable actors. But why must experience be narrativized?

Barbara Myerhoff referred to our species as *Homo narrans*, humankind as storyteller, for she recognized that the universal human inclination to narrativize experience was distinctive and remarkable.[18] Indeed, those "sheer happenings" which refuse narrative form, about which a story cannot be told, have a liminal quality to them. It is as though they occur outside of consensus reality in a mute, formless region that belies our species designation as *Homo sapiens*—recent, as against fossil, human. Consider, for instance: birth, infancy, and very early childhood; madness; intense sexual experiences; near death; also torture, extreme pain, and suffering.

Narratives can be coercive, doing violence to the memories they strive to tame or contain. In the course of telling their life stories, Holocaust survivors often acknowledge the poverty of speech, how words echo hollowly against their remembered pasts. There is no getting beyond those "sheer happenings," to which, finally, no story can do justice. Can deliberate silence be the only alternative to the narrative that belies itself?

2

MY GRANDMOTHER'S SAMOVAR

"Be loyal to the story . . . be eternally and unswervingly loyal to the story," means no less than, Be loyal to life, don't create fiction but accept what life is giving you, show yourself worthy of whatever it may be by recollecting and pondering over it, thus repeating it in imagination; this is the way to remain alive. . . .

"When the storyteller is loyal . . . to the story, there, in the end, silence will speak. Where the story has been betrayed, silence is but emptiness. But we, the faithful, when we have spoken our last word, will hear the voice of silence."

Hannah Arendt, "Isak Dinesen: 1885–1962,"
in *Men in Dark Times*★

I became curious about my family's origins when I was twelve years old. I was writing a report on American immigration for my eighth-grade history class and decided to do some field-work. I distributed a questionnaire to my classmates, asking them to find out why their families had emigrated to America and what countries they had come from. Then I compiled the aggregate data into a pie chart.

I asked my maternal grandmother, Marion ("Nana"), when and why she had come to America. All she told me was that her family had left Russia because of pogroms. In any case, that is what I remember of our conversation. I had never before heard the word *pogrom* and I must have asked my mother to explain what it meant.

Nana died fourteen years later, early on Thanksgiving morning in 1983. She was ninety-seven years old. That spring I had begun inter-viewing Jewish Holocaust survivors. The more I began to learn about other Jewish families, the more I realized how little I knew about my own family's history. What was it like to be an immigrant Jew in America? I wondered. During a trip to Los Angeles to attend my sister's wedding, I sat down with my grandmother and a tape recorder to document her thoughts, feelings, and memories about being Jewish.

When my mother telephoned from Los Angeles to tell me Nana had died, she asked me to bring home the tapes we had recorded five months

★Dinesen's own words appear in quotation marks.

earlier. I wasn't sure whether she wanted to hear her mother's voice one last time or simply to have this record in her possession. Either way, she planted the idea in my mind of sharing Nana's interview with our family. I decided I wanted to give a eulogy at Nana's memorial.[1]

I spent Thanksgiving weekend sitting at the typewriter in my mother's kitchen, transcribing Nana's words and struggling to make sense out of her stream of consciousness. Nana had described childhood memories of her mother's baking in preparation for the Jewish holidays, and we also talked about God and the importance of immigrant Jews remaining observant in America.

It wasn't long before my mother and I began arguing about the accuracy of Nana's memories. "It didn't happen that way at all!" Mother insisted, scanning the transcript over my shoulder. "Nana wasn't an observant Jew." Mother seemed irritated both by my gullibility and by Nana's memory loss during the last months of her life.

In the days before the memorial, Mother and her sisters kept in contact by telephone. Several times, I overheard her complaining about Nana's memory and the fictitious stories I had recorded. These conversations intrigued me, for it seemed that much more was being contested than different versions of "truth." I began to recognize that Nana's memories of the pain of assimilating, and her nostalgia for *Yiddishkeit* ("Jewish culture") and religious observance, posed a particular threat to my mother. Surely, this was a generational hot potato—an unresolved conflict passed from mothers to daughters—waiting to be reckoned with openly.

As in so many Jewish-American families, our ethnic and religious schisms run deep. For my mother's generation, Nana's conflicts about being an assimilated, immigrant Jew are silent. But within my generation—for my sister and my cousins—Jewish ambivalence is clearly evident in high rates of intermarriage and conversion out of Judaism. So conflicted is my family that my mother once tried to convince me that Nana had been born in the United States. In fact, as a young girl she had emigrated from Smolensk, Russia, to America.

It was an exhilarating experience for me to deliver a eulogy at Nana's memorial. Such occasions are times for collective remembering, reflexive rituals when families perform their identities, as if to declare, "This is who she was to me; therefore, this is who I am." Claiming my grandmother's Jewishness as a source in my own life cemented a tie between us that had never really existed during her lifetime. It rooted my Jewishness in soil a century old. Standing at the bema and remembering Nana was one of the few moments in my life when I didn't feel like a marginal member of our family. Indeed, I felt as though I had finally returned home.

Several years after Nana's death, my mother and her sisters broke up her apartment. In one of our weekly long-distance telephone calls, Mother and I were discussing who had staked a claim on Nana's brass samovar. Although I had never actually seen it used, for as far back as I could remember, the samovar had sat majestically on the china cabinet in Nana's dining room. Always polished to a high sheen, through my child's eyes it had been the centerpiece of her apartment.

Mother and I speculated on the samovar's origins. I assumed that Nana's mother, Leah, had brought it with her from Russia, but Mother thought not. "Daddy [my grandfather, Louis Berry] used to bid on odd pieces at auctions. He loved antiques. One evening he brought the samovar home to Mother." "Besides," she added, "Mother was born in this country. After all, she never spoke with an accent."

We argued back and forth about where Nana had been born and I recalled the Russian pogroms I first heard about from her. But Mother had no memories of the conversation that had taken place more than fifteen years earlier. Ethnically, she viewed her mother as one hundred percent American. Indeed, along with many Eastern European immigrants of her generation, Nana had successfully assimilated.

"The *unspoken* . . . becomes the *unspeakable*; . . . the nameless becomes the invisible," wrote feminist poet and theorist Adrienne Rich.[2] It is likely that Nana never spoke to her daughters about leaving Russia or the transatlantic voyage to America. Had she deliberately buried these memories or were they washed away by time? Perhaps the shock of settling in the New World as a young girl and, later in life, bearing six children, had blotted them out.

My great-grandparents, Leah and Bernhardt Hozenpud, were married in Smolensk, Russia, in 1874. This probably was an arranged marriage, for Leah was still a young girl, only fourteen years old. In all likelihood, she and Bernhardt lived apart for several years until she reached adulthood. In 1881, when Leah was twenty-one, their first child was born, a son they named Myer.

As it turned out, this was a historic year for Russian Jewry. Following pogroms that spread across the Ukraine, 1881 marked the beginning of the first major Jewish exodus westward. This wave of emigration lasted for thirty-three years, until 1914, when World War I broke out.

Along with one-third of Eastern European Jewry, my great-grandparents, Leah and Bernhardt, fled Russia. Accompanying them were nine-year-old Myer "and other children born of the[ir] . . . marriage": my grandmother, Marion, a toddler of four years, and her older sister,

Edith, who was about six years old.* They must have made passage in steerage, for they were not people of means.

The Hozenpuds arrived in the port of New York in 1890 or 1891 and eventually settled in Minneapolis. One August day in 1898, Bernhardt was granted citizenship. Leah's affidavit indicates that Bernhardt's naturalization certificate designated him as Bernard Hozenput.[3] There are no citizenship records for Leah among our family documents. I wonder whether she eventually studied to become an American citizen. I never knew either of my grandmother's parents.

In 1910, Marion married Louis Berry, né Berezniack, a young man from Chicago and, like her, a Russian immigrant. Beginning in 1912, Marion gave birth to six daughters. My mother, Berna, the youngest, was named for her grandfather, Bernhardt. Well into her eighties, Marion recalled how fertile she had been as a young woman. With a mixture of irony and pride, she recounted that her husband would merely place his hand on the bedroom doorknob and she'd become pregnant again. According to family lore, she had numerous self-induced abortions.

After my mother's birth in 1925, the Berrys joined the westward migration to Southern California, settling in Los Angeles. My mother, a six-month-old infant, was ensconced in a wicker basket for the journey from Minneapolis. I don't know the actual reason for the Berrys' move.

Louis died when my mother was sixteen, fifteen years before I was born. Eventually, all six of Marion and Louis's children married. The nine Berry grandchildren were born and raised in Los Angeles.

In 1950 my mother married Edwin Robert Linden. Certain biographical details about my father's side of the family remain foggy. My paternal grandfather, Herman Levine, was born in 1889, but his birthplace is uncertain. One family document, my father's birth certificate, lists Odessa, Russia, but Herman's obituary indicates that he was born in Johannesburg, South Africa.[4] Lola Curiel, Herman's niece, told me that "Herman migrated to South Africa as a teenager."[5] Apparently, he belonged to the first boy-scout troop founded in Johannesburg by Sir Robert Baden-Powell. My father carried his father's obituary in his

---

*Family memory holds that Edith died in 1971 at the age of ninety-three. Accordingly, she would have been born in 1878. However, family memory also holds that Myer was Leah and Bernhardt's first child. Edith, presumably, was born between Myer, in 1881, and Marion, in 1886. This five-year range is the closest I can pin down her date of birth. I asked my mother if she could explain the discrepancy between Edith's birth date and the birth order of the Hozenpud children. She suggested that perhaps Leah's affidavit, giving Myer's birth date as 1881, was in error.

wallet, perhaps for the entire twenty-three years between Herman's death and his own. Edwin's death certificate indicates that Herman's "birthplace [is] unknown."

According to one family story, at the age of fifteen, Herman went to England, where he studied medicine. Ten years later, in 1914, he came to America, settling in Philadelphia. Soon after, he moved to New York City where, in 1917, he married Emily Kraemer, a British immigrant. Two years later, their only child, Edwin Robert, was born.

For the next quarter-century, until Herman's death in 1946, he and Emily operated the Economy Department Store in the upper-state New York village of Hancock. Like the earlier generation of Central and Western European Jewish immigrants who ventured from the city to the frontier selling dry goods—first as peddlers, then as merchants—Herman was quite an entrepreneur. Periodically, he also owned stores in the towns of Scranton, Port Jervis, Bainbridge, Greene, Liberty, Sidney, Walton, Oxford, and Delhi.[6] Lola Curiel recalled that "Herman's business kept him away from home much of the time. Mother and son were probably too close, and to Edwin it is possible that Herman's arrival at home was an intrusion. There did seem to be a distancing and lack of warmth. There was also the possibility that Herman would have preferred a daughter."[7]

Emily Kraemer was the third of five daughters. Her mother, Annie Kraemer, was born in the Lithuanian town called Malat in Yiddish (in Lithuanian, Maletai; in Russian, Maljaty). Emily's niece, Lola Curiel, remembered that her grandmother, Annie, had run away from home at the age of thirteen. She landed in London, where she was

> befriended and taken in by the original London anarchists—Rudolf Rocker, David Isakovitz, etc. . . . A man named Noskin was the father of all five daughters. Since they were anarchists, they never married. . . .
>
> [At the turn of the century] Annie brought her kids to America in search of an easier life. They traveled steerage, which didn't cost much and a collection was probably taken up to finance the trip. Anarchists believed in helping each other. She learned Midwifery and supplemented that with some abortions. That's how she fed them all until they were old enough to work ([at age] 12? [or] 14?). What was their life like? Pretty rotten! . . .
>
> In the 1920s, Annie said that the anarchists had outlived their time and she shifted her allegiance to the Communists because they were more active. Adelaide [Annie's second daughter] actually joined the party, was active for several years and then got kicked out over a

disagreement. The remaining four women [Annie's other daughters] were totally apolitical.[8]

Of Emily's four sisters, Adelaide was my favorite. I remember her as a maverick, an independent woman who never married. In our family—perhaps, in any family—a single woman is an anomaly, which must be accounted for. As a child, I was told that Adelaide's sweetheart had been killed in the First World War. Recently, Lola explained to me that Adelaide

> had a married lover who was supposed to eventually divorce his wife. That never happened. This man was somewhat affluent. He financed her, spent afternoons with her . . . and she seems to have adored him. [There was] lots of family dissention over that. I don't know what lit a fire under her when she was in her late forties but she suddenly got a sales job in Gimbles [department store], joined the Union and became active in it. She worked her way up to the top of the Gimble union. . . . I might speculate that she had already joined the [Communist] Party and had been assigned to do exactly that. However, she was good at what she did and gained a lot of respect.[9]

By the time I knew Adelaide, she was well into her sixties and still active as a union leader. Through the eyes of my childhood, I recall her distinctive appearance—huge glasses whose stems extended from the bottom of the frames, giving the appearance of being upside down. I remember her visits to California in the early 1960s and my visit, in 1966, to her efficiency apartment on West 58th Street, a few blocks off Central Park. I deeply regret losing contact with her after my father died, for I loved her dearly.

In the late 1930s my father moved to the South to study at Duke University. He must have been one of a handful of Jews on campus, for in those days, private colleges and universities had admission quotas. In 1939 Edwin filed a petition with the Superior Court of Durham County, North Carolina, which read, in part, that "the interest of said Edwin Robert Levine would best be promoted by changing his name to Edwin Robert Linden." On the day Pearl Harbor was bombed—7 December 1941—Edwin *Linden* moved to Los Angeles. Five years later, after Herman died, Emily relocated to Los Angeles as well. Following Edwin's lead, she also changed her name from Levine to Linden.

Family secrets are often revealed once the keeper of the secret dies. I was twelve years old in 1969, the year my father died. Some time afterward, I stumbled upon a copy of his death certificate, from which I discovered that his father's last name had been Levin. (This document is in error. Herman's last name was Levine, not Levin.) This was how I learned that Linden was a name my father had made up.

I asked my mother why Edwin and his father had different last names. She explained to me that anti-Semitism was rampant during the depression years. Jews struggled hard to find work, and in order to get a job many tried to pass as gentiles.

I don't think I actually believed what Mother said about "passing," perhaps because I had no real understanding or firsthand experience of institutionalized anti-Semitism. I may have wondered how some American Jews retained their names during the 1930s and 1940s yet still managed to work. What would it have felt like to carry the stigma of a "Jewish" name?

More recently, I have wondered what would have happened if I hadn't uncovered my father's death certificate. Would I have discovered otherwise or been told that Linden was a made-up name? Why had Edwin kept his original family name secret from my sister, Tracey, and me? How had Levine, obviously a Jewish name, become "unspeakable"? Can it be a coincidence that he never spoke to us about his father—my grandfather, Herman—about whom I know little more than I can piece together from family documents?

Jews have been living in *galut* since the destruction of the First Temple in Jerusalem in 586 B.C.E. Consequently, most of us know little about the lives our forebears lived. In some cases, names going back as few as three generations have been lost—forgotten. But dispersion and mobility are defining conditions of modernity, for Jews and gentiles alike. Indeed, the modern world *is* the diaspora.

In our own century, liquidation of the Eastern European *shtetlach* ("Jewish hamlets")—heart of the Ashkenazim—severed the roots Jews had laid down over the course of hundreds of years. The near destruction of *Yiddishkeit* by the Nazis precludes the possibility of linking our lives in the present with the homelands of past generations. The places we might have visited have vanished. For most Ashkenazic Jews, there is nowhere even to begin the search. Only in our memories can we make the journey back.

3

"WE DON'T BELIEVE IN 'ORGANIZED RELIGION'"

> *Memory*
> *is the simplest form of prayer.*
> Marge Piercy, "Black Mountain"

Over the years, my feelings about being Jewish have waxed and waned. The world of my youth, Los Angeles's West Side, had a dense Jewish presence. My parents were atheists, although I do not recall their using that term to describe themselves. "We don't believe in 'organized religion,'" they explained to my sister, Tracey, and me when we were very young. For years I was perplexed by the idea of "organized religion." What was disorganized religion? I wondered.

Yet every year without fail, Mother kept us out of school on the first day of Rosh Hashanah. How ironic that we marked the Jewish new year with our annual visit to the eye doctor!

We never attended *shul* ("synagogue") as a family. In fact, I don't believe I ever even entered a synagogue with my father. (The young rabbi who officiated at Edwin's memorial had never met him.) On only a handful of occasions have my mother and I attended shul together: once, for a family bar mitzvah in 1969, the same year my father died; then again, fourteen years later, for my grandmother Marion's memorial and the sabbath preceding it.

Most of my childhood friends were Jewish. But until I graduated from college and moved to San Francisco, I had attended synagogue only once or twice with friends. Jewish liturgy, prayers, and the cycle of festivals were virtually unknown to me.

Debbie Michel was my best friend for several years during elementary school. Her parents, Rhoda and Steven, are Rumanian. They came to America as refugees during the Nazi era, a subject that was never discussed in my presence. In the mid-1960s, the Holocaust was not dinner-table conversation.

Debbie and I loved each other with unselfconscious devotion, as only young girls can. She was the first observant Jew I had ever known well. I recall that when we were about ten years old, she began to teach me to read the Hebrew alphabet.

The first time I ever attended synagogue-was the year Debbie took me to High Holiday services at Sinai Temple, on Wilshire Boulevard in Westwood. My memories of the experience are dim, but I recall that people inside the sanctuary seemed restless. There was a lot of shuffling and moving around, perhaps *davening* ("praying"). We got bored quickly and left. Maybe my parents were right about organized religion being for *other* Jews. . . .

When I was ten and Tracey was twelve, we were sent to New York for the winter holiday, where my grandmother, Emily, was visiting her family. Mother was about to undergo major surgery and our cross-country trip was designed to solve the problem of child care during her hospital stay. Tracey and I found out about Mother's surgery only after returning to California. By then, she was recovering at home.

I vividly remember when Mother told us that she had been in the hospital. Daddy picked us up at the airport and brought us home. "Your Mother is resting," he explained neutrally. "That's why she didn't come along." I walked into my parents' bedroom and sensed immediately that something was wrong.

Mother's bed was covered with a fancy white sheet I had never seen before and Mother, a vigorous woman, was flat on her back. I asked her why and she told us about her operation.

Throughout my childhood, minimal disclosure about matters of illness and death was the rule of thumb my parents followed. As a result, I became extremely sensitive to the fact that grown-ups often deliberately masked the truth with lies. I railed against the power adults wielded over me, especially the power to deceive.

While Tracey and I were in New York, we met Emily's Aunt Fannie and Uncle Louie. These Old World Jews were dismayed to learn that we were not receiving a proper Jewish education. They thought we should be attending Hebrew school.

After we returned to California, I mentioned our visit with Fannie and Louie to my parents. This may also have been when my sister and I asked if we could celebrate Hanukkah rather than Christmas. (At the time, our family only observed Christmas.)

Daddy's response to my request to attend Hebrew school was unequivocal, and I never again broached the subject with him. "Over my dead body" were his final words. Curiously, as though they were striking a compromise with us, Mother bought the family a menorah. The following year, we started lighting Hanukkah candles and making the blessings.

From the time I was a young girl, every year in spring we celebrated Pesach with Mother's five sisters and their families. I remember these seders with fondness. Of all the festivals in the Jewish cycle, Pesach is the one I treasure most.

At our family seders, neither the children nor the adults followed along in the Haggadah, the ritual text. Instead, Aunt Myra typed up individual portions for each of us, which were placed at our assigned seats at the seder table. As the youngest member of the extended family, I was expected to ask the "four questions."★ Aunt Jewel always prepared the chicken soup and *knaidlach* ("matzo balls").

Because of long-standing differences with several of his brothers-in-law, my father chose not to attend these and other family gatherings. This must have been extremely difficult for my mother, but I learned to take his absences for granted. After all, I had never known otherwise.

Beginning when we were young girls, Tracey and I spent part of each summer at Jewish camps. More than any other childhood experience, this nurtured my Jewish identity and love for *Yiddishkeit*. At camp we sang Jewish songs, learned Israeli folk dances, and observed *shabbos* ("sabbath"). Friday night supper was a special meal, for which we would dress in crisp white shirts and navy-blue shorts.

We learned about Zionism, the founding of Israel, and the Holocaust. We were taught to identify with *Eretz Yisroel* ("the land of Israel")—the Jewish state. I was astonished to learn that the Law of Return automat-

---

★In the traditional Haggadah, the youngest child present asks the four questions. In response to these questions, the *Maggid* ("the telling") is recounted:

> Why is this night different from all other nights? On all other nights we eat bread or matzoh. Why, on this night, do we eat only matzoh?
>
> On all other nights we eat all kinds of vegetables. Why, on this night, do we eat bitter herbs?
>
> On all other nights we do not dip our food even once. Why, on this night, do we dip our food twice, once in *charoset* [mixture of nuts and fruit] and once in salt water?
>
> On all other nights we eat either sitting up or reclining. Why, on this night, do we only recline?

ically granted us Israeli citizenship, simply because we were Jews. For the first time, I saw footage of the liberated death camps. My stock images of the Holocaust—piles of emaciated corpses at Dachau and Bergen-Belsen, and children packed into cattle-car transports—date from the summer we were shown the film "Let My People Go."[1]

My "Jewish" memories of summer camp are entangled with fond memories of being in nature for a few weeks each year—hiking in the Angeles National Forest and breathing fresh mountain air—and renewing deep, loving friendships with other campers and counselors. Living in a summer community where religious and cultural life were celebrated nourished my pride in being a Jew. As an emblem of this pride, during most of my childhood, I wore a delicate gold *Magen David* ("star of David") on a chain around my neck, given to me by my grandmother, Emily.

What fragments shall I add to this story? Did I neglect to say that I attended a Presbyterian nursery school? I still remember a song from that time:

> Very softly I will walk.
> Very softly I will talk.
> Into church I go.

Going to church was a regular part of the school's program. I don't recall how I felt about church as a toddler but my guess is that it was a magical sort of place—dark, quiet, and soothing. Recently, I asked my mother why she had sent my sister and me to Christian preschools. "The Presbyterians ran excellent schools," was her reply. What about the Jews? I wondered ironically.

Like so many second-generation American Jews, my parents' ambivalence about their religion and culture caused them to feel conflict about encouraging Jewish identities in my sister and me. These tensions, however, are not unique to their generation, nor to Eastern European Jewish immigrant families.

For many children of the depression—my parents' generational cohort—assimilation and upward mobility became fused. Pressures to blend into the middle class and realize the postwar, suburban American dream seemed overdetermined—beyond individual choice. But my parents' generation was not the first to turn its back on traditions; their parents and grandparents had left the Old World, severing continuity within families—and in many cases, expunging family memories as well. Assimilation was no more—or less—than a single moment in the dialectics of exile, where Jews have dwelled for centuries.

One Saturday morning in June 1983, my sister celebrated her marriage. Tracey is a convert to Catholicism, and her husband, John, is an Episcopal priest. The wedding was held at All Saints Church in Beverly Hills.

Tracey and I have never had an easy relationship, but at the time of her wedding we were deeply estranged. I was uncomfortable at the prospect of entering a church on Saturday, the Jewish sabbath. I felt hurt by the intermarriage and Tracey's identification with Catholicism. I anticipated the occasion with dread.

As it happened, the wedding coincided with a political action I wanted to participate in: a demonstration and blockade at the University of California's Lawrence Livermore Laboratory. Located near Berkeley, the lab is a primary nuclear weapons design contractor for the Department of Defense. Lani Silver, my collaborator on the Holocaust Media Project, and I had discussed the idea of blockading together. I ruminated for a week about whether or not to participate in civil disobedience, risking arrest and short-term detention. In daydreams I telephoned my mother to say I was in jail and wouldn't be able to attend the wedding. But, in the end, a sense of family duty prevailed and I decided to forgo the civil disobedience part of the action.

On Thursday, three days after the demonstration, I flew down to Los Angeles for a long weekend. Lani had been in jail since Monday morning, and there was no telling when she and one thousand other blockaders would be released from Santa Rita Rehabilitation Center, the Alameda County Jail. I expected to have my hands full as Lani's support person, hundreds of miles away from home.

I divided my time in Los Angeles among family obligations, the Holocaust Media Project, and keeping close tabs on the blockaders in jail. Lani and I both recorded diaries during the eleven days she remained in jail. Once the ordeal ended, I interwove our separate accounts into an article juxtaposing perspectives from inside and outside of jail. The following passage, written during the weekend of Tracey's wedding, is excerpted from "Santa Rita Jail Diary."

> I awoke this morning starved for news reports from home. But the Los Angeles media are silent about the "Santa Rita 1,000." I am anxious to talk with family and friends about the Livermore action and the arraignment crisis. It is shocking to find out that no one I've spoken with is aware of the situation or concerned about the threat of nuclear war.

I spend [Friday] . . . afternoon at the Simon Wiesenthal Center. I am scheduled to meet with the executive staff to discuss the Holocaust Media Project's plans. . . . I arrive early and spend a leisurely hour at the Center's museum. Most of the images I see are familiar to me. Even so, I am deeply affected by this dark and somber place. I find a corner with a bench and sob quietly. I still cannot grasp the complicity and complaisance that permitted the rise of Nazism fifty years ago. Then, nobody wanted to believe that European Jewry was slated for mass murder, and today, most people still would prefer to forget the Holocaust.

Denial is denial—whether it concerns the Nazi Holocaust or the threat of nuclear annihilation. It seems most Americans are willing to pay any price to purchase an illusion of safety in the name of "defense." But my sense of sanity is threatened by such illusions. When I cling to the view that all of humankind is not in grave and immediate danger, I feel madness closing in on me.

[Later that evening] Mother and I are preparing dinner side by side, in silence. We had a bitter fight an hour ago, shortly before Tracey and John arrived. Tracey hovers over some of her wedding gifts. I glance up from the counter where I'm chopping garlic and see what appears to be the third china place setting she has opened tonight. I am overcome by a sense of disgust at the opulence of these presents.

Mother makes a last-ditch effort to draw me into the conversation. "Ruth dear," she exclaims, "isn't the china pattern lovely?" I look, but I cannot see the colors, the design. Instead, I only see images of the "Santa Rita 1,000" and tens of thousands of people rotting in American jails and prisons, bag ladies roaming the downtown streets of San Francisco, the gas chambers and crematoria at Birkenau, the Salvadorian *desaparecidos*, the disappeared ones in unmarked graves. Without answering, I storm out of the kitchen feeling terribly confused.[2]

Mother and I prepared to leave for church early the next morning. I was resewing a button on her dress when the telephone rang. I reached for the receiver and an unfamiliar voice mistook me for Berna. "I just want to say *mazel tov*, since it's probably the only time you'll hear it today," my mother's friend declared. I laughed, replying, "Not if I have any say in the matter."

On an occasion that effaced us as Jews, this Yiddish blessing had the reverse effect. It affirmed our roots, making us visible to ourselves. By openly acknowledging the irony of the event—that intermarriage is a mixed blessing—my mother's friend exposed what no one else seemed willing to express. Throughout the day, I cleaved to her words like a talisman.

During the ceremony, "Our Lord Jesus Christ" was repeatedly invoked in benedictions and prayers. At first, I flinched at the very presumption. *My* lord?

In a surrealist montage, startling juxtapositions allow viewers to experience art as a process of selecting and arranging forms—editing reality, so to speak. So it was that the shock of these words reminded me that I was "only" observing a ritual, fashioned and staged according to Christian traditions. Like an injection of novocaine into a main vein, repetitions of this phrase gradually numbed my pain and rage.

I had forgotten that the meanings and values being expressed were Tracey's, not mine. I was no longer her little sister, Robin, youngest member of the extended family. I was Ruth, a biblical name I chose for myself, evoking devoted friendship among women—a name whose meaning is compassion.

We rose and sat, reading aloud from the New Testament. Along with everyone else, I stood, though I did not take a book. Beside me Mother read along, loudly. I was shocked by the volume of her "amens." I thought twice about remaining in my seat while everyone else was on their feet.

I recalled my decision in ninth grade to stop reciting the Pledge of Allegiance. Then, I was still obliged to stand, along with the rest of the class. What a *tsimmes* ("upset") that caused. In a split second, I decided not to make another fuss, at least not then and there. In the row behind me, Tracey's old friend Janet was silently holding a closed book in her arms. A kindred spirit, a sister—another Jew.

After the ceremony, Tracey and John had their pictures taken with family members and friends. I stood off to one side, talking with my cousins. Out of the corner of my eye, I watched the photographer arranging people in small groups, but I was not asked to join in. I wondered whether I was deliberately being excluded.

Eventually I walked toward my mother, who motioned to Tracey for the three of us to be photographed together. Mother's eye caught the *Magen David* I was wearing around my neck. She gave my shoulders a perfunctory pat and unbuttoned my collar another inch to expose the star.

For the second time that morning, my Jewishness was affirmed, making me visible to myself. In the moment we were photographed, I became a keeper of family memories—a reminder that we are Jews. In juxtaposing Tracey and me before the camera, Mother had arranged a living montage, one that exposed the paradox of being an assimilated Jew in the late twentieth century.

In native cultures—among tribal peoples living close to their traditions—religion is an inseparable part of daily life. The sacred permeates the mundane—what counts as food and how it is prepared, what are thinkable thoughts and askable questions, which mysteries of nature require explanations. In indigenous cultures, the categories of religion and ethnicity would be redundant—meaningless. Just as there would be no dichotomy between sacred and secular, neither would ethnicity be problematic, as it is in the West—to be claimed, discovered, recovered, or preserved.

A sense of rootlessness prevails in the West, where Emile Durkheim believed the domain of religion had contracted.[3] Among the middle classes, workshops, "twelve-step" programs, therapies, and New Age spiritualities of various stripes offer severed selves promises of healing. We are driven to extreme alienation by commodity fetishism, while religion (packaged as "spirituality" for the 1980s and 1990s) itself has become a commodity. Inside and outside of Judaism, in the wake of "a vanished world,"[4] assimilated Jews face great challenges and many choices for living our secularized lives.

I cannot see myself as a *ba'alat teshuvah*, "returning" to traditional Jewish observance. There are, after all, many pleasures in the margins. Nor can I imagine making *aliyah*—settling in Israel. I have no desire to transplant myself into a volatile war zone, where I would be considered either an enemy or a traitor—perhaps both. Like my father who changed his name and moved across the country by himself, I also am a renegade, a rebel—breaking other people's rules in order to make my own path.

COMING OF AGE
AS A FEMINIST (1976–77)

More and more, it has seemed to me that the idea of an individual, the idea that there is someone to be known, separate from the relationships, is simply an error. As a relationship is broken or a new one developed, there is a new person. So we create each other, bring each other into being by being part of the matrix in which the other exists. We grope for a sense of a whole person who has departed in order to believe that as whole persons we remain and continue, but torn out of the continuing gestation of our meetings one with another, whoever seems to remain is thrust into a new life.

Mary Catherine Bateson, *With a Daughter's Eye*

atherine Bateson wrote these words about her mother, Margaret Mead, following Margaret's death in 1978. The insight expressed in these lines—that relationships create persons, not the other way around—challenges the notion of personality that lies at the heart of modern Western psychologies. The epigraph opening this chapter occurs at the moment in the text when Catherine reveals her discovery that her mother and her mother's teacher and lifelong friend, Ruth Benedict, had been lovers.

Margaret successfully hid this secret during her lifetime. Yet Catherine rejects the conclusion that, without this information, she had not *really* known her mother—indeed, that no one had really known Margaret—because she had carefully concealed her bisexuality.

This view implies that selves and persons are not isomorphic—on the contrary, an individual is or has multiple selves. During a person's lifetime, as significant relationships are left behind and new ones are entered into, selves die and are born anew. Yet each self is authentic and complete in its own right; no one self is a priori—more "genuine" or "true" than another.

The relational character of selves may be likened to this same property of atomic particles. In order to discover the basic components of atoms and the elementary forces operating among them, high-energy physicists create experimental collisions between bits of matter moving at extremely high velocities. When particles collide, energy is generated—

mostly in the form of new particles.[1] So it is with persons, for moments of "collision" between selves also generate energy in the form of new selves. Just as certain atomic particles are created through interacting with other particles, so selves are born and die in relation to other selves.

My early years in the women's movement were a chain of "collisions" of great velocity. In heady political debates and protracted meetings, old selves died and new selves were born. Like those debates and meetings, my stories meander and drift, for constructing selves is rarely a lineal process akin to placing one foot in front of the other.

Recounting this period in my life—roughly, the years between 1974 and 1980—requires nothing short of remaking myself in the present. Indeed, reflexive acts of remembering and retelling have the power to change a person forever. Reflexive consciousness bends time by collapsing the (culturally constructed) boundaries separating past and present selves. This chapter, then, is a study in how selves make stories and how stories, in turn, make new selves.

I came of age in the second wave of the women's movement. As a high school student during the early 1970s, I was introduced to debates about equal rights and the psychology of sex differences. I read *The Second Sex* and pondered my burgeoning lesbian sexuality, terrified by the forces of desire in my body. From my liberal, middle-class vantage point, I recognized that sexism indeed had shaped the course of other women's lives. But I believed I was among the lucky ones to have been spared.

Other experiences deeply influenced my teenage years: discovering Freud and exploring, in late-night conversations with my friends, the permutations of our minds and hearts; attending the Pentagon Papers trial and learning about the ravages of racism and American imperialism in Vietnam; reading the existential philosophy of Sartre—a beacon in my heady quest for life's meaning; and pondering Gertrude Stein's delightfully irreverent play with language. These were the landscapes of my adolescence.

From the time I learned how to read, books and ideas were my mainstay; they made my life possible and bearable. As a teenager, I forged an identity as an intellectual. I found a resting spot in a life of the mind, but only temporarily.

My childhood was steeped in the ethos of the 1950s. "Drop drills" during elementary school, in case of nuclear attack by the Soviets, inscribed the Cold War on my generation's bodies and minds, and

"Ozzie and Harriet" helped us to visualize the suburban middle-class dream. When our families fell short of the Nelsons, which they did routinely, then we learned that our individual shortcomings were blame-worthy.

Later on, I was deeply affected by the antiwar movement of the 1960s and the counterculture that flourished alongside it. During the late 1960s, I was a committed volunteer in the offices of Another Mother for Peace. At age twelve I smoked marijuana for the first time.

During adolescence, that nebulous developmental period sandwiched between childhood and death, which psychologists claim often extends into midlife, the search for identity becomes self-conscious and all-consuming. If alienation itself—whatever its origins—did not stimulate my Search for Life's Meaning, then it certainly was an outcome of my turning inward. Feminism was the first arena in which I consciously struggled with my identity. During and after college, I embraced several different feminisms: socialist feminism, lesbian feminism, lesbian sep-aratism, and radical feminism.

Distinctions among feminisms were of utmost significance to us, for the women's movement of the 1970s was ideologically segmented. We defined ourselves by what we didn't believe, as much as by our principles, values, and praxis. Making The Revolution was a serious commitment: we lived our lives and did our work urgently and pas-sionately.

In the 1970s feminism was: social world and social movement, community, ideology, weltanschauung, cosmology, and ethnicity.* Somehow, I managed to hold fast—often, only by fine threads—to the role of observer. I seemed slightly out of step with everyone else. Mannheim's description of the intellectual's "socially unattached" posi-tion in modern societies is fitting.[2] I remained on the outskirts—marginal—even though, in other ways, I was a true believer.

The Thorn Collective was my first women's group. When we started meeting in January of 1976, all ten of us were students at the University of California, Santa Cruz. Eight of us were in our early twenties; two women were close to thirty. The name we chose for ourselves expressed

---

Webster's New Collegiate Dictionary defines *ethnic* as: "1: neither Christian nor Jewish: heathen 2: of or relating to races or large groups of people classed according to common traits and customs." My use of the term *ethnic* follows the second definition, although the "common traits and customs" I am referring to are not usually viewed in this way.

our intention of becoming a thorn in the side of the university administration.

Several women who had been active in the Women's Studies Collective conceived the idea for the group. The Collective (as the women's studies group was called) was the locus of feminist political activity on campus and the governing body of UCSC's newly founded women's studies program. These women had become dissident members of the Collective, disillusioned with academic politics. They envisioned a different kind of group, but one that incorporated the Collective's principles of internal democracy, consensus decision-making, and criticism/self-criticism.

I was a member of the Thorn Collective for twenty months. It seems to me that, for most of this time, defining the group's identity was our underlying project. We knew we were oppressed as women and as students. What sort of group could most effectively transform our condition? Would our focus be political action, problem-solving, consciousness-raising, or study?

We needed to know who we were in order to build mutual trust and commitments, and to set goals and priorities for the group. And in order to work within and be accountable to the Santa Cruz political community, group members needed to have a reasonably consistent sense of purpose.

The Thorn Collective's most memorable accomplishment may have been the passion with which we combined our quest for group identity with an awareness of group process as praxis. Group process meant much more to us than dispatching agenda items in a timely and efficient manner. Rather, we viewed our meetings as a laboratory for practicing the skills necessary to transform society.

Members of the Thorn Collective recognized the revolutionary character of collective process. We believed that:

> working collectively is a process in which we encourage each other to develop our individual talents and energies in ways we find fulfilling, yet keeping in mind the needs and desires of others. Equal participation is encouraged by the elimination of a hierarchical power structure (one person having authority over others). Consensual decision-making seeks to incorporate the opinions of all members rather than suppressing dissention through "majority rule." This encourages development of the abilities to articulate our feelings, to listen to each other, to give and receive criticism (both positive and negative), and to learn together.[3]

Collective process is a form of pure democracy. It is often cumbersome, time-consuming, and frustrating. Collective "struggle"* was the method of our revolution, our strategy for making new selves and new social structures. Our greatest challenge was learning to channel the energies it generated into personal and social change.

Our first activity as a group was to produce a newsletter, which we called *Thornside*, consisting of two lengthy articles about student oppression at UCSC.[4] During the 1970s, UCSC was generally viewed as the most liberal—even radical—of the nine University of California campuses. The irony of indicting the downside of many of its permissive practices did not escape our group.

We only published one issue of *Thornside*, which we distributed at a campus-wide forum on student activism during the 1960s. Rereading *Thornside* today, fifteen years later, I am still impressed by our analysis of the university as an institution of social control. We recognized that as students we were being indoctrinated—prepared for productive roles in the work force, encouraged to consume exotica, and suppressed from expressing dissent.

In honor of International Women's Day (8 May) and the American Bicentennial, the Thorn Collective undertook our second project. This involved spray painting a highly visible billboard at the southern edge of the city with the following message:

STOP TWO HUNDRED YEARS OF OPPRESSION
SOCIALIST-FEMINIST REVOLUTION NOW!

The preceding weekend, we constructed huge, brown-paper stencils of letters and symbols of women's power—a raised fist encircled by the sign for woman.† Our guerrilla action also was an initiation rite—scru-

---

*The term *struggle* is commonly used by Marxist revolutionary/liberation movements. In the 1960s and 1970s, it was appropriated by the New Left and socialist feminists. Struggle was an ongoing, often agonizing process of confronting, challenging, and criticizing/being confronted, challenged, and criticized. It required great strength, openness, and the courage to make new discoveries about oneself and others. Issues emerging in the course of struggle could be resolved by analyzing their personal, political, and historical roots. Historically, criticism/self-criticism has been a significant tool in many revolutionary movements. It was developed most intensively in the Chinese Revolution.

†Since the 1960s, the semiotics of power have changed dramatically. Feminists used to speak of power as though it were a verb, as pure energy. Today, power has been transformed into empowerment, a noun—a passive, psychological state of being. Webs and matrices are the icons of empowerment—embedded images with entirely different connotations than the call to action of a raised fist.

---

pulously planned and timed, risky and secret. As in traditional rites of passage, our identities, as individuals and a group, would be transfigured.

None of us welcomed the possibility of being arrested, so we found out when, during the early morning hours, the police would patrol the area where the billboard was located. Of all the Thorn women, I believe my fears were strongest—at least I expressed them more vociferously than the others. I was beset by images of being carted off and confined in jail, until my friend Joyce (who was not a member of Thorn) managed to reassure me. If we were actually arrested, she promised to call her friend, the district attorney for Santa Cruz County, to come to our aid, regardless of the hour. These worries resurface every time I consider taking part in civil disobedience, though I don't recall how I interpreted them at the time of the billboard action. Today, I link them to my sense of vulnerability as a Jew and my identification with Holocaust survivors— "deportation anxiety," so to speak.

As it turned out, my fears of being arrested were for naught. We did our work quickly and efficiently sometime around 1 A.M., and no one bothered us. In the morning, we brimmed with pride—secretly, of course—responding nonchalantly when our friends asked whether we'd seen the billboard at the foot of High Street. Later in the day, we photographed our handiwork—a good thing too, since the billboard was defaced before the end of the week.

During the spring months, the ten of us worked on various campus-wide projects. Jill was active in efforts to start a student union at UCSC, an idea that grew out of the winter forum on student activism in which the Thorn Collective had participated. "No, we're not planning to build an on-campus bowling alley (à la UCLA or UCB[erkeley]) and we're not planning to produce major rock star concerts," read an article in the first issue of the *Student Union News*, a publication she and Ellen, also a Thorn member, helped to edit.[5]

During spring quarter, Dorothy and I taught "Female Physiology and Gynecology," an extremely popular course that enrolled more than three hundred students. In those days, undergraduates were permitted to teach full-credit courses with minimal faculty supervision. This was one of UCSC's many progressive policies with an exploitive edge, for the administration surely recognized the cost-efficiency of employing unpaid teaching staff.

Two years earlier, in 1974, Laurie Garrett, a UCSC senior, had developed and taught "Female Physiology and Gynecology" as a "student-directed seminar." Enrollments in such courses were normally limited to twenty-five. But one hundred students turned out on the first day of class and demanded that the administration waive the restriction. The next year Laurie was hired as an instructor to teach the course.

In 1976 we again offered "Female Physiology" as a student-directed seminar. The following year, Dorothy, who had finished her course work, was hired as an instructor and paid to teach the course. In subsequent years, "Female Physiology" was taught by a physician on an adjunct basis. I do not know whether it has become a permanent part of the UCSC curriculum.

At about this time, Rhonda, one of the older group members, got pregnant. She planned to raise the baby on her own. Throughout the summer and fall, we discussed what Thorn's relationships with Rhonda and the baby could be.

As an alternative to both the nuclear family and single motherhood, we envisioned a new institution, which we called "collective motherhood." This was a natural extension of our view of group process as praxis. Here was our opportunity to refigure the fetishized relations of the nuclear family that damaged mothers and children alike through isolation, violence, and narcissistic, dyadic dependence.

Rhonda and I had never been close. At best, we tolerated each other; at worst, there was misunderstanding and antagonism between us. I chafed against her New Age spirituality. My middle-class decorum clashed with her matter-of-fact, working-class style.

Silently, I sat through several months of meetings. I was confused, resentful, and growing isolated from the group, afraid of dissenting from Thorn's "decision" to have a baby. Following our meetings, Kirsten and I would debrief by telephone. I was furious in those conversations. "No one consulted me about having this baby in the first place. If they had, I would have said 'no.'" Kirsten seemed to share these feelings, but we kept them between us.

It was difficult for me to acknowledge that I had no interest in helping to parent Rhonda's child. Did I feel this way because of Rhonda's and my poor relationship or was I temperamentally unsuited for motherhood? I must have feared being ostracized. Would other members of Thorn challenge my commitment to the group? Would I be viewed as "politically incorrect"? It was a huge burden to bear my belief that when my political commitments conflicted with my feelings, then somehow I was at fault.

I managed to steer clear of Rhonda, the baby, whom she called Cedar (born in February 1977), and soiled diapers. My sole contribution to the collective motherhood project was occasionally working a shift at

"Mother Right," Santa Cruz's first feminist bookstore. Rhonda and Jill had opened the store in the fall of 1976.

Cedar is now a teenager. Ellen and I used to be neighbors in North Cambridge, but we lost touch when she moved. Several summers ago in San Francisco, I visited with Lauren and her baby, Jennifer, and Lynne and her daughter, Sara, who is now a young woman the same age as many of my students. Nancy and I bumped into each other some years back, headed for MIT on the #1 Dudley bus. I haven't seen Kirsten since I moved to the East Coast but Lynne told me her brother, David, had died.

Of all the Thorn Collective women, I have stayed in closest contact with Jill. Seeing her during my sporadic visits to Los Angeles is always a pleasure. Thinking of Jill, I am filled with memories of strolling arm-in-arm through the Fairfax district, a Jewish quarter in the center of the city; attending a *shabbos* service at Congregation Beth Chayim Chadashim, L. A.'s lesbian and gay shul, followed by *oneg shabbat* at the trendy City Café (the service was banal and we were disappointed); and leisurely lunches at Cantor's, an old-fashioned Jewish deli.

Thorn Collective meetings followed a strict format. Their structure never varied without prior discussion and, of course, group consensus. For every meeting, we designated a facilitator and note-taker, agreed upon an ending time, and set and prioritized an agenda. Often, a specific amount of time was allocated for each agenda item. Then, each member of the group "checked in" briefly (called "space check," "weather report," or simply "check-in"). We never timed this part of our meetings.

As we progressed through an agenda, proposals would be introduced by an individual and discussed by the whole group. Any objections to a proposal would be raised and debated. Then, one of three things might happen. If there were no objections, or after objections were resolved, the facilitator would ask for the group's consensus on a proposal. On the other hand, if objections seemed irresolvable, a proposal would be thrown out. When this happened, an alternate proposal on the same issue would be introduced.

A third possibility frequently occurred. In the course of discussing and debating a proposal, issues could become too complicated for resolution in the allotted time. Then, we would continue discussing the agenda item at our next meeting.

Ordinarily, the Thorn Collective practiced criticism/self-criticism at the close of each meeting. This was time designated for evaluating the session while it was still fresh in all of our minds. Its aim was to help us learn to notice and express appreciation for each others' contributions to the group process, and for our own good efforts. Criticism/self-criticism was also a time for airing discomfort, disappointment, and anger when they arose, rather than storing up a litany of resentments and complaints.

> We take up the weapon of criticism to get rid of the attitudes and ideas from our culture and daily existence that keep us from uniting to throw over the old order and build up a new one. This makes criticism very different from encounter groups or conventional therapy, where the purpose is to increase each individual's well-being or ability to adjust. We decide to do criticism not because it is best or most comfortable for us as individuals or as small groups, but because we think it will advance the whole—the whole group, the whole organization, the whole working class—ourselves included.[6]

Toward the end of our first year together as a group, the Thorn Collective planned an intensive criticism/self-criticism session. We envisioned this as an opportunity for each group member to speak to every other member as directly and honestly as she could. We hoped to strengthen relationships within the group and to acknowledge our collective gains. We wanted to know how others perceived our strengths and talents, and where they thought we stood in our own way.

Our desire for an intensive form of criticism/self-criticism reflected deep hopes for recognition: to be known by the other members of the group and, in turn, to know them. In order to continue the work of making ourselves and remaking the world, we needed an occasion for "performing" our individual and collective identities. As Barbara Myerhoff explained, a "group's shared and unquestionable truths [are] made unquestionable by being performed." Myerhoff coined the term "definitional ceremonies" to describe ritual "performances of identity, sanctified to the level of myth."[7] Ours would be a secular ritual grounded in routine, yet defamiliarized, practices.[8]

We planned the criticism session over a period of several weeks. My memories of the event itself have blurred, so I telephoned Jill for help in remembering. Together, we recalled convening over a two-day period, at least ten hours each day, at the Laguna Street house where Jill, Dorothy, and Ellen had lived. Jill remembered the session as a test of our courage and strength, as individuals and a group.

Who took the first turn and how did we decide? What was it like to take my turn? I've long forgotten these details, but what I vividly recall is that one woman stormed out of the room in the middle of the session, deeply hurt by words that were spoken to her. I am not sure whether she ever returned to the group.

I cannot speculate about the consequences of the criticism/self-criticism session for the Thorn Collective, or its meanings for individual members of the group. I have no retrospective data, nor did I record notes during or following the ritual. Moreover, because rituals are liminal events, assessing their outcomes raises complex empirical questions.[9] However, I am certain that Thorn members participated in the session as credible and believing subjects. Regardless of whether or not the session achieved its stated goals of deepening our lines of communication and encouraging group solidarity, it was an effective definitional ceremony — a fitting group rite of passage in the months before Rhonda's baby was born.

All ten members of the Thorn Collective were white women. We were evenly divided between working-class and middle-class backgrounds. At the time, perhaps three of us considered ourselves lesbians; other members of the group either identified themselves as heterosexual or did not define themselves one way or another.

Four members of the group were Jews, but I don't recall a conscious sense of Jewish solidarity among us. Only one occasion comes to mind when we spoke of being Jewish. This was a passing conversation — insignificant and long-forgotten — probably occurring during our first six months together as a group.

During the 1970s, as I came of age as a feminist, my connection to Judaism and Jewish culture was suppressed. Still, as a metaphor for genocide and terror, the Holocaust lingered at the surface of my consciousness.[10] After reading Philip Levine's poem, "For the Poets of Chile,"[11] I wrote the following passage in my journal:

> The coup, 11 September 1973, has been an important political lesson for me. It is a frightening reminder of the phenomenology of terror — like the destruction of six million Jews but different because it is happening right now, in the present. And no matter how much money I send, how many letters I write, signatures I gather, or *peñas* I attend, people are being tortured and murdered daily. And there is really nothing that I can do to stop the killings.
>
> "Someone must remember it over and over . . ." Levine is talking about a kind of resistance — the dialectic between the burden of remembering and the recognition that we must remember. . . . We all must remember so as to carry on, to resist, to survive.[12]

Those were the years when feminism affirmed our commonality and solidarity as women, with *all* women. Differences among members of the Thorn Collective were silenced. The same process was occurring within the movement at large, among women with backgrounds far more diverse than ours. Feminists hadn't yet developed a language for articulating our differences.

Feminist constructions of identity were singular and one-dimensional. Our individual identities were rooted in the movement; thus, any distinction that set women apart from each other could be viewed as divisive—a betrayal of sorts. We believed that we were women "first," then Jews and lesbians, students and mothers, and so on.

Consequently, I have few Jewish memories from the 1970s. One that comes to mind, tinged with unpleasantness, concerns a housemate of mine who became a *ba'alat teshuvah*, "returning" to traditional Judaism. I remember feeling uncomfortable with the rituals she practiced— lighting *shabbos* candles and struggling to keep kosher in our *trayf* ("unkosher") kitchen. As far as I could tell, her observances had nothing to do with me or my Jewishness. In my eyes, she became an "other," backward and strange—out of step with "reality."

Yet UC Santa Cruz was an assimilated Jewish community of sorts. Jews comprised a large proportion of the student body, though most of us were unselfconsciously Jewish. For feminists who also were Jewish, there were not yet any political or spiritual contexts for exploring our religion or celebrating our culture.

In May of 1977 the Thorn Collective decided to stop meeting temporarily. We had been together for just under eighteen months. This was a trial separation; we didn't know whether we wanted to continue the group. Many of us felt shocked and afraid of losing each other.

The conflicts facing the Thorn Collective were not unusual. Groups often question whether they can continue to meet or work together, and some even routinely struggle with this issue. At a time when American feminism was beginning to segment along lines of differences, we attributed the group's problems to the dissolving of our common ties.

After a brief summer recess, we resumed our meetings, but in August I left the group. The following passage about unity and differences among Thorn Collective members is excerpted from Kirsten's journal.

> Over a year ago . . . I remember thinking how incredible it was to
> find nine women so focused on the "commonness" between them. It

seemed to me that never before had nine people had so much in common. The same thought patterns, . . . wanting the same things, needing the same things. . . .

In a year's time changes occur in our everyday existence. One year ago, one of us was a mother, now there are two; all nine of us were students, now there will be only two; seven of us are now working women. . . . But these are only differences in our external existence. Are we not basically the same women today that we were then? How have we changed internally? What changed so much that we can no longer communicate our changes? Are we tired of being closed in by our "commonness," which at the time was our strength? . . .

If it is true that our focus has shifted from our commonness to our differences, then why can't we seem to deal with the differences? We seem to recognize them. It is true that we have made some effort toward recognizing them, but it is again fading away. . . .[13]

During the late 1970s, recognition of differences in the North American women's movement reached a threshold. From multiply marginalized locations, feminists of color began to analyze how liberal and radical feminists' essentialist constructions of the category "woman" had effaced their lives and experiences. Far from being inclusive, North American feminism had evolved as a white, middle-class movement. On the whole, white feminists have been slow to recognize our stakes in confronting the movement's racism.

In increasing numbers, feminists of color began writing about their multiple identities.[14] They recognized—as white women did not—that race, ethnicity, and gender are indissoluble and codeterminant. One source of oppression could not be reduced to another: they were oppressed because they were African Americans, Latinas, or Asians living in a racist society (also, in many cases, because they were lesbians, poor, disabled, and/or old) *and* because they were women. These early writings by feminists of color have come to be known as identity politics because they analyzed the politics of identity through lived experiences of multiple oppressions and resistances.

Feminists of color developed identity politics as a political strategy. But as the women's movement rapidly segmented into distinct subworlds, identity politics was appropriated by other marginalized groups.[15] During the past decade, Jewish lesbians, disabled women, older women, recovering alcoholics, incest survivors, and many others also have produced oppositional accounts of their multiple oppressions and resistances. Now we speak not of feminism but of feminism*s* in the plural.

In the mid-1980s, feminist analyses of differences took a global turn. Rather than dividing women from each other or rendering our lives unintelligible to one another, some feminists began to regard differences as a link among women everywhere.[16] *Global feminism* addresses the common needs, common oppressions, and common resistance strategies of women in postcolonial societies, indigenous cultures, and the industrialized world.

Ecofeminism enlarges the vision of global feminism by de-privileging the priority of human lives over other species. Echoing native and Buddhist teachings, ecofeminism refigures women as of—not apart from—"nature." Thus, destruction of the earth's rain forests and ozone layer, and of the tens of thousands of plant and animal species with whom we share our planet, is considered the annihilation of women's very selves.

As segmentation deepened during the early 1980s, lines were drawn between contesting feminist factions. It seemed to me that the women's movement had turned on itself. During those years I felt deep confusion and despair. My dreams of making a revolution faded away, along with the social movement in which I had come of age.

5

REINVENTING ETHNICITY (1978–84)

Ethnicity (as well as other similar dimensions of regional, gender, religious, class, and generational identity) is something reinvented and reinterpreted in every generation by each individual.

Michael M. J. Fischer, in *Anthropology as Cultural Critique*

In the autumn of 1978 I moved from Santa Cruz to San Francisco, a spectacular ninety-minute drive north on coastal Route 1. For nearly six years I lived in the Castro district of the city, in a sunny studio apartment nestled between elegant Victorian homes. I loved walking in my new neighborhood, up and down the foothills of Twin Peaks, to shop and do errands on Castro Street. Through the window over my desk, a southern exposure, I saw a breathtaking panorama of the city.

I was settling into my new apartment when Dan White murdered Supervisor Harvey Milk and Mayor George Moscone. I first heard the news at midday, on television monitors set up in a lobby at UC San Francisco. That night, alongside thousands of our grief-stricken neighbors, my friend Leigh and I marched across town in a candlelight procession.

Early in 1979 I began working as publications coordinator at the Western Gerontological Society. I stayed at that job for just over a year. Then, until I left California in 1984, I worked as a free-lance writer, editor, and research consultant.

This was a time of drifting. My life felt deeply fragmented and unmoored. I was waiting—but for what I did not know.

In the summer of 1980 Leigh Star and I wrote an essay about Fay Stender, a civil rights lawyer who became renowned when she defended Black Panther leader Huey P. Newton and Soledad Brother George Jackson.[1] Fay had committed suicide in May of 1980. Fourteen months earlier, a young Black man named Edward Glenn Brooks had forcibly entered her home and shot her six times at point-blank range. Brooks's attempt to kill Fay had left her paralyzed from the waist down and in severe chronic pain.[2]

Leigh and I had met Fay a few months before she was shot. News of her suicide left us with many unanswered questions about her life and the meanings of her death in our lives. Fay's death catalyzed extended conversations between Leigh and me about violence, assimilation and passing, marginality and our own mortality—conversations that continue to this day.

I am leafing through a manila folder thick with photocopies and yellowed pages of newsprint. Its green label, carefully pasted in the upper right-hand corner, reads: "Survived by Her Silence: For the Memory of Fay Abrahams Stender." Inside the folder are several drafts of Leigh's and my essay. The first draft is dated 10 July 1980, just over a decade ago.

Various obituaries from California newspapers are tucked into the file. Among them is "Requiem for a Radical," an incendiary article about Fay's role in the prison reform movement during the early 1970s. "Requiem" "created a storm of controversy in the progressive media community."[3] In the front of the folder are copies of the last photos of Fay and her lover, taken in Fay's Berkeley home. Fay looks frail but happy to be alive.

A thick wad of correspondence falls into my lap, including Fay's lover's notes to me, and letters back and forth between half a dozen prospective editors and publishers. Evelyn Beck planned to include "Survived by Her Silence" in *Nice Jewish Girls*, a collection of writings by Jewish lesbian-feminists, and we signed a contract with her and Persephone Press.[4] But at the eleventh hour, "Survived" was cut from the manuscript.

"Survived by Her Silence" was an experiment in collaborative autobiographical writing. As Leigh and I wrestled with the meanings of being Jewish and lesbian in our own lives, we tried to reconstruct what being Jewish and lesbian might have meant to Fay. Writing was a reflexive act: as we remembered Fay and reconstructed her life, her story became our stories.

"Survived" was rejected for publication four times. I grew worried. Right before my eyes, it seemed that the details of Fay's remarkable life were being erased. Only a handful of friends had known Fay had a woman lover in the years before she died. Would future biographers cover up or trivialize her lesbianism? As a safeguard against biographical revisionism (a vexing problem for lesbian and gay historians), publishing "Survived by Her Silence" seemed urgent.

I wanted Fay's life and death to be registered and remembered by the Jewish-feminist community. But, in the end, I couldn't interest an editor or publisher in our essay. I was indignant at this insult to Fay's memory. In January of 1982, feeling resigned about the politics of feminist publishing, I wrote to Evelyn Beck, "I don't feel that I will ever write for the feminist press again."[5]

More and more, I felt invisible and displaced among feminists. The movement was fragmenting in unexpectedly painful ways, and in response, I gradually withdrew from the women's community. Feminism had anchored my life for years and the losses I felt were excruciating. They cut as deeply as any death I've ever mourned, except this time the death felt as though it was my own.

In 1980 lesbian sadomasochism emerged as an issue in the Bay Area women's community. What did it mean for feminists to argue that pain, power, and powerlessness could be sources of erotic pleasure and sexual liberation? Leigh Star, Diana Russell, Darlene Pagano, and I were troubled by claims that valorized lesbian sadomasochism, and we decided to edit a book exploring the debate.[6]

We met together for many months, fleshing out the project and soliciting articles. Eventually, we accepted work from more than two dozen authors. During the summer and fall of 1981, I prepared the manuscript for publication.

The sadomasochism question fomented an all-consuming battle. However, this was not the first time feminist communities had divided along ideological lines. Recent debates about pornography, racism, and transsexualism had already polarized the movement. By now, it seemed as though paralyzing conflicts were practically routine.

The sadomasochism controversy revolved around dread, mistrust, and moral righteousness. Given the nature of the issues—the politics of desires—it was inevitable that deep emotions would be stirred up. I had hoped *Against Sadomasochism* would not exacerbate extant splits in the movement but, in fact, deeper segmentation followed publication of the book.

The lesbian sadomasochism debate deepened my despair about the state of feminism. It was clear to me then, as it is clear to me now, that binding and beating one's sexual partners and eroticized humiliation and degradation are unacceptable practices, whoever engages in them. In my heart, I believed that sadomasochism is harmful and I resented the substitution of ideology for discussions about feminist ethics.

Black lesbian poet and essayist Audre Lorde posed the question, "Who profits from lesbians beating each other?"[7] Indeed, the sadomasochism question distracted us from matters of survival at home and abroad—the Euromissiles, sexual violence, and American collaboration with apartheid in South Africa.

Publication of *Against Sadomasochism* in the summer of 1982 turned out to be a disappointment. After more than two years of working on the book, the debate had consumed my intellectual and political energies. I felt trapped. By the July release date, I felt the less was said about the issue, the better off we'd all be.

Still, a party was planned at A Woman's Place Bookstore in Oakland to celebrate publication of *Against Sadomasochism*. As it turned out, on the night of the event the bookstore collective was splitting up. We were caught in the middle of their strife, as one faction of the staff contested the other faction's right to keep the store open. I couldn't bring myself to enter yet another feminist battle zone. At the last minute, I decided to stay home.

Against Sadomasochism was reviewed in *The Nation*, *Village Voice*, *Gay Community News*, and *Off Our Backs*, among other publications. *Ms.* magazine listed the book as a best-seller in American women's bookstores, and in London it made the alternative best-seller list. Most reviews published by the left and gay presses were hostile. Either they trivialized the issue (one reviewer described the book as "ideological overkill") or they portrayed the book as advocating censorship and sexual repression. Overall, reviewers in feminist magazines and newspapers were sympathetic. A decade later, *Against Sadomasochism* is still in print and continues to sell, slowly but steadily.

Rosh Hashanah 5742/1981 was one of the first years I made a point of observing the High Holidays. I invited a few friends for supper and then we went to shul. This was when the Holocaust began tugging at me. I had read a lengthy article in *Atlantic*, "The Kingdom of Auschwitz,"[8] and after finishing the piece, I was unable to sleep for several days. Then I began reading *Eichmann in Jerusalem*, but I found the book so upsetting I had to put it down.[9]

My Jewish consciousness was changing. In the spring, Burton Bernstein's memoir, "Personal History," was serialized in *The New Yorker*.[10] I found his stories riveting. They brought me the same sense of fullness I had experienced as a child, when books alone were my lifeline.

Bernstein's portraits of his parents—immigrants from Eastern Europe struggling to accommodate to life in America—transported me to times and places far away from the assimilated Jewish communities where I had always lived. His childhood memories brought to life the smells, tastes, and sounds of *Yiddishkeit*.

In an unforgettable passage recalling a research trip to the YIVO Institute for Jewish Research in New York City, Bernstein discovered a death roster of twenty-seven relatives whom he had never known, the Bernsteins of the Ukrainian *shtetl* of Korets. They were murdered by the *Einsatzgruppen*, the roving death squads following behind the German troops that occupied Poland and Russia. Only then did he understand the meaning of the Holocaust and what his family was.

I continued reading Jewish books during the spring. Anne Roiphe's reflections on being an assimilated American Jew, *Generation Without Memory*,[11] moved me deeply, and I recognized pieces of myself in her story.

Then, on 6 June, Israel invaded southern Lebanon. Along with many American Jews, I was shocked by reports of Israeli massacres of civilians living in refugee camps and ongoing mistreatment of soldiers taken as prisoners. My friend Martha and I eagerly attended a lecture sponsored by the Anti-Defamation League that promised to set the record straight.

The ADL representative told us that the reports we had read weren't reliable because they were tainted by anti-Semitism. He assured us that Israel would never harm a civilian population in the name of self-defense or retaliation. He insisted that no human rights violations had occurred. Besides, wasn't it a just cause to defend Israel's borders at any price? Although I was ill informed about Middle East politics, this simplistic view of the war aroused my suspicions. We left frustrated and disappointed.

Yet I wanted to be reassured. I wanted to believe that Israel was beyond reproach, that protecting her borders could be justified by any means necessary. Like the ADL representative, I also equated any criticism of Israel with anti-Semitism.

The summer months were marked by ongoing debates about Israel's war in Lebanon. Several coalitions of Jewish feminists circulated statements criticizing both the reactionary "defense" policies of the Israeli government and leftists' anti-Semitic diatribes against Israel. These position papers affirmed Israel's right to exist alongside the Palestinians' right to a national homeland. I learned it was possible to oppose policies of the Israeli government while also affirming Israel's right to exist inside safe boundaries. In time, I came to support the Palestinians' claim to an independent state.

I attended the first Bay Area conference on Jewish feminism, hoping it would be a place I could feel at home. I even planned to lead workshops on Jewish identity twice during the weekend.

The mood of the conference was celebratory. Several hundred women—mostly Jews and lesbians, it seemed—were thrilled to be together, but I felt gloomy and isolated. I was ready to leave after the first hour.

As it turned out, my workshop never met. It was preempted by a panel on the Middle East, attended by most of the conference participants. I felt both disappointed and relieved to have an excuse to leave early. I decided not to return for the second day of the conference, canceled the workshop I was scheduled to lead on Sunday, and stayed home.

During the summer of 1982, I also attended the second annual San Francisco Jewish Film Festival. I loved watching films about Jews and Jewish communities all over the world late into the night. Since leaving San Francisco in 1984, I've planned many summer trips home to coincide with the festival.

The festival draws a devoted following from inside the Jewish community and from its unaffiliated margins as well. One reason for this immense popularity is expressed in the festival's subtitle, "Independent Filmmakers: Looking at Ourselves." Film is a reflexive medium[12] and for many Jews who attend the festival, seeing their (our) lives, histories, and cultures through a camera's lens is a reflexive ritual of sorts. Like other celebrations that mark the annual Jewish cycle, the film festival, falling between Shavuot ("Feast of Weeks") and Tisha b'Av ("Mourning of Destruction of the First and Second Temples"), has become a local tradition.

Later that fall, my friend Lili and I attended a lecture given by Simon Wiesenthal, a Holocaust survivor and world-renowned Nazi hunter. Wiesenthal's talk was entitled "Murderers among Us," though I hardly remember what it was about.

My memories of the evening are surrounded by a feeling of destiny, for torrential rains were flooding the city and driving was dangerous. Common sense dictated that we stay home. But this was my first opportunity to hear a Holocaust survivor speak and I insisted that we make the trip to San Rafael.

In 1982 I began calling myself Ruth and asked my friends and family to do the same. Ruth is the middle name I was given at birth. I was named Robin after my father, Edwin Robert, and Ruth for my father's cousin, who died as a young woman before I was born. I asked Ruth's sister, my cousin, Lola Curiel, about Ruth's death. She explained:

> Ruth became seriously diabetic when she was fourteen. She couldn't tolerate insulin and [the diabetes] had to be controlled with diet alone.

When Ruth was seventeen, she married an artist, Jack Silvay, and went to Paris. This was 1927–28, an extremely cold and icy winter. "La Flu" was rampant and the ice prevented fresh food from coming up from the South. Jack thought Ruth was not doing well so he took her South to St. Tropez (long before it became chic). However, it was too late because she died in a small Catholic hospital on March 14, 1928, one week before her eighteenth birthday.

Ruth was buried in a small churchyard. I lost my sister when I was twelve. My father, Harry Serwer, went there in 1931. He gave the church a substantial amount of money for perpetual care. My half-brother, Jimmy, went there after World War II and found nothing—all bombed to hell. These are just vital statistics and tell nothing about Ruth, except that she was precocious. She was also beautiful, loving, intelligent, poetic and very sweet.[13]

I can find no record of the exact date I changed my name to Ruth. Perhaps because I had always been Robin Ruth, this did not seem like a significant shift. On the contrary, taking Ruth as my first name seemed perfectly natural, as though it was *bashert* ("inevitable, predestined"). In traditional cultures, many life transitions are marked by taking a new name. Similarly, in the West rites of passage may be accompanied by namings: births, christenings, confirmations, marriages, divorces, and so on. By taking the name of Ruth, I signified to myself and others my desire to explore what it means to be a Jew and to live Jewishly.

At about this time I asked my sister, Tracey, about her relationship to Catholicism and she told me she had converted. With my new name—a Jewish name—I had chosen a path my sister rejected. Tracey's indifference to Judaism deepened my sense of urgency about being visible as a Jew.

No single factor accounts for my gradual turn toward Judaism and Jewish culture—not my sister's conversion to Catholicism, nor Israel's invasion of Lebanon, nor my grandmother Marion's death, nor the loss of feminists as my reference group. Yet each of these factors heightened my self-awareness as a Jew. Taken together, they radically "repositioned" my life.[14] But in 1982, I couldn't have imagined the changes that taking the name of Ruth would set in motion.

For Pesach 5743/1983 my friend Alice and I decided to host a seder together. Pesach, the Jewish festival of freedom, celebrates the Israelites' redemption from slavery in Egypt. We wanted our seder to be traditional, yet connected with contemporary struggles for liberation.

The Haggadah (ritual for the seder) is a mirror of our lives—a reflexive text. Its words are magical incantations with the power to telescope through time.[15] We modeled our Haggadah on a secular, Yiddish and English text written by the Erev Shabbos Discussion Group, of which Alice's parents are members. Alice's family's Haggadah didn't mention God or contain a word of Hebrew, and neither did ours.

We spent the day of the first seder preparing the Haggadah, cleaning house, and cooking. Traditionally, the seder is an elaborate meal, consisting of many courses. Cooking side-by-side is a kind of dance—intimate, exacting, and sometimes frustrating. It was touch and go when we ran out of walnuts in the middle of making *charoset*, just as our guests were arriving and neither one of us was dressed.

Close to twenty friends were coming for dinner. Alice had turned her art studio, an L-shaped room, into a dining room. Two carefully set tables filled the entire space.

Some of my friends were meeting for the first time. I was thrilled to be introducing them to each other. People arrived carrying huge bundles—side courses, extra folding chairs, and flowers. Martha brought her mother's silver. I worried that there might not be enough food, but it turned out we had more leftovers than our guests could carry home.

After dinner some of our guests hurried off; others lingered over coffee and dessert. I busied myself rinsing dishes and wrapping up leftovers. Every now and then, I left my post at the kitchen sink and poked my head inside the dining room.

At one point, I paused by the door. Standing quietly, still in my apron, I looked out into the room. A wine glass here, a spoon there, and scattered cups of cold tea and coffee waited to be cleared from the tables. Leigh and Julie were locked in animated conversation. Other friends sat together in small clusters. No one seemed to notice me noticing them.

A wave of fullness washed over me—the sense of peace that comes from being utterly present, with no memories of the past or concerns about the future. Tonight, I thought, bears witness to Alice's and my friendship and our friendships with each of our guests as we celebrate the miracle of the Exodus, the miracle of our lives. Then I understood what Jews have known for centuries: that our freedom is the greatest gift life has to offer. I recognized grace in that moment.

I ran into Lani Silver on a January evening in 1983, after a concert by the Bay Area Women's Philharmonic. Over the years, our paths had crossed repeatedly. At a party the previous summer, she had told me about her interviews with Holocaust survivors in Israel and a documentary she was producing for National Public Radio. Lani joined my friends and me for a late supper. When we parted, she promised to let me know when her programs would air.

In late March Lani telephoned to say that her series was nearly finished. But the interviews she had conducted in Jerusalem were only a beginning. In a few weeks, she planned to collect more life histories at the American Gathering of Jewish Holocaust Survivors in Washington, D.C. This time, she was organizing a team of interviewers to work with her.

By now, no subject was more compelling to me than the Holocaust. I wanted to know more about it and about Lani's projects. My consulting practice was in a lull, and I offered to help her finish the documentaries and prepare for the Washington conference. She agreed.

During the next few weeks, I solicited cash contributions and in-kind donations of audio cassettes and other needed supplies, made routine telephone calls, dubbed tapes, and performed simple engineering tasks. Shortly before Lani left for Washington, she invited me to come along as an interviewer. Right away, I knew this was an opportunity I could not pass by. Terrified and excited, I said yes and immediately began preparing for the trip.

When I boarded the plane for Dulles Airport, I worried about being an inexperienced interviewer. How would I know what to ask? What would happen if I asked the "wrong" questions? Could I unlock a Pandora's box of dangerous memories?

I now know that it is perfectly natural for interviewers to wonder whether their questions could have damaging consequences for interview subjects. But less often are interviewers concerned about protecting themselves. Yet I wondered whether I might be harmed by eliciting survivors' memories of the Holocaust—memories that might rouse my own unnamed terrors.

I could scarcely speak of these terrors. Paralyzing terrors stirred by reading *Eichmann in Jerusalem* and "The Kingdom of Auschwitz." Terrors that quickened late into the night. Terrors easier to bear than the nightmares I feared would come when I fell asleep. Why had I walked into these terrors with my eyes open? Why did I feel obliged to face them?

I arrived in Washington late on a Saturday afternoon. On Sunday Lani and I met at the convention center, but there wasn't much for us to do until the conference opened on Monday.

Later that evening I met Carol Bernson and Stephen Shames, photographers from New York. While Lani was interviewing Holocaust survivors in Jerusalem, they had been taking studio portraits. The three of them had formed a loose partnership to edit a book of life stories and photographs. Now we were a foursome. Since I was an experienced editor, I agreed to shepherd the book through to publication.

Beginning the next morning and continuing for four days, I interviewed more than two dozen survivors. This was, by far, the most intense experience of my life. Shuttling back and forth between Holocaust time and tape-recorded time distorted my sense of "real" (linear) time. I didn't have a spare moment in which to record interview notes. Consequently, my memories of this period, like my experiences at the conference itself, are tangled and compressed.

The next chapter, "Bearing Witness: Reflections on Interviewing Jewish Holocaust Survivors," represents Lani's and my joint effort to weave our memories of the conference into a story with a beginning, middle, and end. But no one account can render the emergent, open-ended character of lived experiences. As Barbara Myerhoff and Deena Metzger observed: "All single reflections are distortions. True reflections can only come from many images, a selection offered among which one chooses, discards, makes corrections."[16]

Indeed, the next part of the book may be read as a series of inscriptions of the conference. Each chapter experiments with different narrative strategies for making memory fragments into stories. By positioning — then repositioning — Holocaust survivors and myself, meanings of past events are reconstructed and reinterpreted. As the past is refigured, so the present is made. This is how selves make stories and stories, in turn, make new selves.

CODA

When Lani and I returned to San Francisco, we founded the Holocaust Media Project. The project's aims were to produce another set of radio documentaries, a book of portraits and interviews, and a series of portraits and text panels for national exhibition. We also planned to continue collecting oral histories.

I began writing funding proposals, and in June 1983 we were awarded a small planning grant from the California Council for the Humanities. Frances Goldin, a literary agent in New York City, agreed to help us find a publisher, and Lani and I began editing interviews. Now and then, we gave lectures and media interviews about our work, and met with leaders of the Jewish community to discuss the project's fiscal needs.

Codirecting the project was a challenge. Funding was scarce and the future didn't look encouraging. By the fall of 1983, I realized my administrative commitment to the project could only be short-term.

As it turned out, I worked on the book sporadically for five years. By 1988 many publishers had rejected our proposals and our literary agent had left the project. I had come to view the documentary as a problematic genre for representing the Holocaust and I withdrew as a coeditor of the book.

Each year since college I had deliberated about going to graduate school. But this year was different. I had changed. I had dozens of questions about the interviews we were collecting but neither the time nor analytic skills to explore them. What impelled so many survivors to tell their life stories? Why did other survivors remain silent about their experiences during the war? The sheer quantity of our interviews was overwhelming. I had no idea where to begin.

In August of 1984 I resigned from the Holocaust Media Project. This was a painful parting, but I was excited to be returning to school with a clear purpose and plenty of data in hand.

To a native Californian, New England has an exotic lure. During the years I lived in Cambridge, Massachusetts, where most of this book was written, I felt like an ethnographer working in another culture. Often, it seemed like I was living in a world of strangers—people with whom I had no shared histories.

Moving across the country allowed me to defamiliarize myself. And becoming a stranger to myself laid the foundation for the experimental approach to life stories developed in this book.

II

TOWARD A SOCIOLOGY
OF THE HOLOCAUST

I have never been able to do research and think in a way other than, if I may so put it, in a theological sense — namely, in accordance with the Talmudic teaching of the forty-nine levels of meaning in every passage in the Torah.

Walter Benjamin, *Briefe 2*

6

BEARING WITNESS
Reflections on Interviewing
Jewish Holocaust Survivors
(with Lani Silver)

Lani

I was living in Jerusalem in the spring of 1981, interviewing Israeli scholars and political activists for my doctoral research. When I learned that the World Gathering of Jewish Holocaust Survivors would be held later that summer in Jerusalem—the first gathering of Holocaust survivors since the war—I decided to extend my stay abroad to interview survivors and their families and to document the conference.

I planned to produce a documentary series for public radio. The series, "Children of the Holocaust," aired during the spring of 1983 on stations across the country. The experience of interviewing Holocaust survivors and the two intervening years since then, when I lived with the survivors' stories and produced "Children of the Holocaust," have presented the greatest personal and professional challenge I have ever known.

June 1981, Jerusalem As I prepared to attend the World Gathering of Jewish Holocaust Survivors, I experienced a sense of trepidation: Who am I to be recording accounts of the most unspeakable *and* unspoken atrocities of human history? Would I not bring more pain to the people I interviewed by asking them to dredge up their memories of concentration camps and hidings? Would they be racked with pain? Would they even be able to speak at all?

When I arrived at the Gathering, which was attended by five thousand survivors and their families, I was reassured to find that most of the conference participants—survivors and their children—wanted to talk with me and other members of the press about the Holocaust. Many survivors described the slow anguish that had brewed during the thirty-five years since liberation when no one cared to listen to or wanted to know their stories. But here in Jerusalem three hundred press people were prepared to bear witness.

I interviewed survivors from 8:30 A.M. until 11 P.M. I rarely left my post—two folding chairs in a quiet corner—for six days. There was no time for me to assimilate the stories I heard. The opportunity to reflect emotionally and intellectually on this experience had to await my return to the States.

The Gathering was no place for sentimentalists or people with weak stomachs. My first interview was with a man who described seeing his baby thrown into the air by an SS officer, then caught on the blade of a bayonet and shot to death. The second woman I talked with had lived with three relatives in an underground "grave" for three years. My third interview was with a woman who was immediately separated from her mother upon arriving at Auschwitz. Her mother's fate was a common one: the infamous Dr. Mengele selected her for the gas chambers.

I interviewed one of the four women who smuggled the explosives into Auschwitz/Birkenau that were used to blow up Crematorium Three. There was Leesha Rose, a nurse and Dutch Resistance fighter, who escaped deportation three times and saved the lives of hundreds of Jews in hiding. And William Lowenberg, who carried away dead bodies from the devastated ruins of the Warsaw Ghetto. A man who looked exactly like my grandfather, known during the War as "Comrade Z," described the years he fought with the partisans. During fifty interviews, I was immersed in the most remarkable stories of courage. At the same time, I felt anguish beyond words.

The survivors cried and so did I. Yet the pain relived in revisiting the past was balanced by indomitable strength, laughter, and warmth. The survivors' fighting spirits and tenderness have a tangible quality. Bearing witness to their lives will profoundly change your hold on the present.

Virtually none of the survivors had parents. Indeed, most had watched their grandparents, mothers, and fathers being marched to the gas chambers. This means that the second generation, the children of survivors, has almost no extended family—no grandparents, and few uncles, aunts, and cousins. One-third of an entire culture was annihilated.

On the first day of the Gathering I took a late afternoon break. By chance, I met Stephen Shames, an American photographer who was taking portraits of survivors and their families. He introduced me to his three partners: Carol Bernson, Jerry Bergman, and Peter Tatiner. They

Lani Silver. Photo by Ron Greene.

were New Yorkers—charming and warm—and we all felt an immediate sense of *mishpokheh* ("family"). Before long, we had a simultaneous brainstorm: I would interview the survivors they photographed, and together we would produce a book of matching portraits and interviews. The photo-essay we envisioned seemed like the perfect complement to the radio series I had in mind.

July 1981, San Francisco   My plane landed at 8:00 A.M. on a Friday. By noon I had queried five magazines about doing a story on the World Gathering. I got a mildly encouraging response and set to work writing. The two magazines that had expressed interest subsequently decided against using my article. No kill fee. I was back where I had started, and the World Gathering, like the Holocaust itself, was fast becoming old news.

This marked the beginning of a long downward spiral. You may recognize your own experience in my story. It is a familiar one to every free-lance journalist and radio producer. Not one magazine, national or local, wanted a story on the World Gathering. I sent out one hundred queries, and by the end of summer I had received one hundred rejection letters. During the fall I wrote five grant proposals to produce a radio series and contacted three literary agents and four publishers. At best, I was greeted with cordial uninterest.

But I believed my seven years of experience as an independent public radio producer would stand me in good stead when I contacted the two major public radio networks that had syndicated my programs in the past. So you can imagine my surprise when one programming executive told me that he was "sick to death of the Holocaust." The other network spokesperson was not interested in Holocaust programming because, as he put it, "There has been too much on Lebanon lately." Thankfully, I had the presence of mind to ask what the invasion of Lebanon had to do with the Holocaust. But my disappointment and rage deafened me and I'll never know what, if anything, he replied.

I have felt deeply discouraged at times. But I never gave up. What saddened me most was the repetition of indifference toward the Holocaust and Holocaust survivors.

March 1983   I continued to work on the three-part documentary series, "Children of the Holocaust," and a program on the World Gathering. The Jerusalem tape won an award from a local press club, and the National Federation of Community Broadcasters featured it in its monthly catalog. The publisher W. H. Freeman seriously considered taking on the book and provided funding for film processing and tape transcription. But by the summer of 1982, the economy had so damaged the book market that Freeman was forced to withdraw interest in the project.

With no luck at National Public Radio or the Canadian Broadcasting Corporation, we independently released the four programs via the satellite during early April, to coincide with *Yom ha-Shoah*—the day of Holocaust remembrance. In the meantime, I was preparing to attend the American Gathering of Jewish Holocaust Survivors in Washington, D.C., to conduct more interviews. Carol Bernson and Stephen Shames, two of the photographers I had met in Jerusalem, were going to set up a photography studio again, and we arranged to work together.

There were dozens of details to attend to and either project—putting the tapes up on the satellite or preparing to interview at the American Gathering—was more than one person realistically could handle. But I had a lot of support, and a few miracles even occurred. Konnilyn Feig, historian, author of *Hitler's Death Camps* and a board member of the San Francisco Holocaust Library and Research Center, facilitated a grant from the Holocaust Library for satellite fees and partial airfare to Washington, D.C. Lynn Chadwick, managing director of Western Public Radio, dear friend and engineer par excellence, was an ideal technical consultant.

I organized a "cassette-a-thon" to solicit donations of audio tape for recording interviews at the American Gathering. My plan was simple: I mailed a flyer to fifty friends and contacted ten local radio stations and several neighborhood merchants. The response I received was well beyond my expectations—one thousand cassette tapes were donated.

Ruth Linden, an acquaintance, was among those who responded to the cassette-a-thon. She offered to help me finish "Children of the Holocaust" and prepare for the American Gathering in any way she could. Several weeks before I left for the conference we began working together. She assisted with every imaginable detail, from composing the legal release and reconstructing narration for one of the programs when a production assistant disappeared with the only copy of the script, to delivering posters and dubbing tapes. I asked her to come with me to Washington, D.C., and she accepted.

Ten thousand survivors were expected to attend the American Gathering and I wanted to put together a team of interviewers. Five, ten, or twenty people could cover more ground more intensively than Ruth and I could manage together. Based on suggestions from Nan Rubin and Jim Gleeson of the National Federation of Community Broadcasters, and staff at Washington, D.C., Pacifica station WPFW, I drew up a list of twenty-five public radio reporters in the D.C. area who might be interested in interviewing survivors. I telephoned each of them, and twenty-three agreed to work with us at the conference. Their enthusiasm and generous spirit were stunning. But this was only the beginning.

April 1983, Washington, D.C. Several days before the conference opened, twenty interviewers met as a group. We discussed having mixed emotions about documenting the survivors' lives—feeling a deep sense of responsibility and, simultaneously, a nameless apprehension. I distributed a list of interview guidelines and suggested questions they might ask.

At any given moment, seven or eight interviews were being conducted. We used Carol and Steve's photography studio as a reception area and interviewed survivors for five days, from early morning until late at night. Each interviewer signed up in advance to work shifts that fit their schedule. Some people took a few days off from their jobs and others joined us after work. Two survivors, Gloria Lyon and Harry Frankell, conducted interviews themselves. We recorded more than 230 interviews, many of which are more than an hour long.

The group worked together beautifully. Everyone took responsibility for the equipment, logging and labeling the tapes, obtaining consent and completing release forms, and coordinating with the photographers. Sometimes we were shorthanded, and a crowd of impatient survivors would descend on us, wanting to be photographed and interviewed on the spot. But crises were always averted. The interviewers calmed frazzled nerves and explained the situation, no matter that they were tired themselves and hadn't had a break in hours. They acted toward the survivors and each other with deep warmth, kindness, and gentleness. This spirit of cooperation and respect among strangers was one of the peak experiences of my life.

Following the conference, a group of interviewers met to share our experiences. Everyone described being deeply affected by the survivors they interviewed and the spirit of the conference. Bearing witness to the survivors' stories forged our commitment never to forget the horror of the Final Solution and the six million who were murdered before they could tell the world the terrible truth.

Upon our return to San Francisco, Ruth and I founded the Holocaust Media Project for the purpose of producing a ten-part radio documentary series on the Holocaust, and a museum exhibit and book based on interviews and matching portraits of survivors. In June 1983 we received our first grant award, from the Joint Fund of the California Humanities Council and the California Public Broadcasting Commission (CPBC), to plan two radio documentaries. Several weeks later, the governor of California, George Deukmejian, cut the CPBC from the state budget. With this move, California's independent radio producers lost a vital source of support.

August 1990 In 1984 the name of the project was changed to the Holocaust Oral History Project. Our primary task became interviewing Bay Area survivors. More than five hundred volunteers have worked with us during the past six years. Three hundred in-depth interviews have been completed, 170 of which have been videotaped. The project also produces a television series for Bay Area cable stations.

Funding the activities of the Holocaust Oral History Project is a serious challenge in the current political climate of retrenchment. But in spite of many constraints, our commitment to interviewing survivors and producing high-quality programming on the impact of Nazism, the Holocaust, and the politics of genocide remains undaunted.

POSTSCRIPT TO THE AMERICAN GATHERING

Ruth

April 1983, San Francisco My ears still ring with thick Polish-Jewish, Czech, and French accents. My heart is heavy with stories of ghettos; transports; arrivals at Auschwitz (the first things one saw and smelled were great billows of black smoke and the stench of burned human flesh) and dozens of other concentration, labor, and extermination camps; hidings in forests; and miraculous escapes from death sentences. I feel the deepest grief I have ever known — pain I cannot comprehend because, in the final analysis, there is no sense to grasp hold of. But my heart also resonates with love, respect, and *nakhes* ("pride") for the survivors who have taught me, over the course of a few days, how a people resisted being dehumanized and degraded in the midst of overwhelming adversity.

I began each interview with the same questions: "Would you tell me your name? Where were you born? In what year? What happened when the Germans entered your town?" I realize now that as I asked these questions, I made a mental comparison between every survivor's birth date and my parents' years of birth. I remember blurting into the microphone during an early interview with a woman born in 1919, "That's the year my father was born." When I interviewed Helena (born in 1930) and her daughter, Sandra (a woman in her early twenties), I thought: "She could be my mother. I could be her daughter." It was unthinkable for me to maintain a "safe" emotional distance during the interviews. I didn't need to guard my vulnerability. I didn't want to.

The interviews were emotional for everyone: the survivors and interviewers, as well as the family members and friends who occasionally joined us. Often, I wept along with the people telling me their stories, clasping their hands in my one free hand, while holding the microphone

Ruth Linden. Photo by Jon Chase.

steady in the other. As I listened to memories of the liberation of Dachau and Bergen-Belsen, I wept joyous tears. And I wept when the survivors I interviewed recalled searching for traces of their families after the war. One woman told me she wandered through the cities of Eastern Europe for six months before she found her sister. They had been separated three years earlier. Sometimes my tears signified the sheer weight of the moment, but mostly they expressed my deep sadness.

I was astonished to realize how easily these people could have been my parents or grandparents; aunts, uncles, or cousins. It is only an accident of history that my great-grandparents and grandparents left Europe several decades before Hitler came to power. One day during the Gathering, I realized that some of my distant relatives, whose names I will never know, must have died in the ghettos, camps, and gas chambers. This was the first time I registered my direct, personal link to the Holocaust.

The Jewish spirit persisted amid unspeakable acts of sadism, whose full meanings we are protected from grasping because we were not there. Acts of kindness and courage—and risks most of us cannot imagine taking ourselves—were commonplace among Jews in the ghettos and the camps. When I would ask a survivor, "How did you find the courage to run, to escape, to beg for mercy?" a frequent response was, "What did I have to lose?" There was even humor. Marilyn Reis, one of the interviewers on our team, told us about a survivor who recounted this story to her: "So I got off the transport at Auschwitz and I looked all around me. I said to myself, 'This place is not for me!' Then, I escaped."

As important as bearing witness with compassion during an hour or two of reliving and retelling (and for some, telling for the first time) was letting each survivor know that her or his story would not be forgotten. Nearly every survivor I spoke with expressed the wish that her story, and the stories of those who were murdered, be remembered. They prayed for human beings to use their intelligence and sense of justice to prevent the repetition of history. This is both a burden and a privilege of being a Jew and living Jewishly that I accept, gratefully.

Documenting the legacy of the Holocaust plunged us into history, our histories as Jews. We can no longer view the Holocaust as a single event merely to be retold or recorded for future generations. Instead, we experience every moment that has come before and each one that will follow through live, fluid connections: the richness of language, sensibilities of the heart, and spirit of resistance. Our ongoing commitments to social change and our vision of a just world have been transformed by survivors' lives and the stories to which we have borne witness.

REFLECTIONS ON "BEARING WITNESS"

The anthropologist is a witness, must bear witness, when no one else is available.
Barbara Myerhoff, in *Between Two Worlds*

Each of us has experienced moments in our lives when we know we are in the right place, doing just what needs to be done. Thoughts of ambivalence, uncertainties, the "what ifs" that can be paralyzing, fall away. We inhabit ourselves fully, rising to the occasion at hand. Some people believe such moments are filled with grace.

This is how I felt at Pesach 5743/1983, during the seder Alice and I prepared together; and in June 1984, when we demonstrated against nuclear weapons production at Lawrence Livermore Laboratories. These feelings return to me when I teach about the Holocaust. As I recount survivors' stories from the podium, I often notice how listeners' eyes convey what their words cannot. Their need to hear about the Holocaust runs as deep as my need to speak about it, and thus the chain of bearing witness continues.

In the summer of 1983 Lani Silver and I wrote "Bearing Witness: Reflections on Interviewing Jewish Holocaust Survivors." In April of that year, the radio documentary Lani had produced, "Children of the Holocaust," aired on National Public Radio. It was well received, and *Soundwaves*, a trade magazine for independent radio producers, asked us to write an article about interviewing survivors.

Lani and I drafted two separate accounts, which we juxtaposed in a single article.[1] She asked me to help polish her piece and I ended up rewriting it line-by-line. Feeling uneasy, I returned the new version to Lani for her corrections and approval. Although she accepted all of my changes, I worried that perhaps I had silenced her voice, like Gertrude Stein writing Alice B. Toklas's autobiography.[2] To whom did the "I" belong? Whose story was I referring to when I changed a sentence to read, "You may recognize your own experience in *my* story"?

In retrospect, I think it is presumptuous for one person to assume she can speak for another, as I spoke for Lani in "Bearing Witness." Admittedly, editors, ghost writers, and social scientists do speak for others as a matter of course. I rationalized my rewriting of Lani's piece on account of our imminent deadline and the exigencies of publishing.

In Lani's and my definition of our collaboration, all of our work was shared. Indeed, for a period of nearly a year, we worked together so closely that I often felt I actually could speak for her. These blurred boundaries are inscribed in the article we submitted to *Soundwaves* for publication. (Soon after we received page proofs of the article, we were notified that *Soundwaves* had folded. "Bearing Witness" is published here for the first time.)

Interviewing survivors had changed my life, radically repositioning me as a Jew and a social scientist. I can think of no single experience up to this point in my life that registered such a decisive impact on my identity. "Bearing Witness" records this grace-filled moment, a phase in my work spanning about twenty months. This period began when I conducted my first interviews with survivors in April 1983. It continued during my collaboration with Lani on the Holocaust Media Project. It ended when I began analyzing interview data in January 1985 in preparation for writing "The Phenomenology of Surviving."

As I reread "Bearing Witness" and reflect on the interviews themselves, I recall the ease with which I talked with survivors, especially women. Women significantly outnumbered men in the sample of interviews I conducted myself (n = 31). Seventy-four percent (n = 23) of my respondents were women and 26 percent (n = 8) were men. I interviewed five of the eight men in my sample along with their wives. In three cases, both wives and children were present.

The primary respondent(s) in these interviews varied from family to family. Sometimes both survivor-partners were interviewed, while in other family interviews I recorded the stories of only one spouse. These differences depended on each family's preferences and the amount of time they wanted to spend talking with me.

Under our auspices more than two hundred survivors were interviewed in Washington, D.C. By entrusting Lani and me with their stories, these people had authorized us to represent them.[3] Representing "others" is what many social scientists and journalists endeavor to do. At the time, however, I did not define this project as social science research. Nor did I identify myself as a journalist. I do not remember in what role, if any, I believed I was acting.

"Giving voice" to survivors was a main objective of the Holocaust Media Project. Yet, for the first few years of this study, I did not recognize the problems inherent in constructing representations. I didn't understand that "representations are social facts"[4] with epistemological and political consequences. Rather, I assumed that representing survivors and retelling their stories was a straightforward project.

In America and abroad, hundreds of survivors have taken on the challenge of representing themselves by publishing memoirs and speaking out in public. Consider, for example, my friend Gloria Lyon in San Francisco. She devotes herself full-time to lecturing, giving interviews, and performing community service on survivors' behalf. In a given week, Gloria's calendar may include speaking to groups of students at two or three different public schools; addressing a church on Sunday morning; and attending a board of directors meeting at the local Holocaust library or planning special events, such as the annual Yom ha-Shoah commemoration. She is also producing a film about her work as a survivor-activist.

Gloria is an extraordinary woman and, like many other survivors, she is indeed capable of representing herself. Yet few survivors can tolerate being in the public eye, as she does, with genuine dignity and grace. And few people of any age or background have her seemingly boundless reserves of stamina, magnetism, and poise.

In fact, only a small fraction of survivors have written books about the Holocaust. (Even fewer survivors have made videos or films.) For every account that has been published, there are dozens of remarkable yet untold stories. Over the past decade, publishing (and film) markets for survivor memoirs have expanded. This trend is connected to a wider interest in the Holocaust, generally, by scholars and the book-buying public. Yet according to some acquisitions editors and publishers, by the mid-1980s the market was glutted. "Enough is enough. We already have a Holocaust book on this year's list," is a sentiment I have sometimes heard.

To a significant degree, book sales are determined by mass-market promotional tactics; readers' tastes and interests only indirectly influence demand. If there is a glut of Holocaust books, then this reflects the strategies and budgets of advertising campaigns and other cultural processes shaping literary consumption patterns. We might ask *why* the market is saturated. How and by whom is a "glutted market" constructed?

The challenges of self-representation facing Holocaust survivors are complex and multifaceted: personal, political, economic, and historical. The Holocaust Media Project and other community-based projects were founded precisely because of the formidable obstacles to self-representation. But what are the consequences for Holocaust survivors of being represented by oral historians, social scientists, and journalists—in short, people like Lani and me, and projects like the Holocaust Media Project/Holocaust Oral History Project? To what extent do survivors depend on a remembrance "industry" to represent them to the media and the American public? Are we enhancing survivors' well-being (according to their own subjective appraisals) by providing a "service" to them and their communities?

Over the years, I have answered these questions in different ways. During the phase of my research that "Bearing Witness" represents, I unquestioningly accepted the view that the survivors we interviewed want the attention of researchers, the media, and the public. They want their stories to circulate—to be told, retold, and remembered. Many survivors have responded enthusiastically to our project precisely because it has given them an opportunity to tell their stories to people outside of survivor communities.

But what will be the long-term impact of the remembrance "industry" on survivors as a community? How has it constructed and reconstructed the Nazi era? How does it reckon with the persistence of genocide in our own time? By remembrance "industry," I am referring to dozens of grass-roots oral history projects, mostly funded on shoestring budgets (including the Holocaust Oral History Project); community Holocaust libraries and memorials; as well as more generously endowed national projects, such as the Simon Wiesenthal Center in Los Angeles (heavily supported by the Hollywood film industry) and the Yale Video Archives.

My use of the term *remembrance industry* may shock or offend some readers. Indeed, it is a bleak commentary on our society that survivors' memories have become commodities. I have coined the term *remembrance industry* because it highlights the inherently politico-economic nature of the work of remembering, documenting, and commemorating.[5]

Nowhere is the politics of memories played out more intensely than in communities making plans to construct Holocaust memorials. In San Francisco, Boston, and the Washington, D.C./Baltimore area, bitter controversies have erupted over how to remember the Holocaust.[6] In the late 1980s, a group of Capitol-area survivors were distressed about plans to build a United States Holocaust Memorial on the Mall. Their foremost concern was that various parts of the museum might be named in honor of donors who are not themselves Holocaust survivors.

In Boston, a monument to be placed in the immediate area of City Hall Plaza was the focus of local dissent. In 1987, an ad hoc group called

Freedom Memorial Inc. initiated this project. Its aim was "to erect a permanent memorial to the GIs who liberated those in the Nazi camps. Also to be memorialized are the resistance fighters, the Holocaust survivors, and millions who did not survive."[7]

Freedom Memorial Inc. proposed building a monument in Boston inspired by "Liberation," a statue that stands in Liberty Park, New Jersey. "Liberation" depicts an American GI holding an emaciated survivor in his arms. Steven Ross, the survivor spearheading construction of the Boston memorial, explained that "this would send a message to Holocaust revisionists that they have to deal with the American army."[8]

Many Boston-area concentration-camp survivors contested this design. They believed it would give the false impression that the United States entered the war in order to save European Jewry. According to Regine Barshak, chair of the Brookline Holocaust Memorial Committee, "It is the *juxtaposition* of the projected statue of a GI (carrying a victim of [a] Nazi death camp), *together* with a projected museum of the Holocaust, which is the object of concern, grief and . . . [painful] interpersonal conflicts in the small community of Holocaust survivors in Greater Boston."[9]

Some survivors hold the view expressed by Joan Bond Sax. In a letter to the president of Freedom Memorial Inc., she expressed her opposition to borrowing the concept of the "Liberation" statue for the Boston Holocaust memorial: "To imply that [saving Jews] . . . was part of a concerted effort [by the American military] is to admit to dismal failure. The majority of European Jews were liberated by death."[10]

Debate over the proposed monument prompted Freedom Memorial Inc. to institute several changes. First, design of the statue will be decided by juried competition. Second, the group has renamed itself the New England Holocaust Memorial Committee. Accordingly, the memorial's focus has shifted to Jewish Holocaust victims. Third, the group has expanded its membership to include Holocaust survivors, educators, and scholars.

Still, local survivors remain wary of "issues of accountability and community involvement."[11] They wonder whether these changes reflect an actual shift in the aims of the project, and they continue to be concerned that the monument could distort historical facts, along with the memory of the six million Jews murdered by Hitler.

According to Dennis B. Klein, director of the International Center for Holocaust Studies of the Anti-Defamation League of B'nai B'rith, Holocaust memorials "often serve as evasions of the real issues." They tend to "distort or erase the past under the guise of memorializing it, [because] any reconstruction of the past mediates if not erases history."[12]

Indeed, both interviews and memorials construct and reconstruct the past. Authority to fashion such reconstructions through interviews, "to ask, respond, present and edit a life,"[13] is becoming professionalized by a small cadre of "experts." The emergence of experts, in turn, has consequences for the stories that survivors tell.

Professionalization of the work of documenting the Holocaust poses many questions for life historians. How is control of interviews negotiated between interviewers and respondents? What count as appropriate and interesting topics of discussion, and who decides? What happens when respondents "use" and "manipulate" interviewers, as we are accustomed to "using" and "manipulating" our respondents? How shall we respond when survivors challenge our authority, insisting that we conform to *their* scripts instead of the reverse? Although I have no clear-cut answers to these questions, I do have a story to tell you about the interview that provoked them.

It was a hot Saturday afternoon in May of 1984. The telephone rang and Gloria Lyon was on the other end of the line. "Are you busy today?" she asked. "There's someone I'd like you to interview." Helen Chalef was visiting San Francisco for the weekend and Gloria wanted to record her life story. I agreed to help.

Some months earlier, Helen's daughter, Susan, had come to San Francisco on business. She stayed at the bed-and-breakfast inn Gloria keeps on the first floor of her home. The two women got to talking, and soon they realized that Gloria and Susan's mother were from the same area near the Carpathian Mountains in eastern Czechoslovakia. Gloria wanted to meet Helen, a *Landsmännin* ("compatriot"), so Susan arranged for her mother's visit over Mother's Day weekend.

Indeed, Gloria and Helen discovered they had a great deal in common. They were nearly the same age, and in the spring of 1944 both women had been deported to Auschwitz from the ghetto in Beregszasz. It was as if their visit was a reunion between long-lost sisters.

Soon after we hung up the telephone, Gloria's husband, Karl, picked me up and we drove the short distance to their home. When I walked into Gloria's living room, a small throng of people was milling around. Gloria immediately introduced me to Helen and Helen's daughter, Susan. Jameson Goldner, who was directing a documentary about Gloria, had stopped by with a film crew. They planned to shoot some footage of Helen and Gloria that afternoon. One of the Lyon grandchildren was also visiting. She played happily by herself amid the grown-ups and the film equipment.

People came and left all afternoon, shuffling around cameras, mikes, lights, and cables. I felt as though I were a prop in a scene Gloria had staged. Although I had gladly agreed to play the role she assigned to me, the situation soon began to make me uncomfortable.

I was surprised to discover how actively Gloria intended to participate in the interview. For instance, she acted as a translator when Helen couldn't explain certain Hungarian words in English:

HELEN: And my next memory—I—forget an awful lot of things. I remember my father was drafted just before. And my mother ran a *korcsma*. It's more than an inn, but—

GLORIA: It's a liquor store, like a liquor—it's an inn. Like an inn is what it is.

HELEN: It's an inn, a small inn—

GLORIA: People stop by to have a drink.

HELEN: And have some, you know, like pretzels and *kifli*—crescents with butter and cheese and, you know, that type of—coffee. (Chalef transcript, p. 4)

At other times, Gloria directly addressed questions to Helen:

HELEN [*describing her siblings*]: There were—I had a brother and then the baby was born. So there were three of us [*inaudible*]. My brother was five years younger than me.

RUTH: What's his name?

HELEN: Sandor, Shmuel.

RUTH: And the baby [*inaudible*]?

HELEN: The baby was three weeks old. She died when she was five weeks old [*inaudible*]. My mother became ill and I was taking care of her, and I think I forgot she was in the [*inaudible*], and I waited a little too

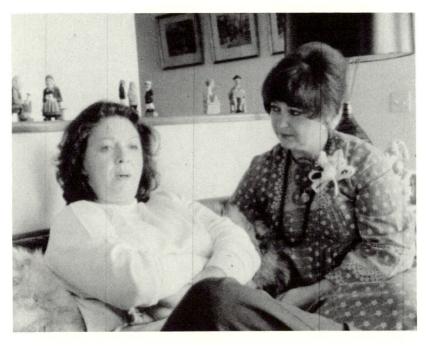

Helen Chalef (left) and Gloria Lyon, San Francisco, 1984. Photo courtesy of the Gloria Hollander Lyon film project, Jameson Goldner, cinematographer.

long. The baby was a little too long in the water; she got pneumonia and died.

GLORIA: I'm sure not—

HELEN: [*inaudible*] That's one baby I wanted desperately not to [*inaudible*]. And when my daughter was born, she looked exactly like my sister, and I always had the feeling that she was my reward, she was my sister coming back.

GLORIA: So tell us about your—the threat of being taken away and how you ended up and where you ended up just before the Holocaust. . . . This is very important. . . . What happened? (Chalef transcript, pp. 10–11)

Helen would turn to Gloria to verify her memories, asking, "You remember that?" At one point, the two women compared their recollections of the same event:

HELEN: And I remember that in front of the troop marching in, the soldiers, there were leather-jacketed men, not uniformed, but in leather jackets and tall leather boots. [*To Gloria*] You remember that?

GLORIA: Well, you go ahead. It was a little different in our area. You lived in a border area, so—

HELEN: No, this was in Beregszasz.

GLORIA: In Beregszasz?

HELEN: This was right in Beregszasz. They had come off the station. We lived by the small—a railroad station, and they had come off the train—

RUTH: Um-hum.

HELEN: [*continuing*] —and were walking through the town, so we were really the first recipients of this wonder. . . . (Chalef transcript, pp. 2–3)

Sometimes Gloria clarified or explicated Helen's memories:

HELEN: But we had people who started coming in and they would come late at night and I remember we were put to sleep, and they expected the children to sleep so soundly that they hear nothing. And I remember stories being told of massacres and drownings. . . .

GLORIA: What, in fact, Helen is talking about is equal to the men who went from town to town, having crossed the Carpathian Mountains [the Polish border], to warn the Jewish population of the towns about what's happening in Poland and elsewhere.

Helen is now describing how she heard about the atrocities of the Jews in neighboring countries, and since she lived right by the—at this point, in Hungary but just on this side of the border from Poland—and how she heard about it as a young girl of twelve. (Chalef transcript, pp. 6–7)

Jim Goldner was growing impatient from behind the camera, and so was I. We wanted Helen to continue telling her story without being interrupted. Jim jumped in first to try to get her back on track. As I listen to the interview on tape, I sound exasperated with the situation:

JIM: Could we start with [*inaudible*] telling the story?

RUTH: Yeah, I would like you just to continue, and you'll be able to pick it up. But I don't want you to keep repeating what you've already said.

GLORIA: She can—

RUTH: Just pick up where you left off. (Chalef transcript, p. 7)

Helen and Gloria had sat up together into the early morning hours, sharing their memories of Beregszasz and the camps. Helen had told Gloria a story about passing as a gentile at a school from which Jews had been barred. Now Gloria wanted her to recount the incident for the camera. She was searching for a probe that would jog Helen's memories from the night before.

By this time, however, I was at my wits' end from struggling with Gloria for control of the interview and I asked her to let Helen tell her own story. Unfortunately, the subtleties of our exchange disappear in the transcript; you also need to hear the inflections in our voices. The story picks up when Gloria changes the subject to ask Helen a question about the "passing" incident.

GLORIA: So tell us about your—the threat of being taken away and how you ended up and where you ended up just before the Holocaust. . . . This is very important. What happened? [*inaudible*]

HELEN: With the schools or—

GLORIA: Where were you—were you— [*inaudible*].

RUTH: Gloria, you're asking very—

GLORIA: I shouldn't—

RUTH: It's very—

GLORIA: I'll tell you why.

HELEN: The difference [between] what happened to me and others . . . [was that] I spoke Hungarian and Jewish and Czech. [*She continues to tell the story for which Gloria had been probing.*] (Chalef transcript, pp. 10–11)

I was caught off guard when Gloria began asking questions because I hadn't realized that she intended for both of us to interview Helen. With a little planning, the taping could have proceeded smoothly, but we had never discussed how we would work together, or even *that* we would work together.

I understood gradually that I was being manipulated. Indeed, Gloria had asked me to come over simply because my presence, apart from anything I actually said or did, sanctioned a "legitimate" interview. Gloria's and my struggle over who was playing which role—who was conducting the interview and who was observing it—is the interview's subtext.

During most of the interview, I confined myself to making sympathetic gestures and sounds. Occasionally, I would repeat something Helen had said to help sustain the flow of memories, or ask her to clarify ambiguous statements. (How long were you there? Who told you that?) I encouraged her to speak at a comfortable pace about what *she* deemed was important. I tried my best to let her control the interview.

This was the first time Helen had told anyone—even her children—about her year in concentration camps. Thus, it was especially crucial that she construct her life history on her own terms. Only after she had completed the narrative corpus—the story from start to finish—did I pose questions that had occurred to me during the interview.

Several months later, I attended a screening of the footage Jim Goldner had shot on Mother's Day weekend. As I watched Helen on film and listened to her voice, it seemed to me she had entered something like an altered state of consciousness, a state of trance. Helen summoned each memory with such emotional force that it appeared as though she was actually reliving experiences as she recounted them.

As Helen's memories spontaneously surfaced on film—rather, as Helen actively constructed them—I noticed a transformation in her bearing. She became more fully present, more embodied. I realized, too, that any attempt on my part to redirect her remembering could have been experienced as an intrusion, even a violation.

I recall feeling protective toward Helen while she was telling her story, wanting to shield her from Gloria's questions. Last year I asked Helen whether she had felt her story was being manipulated, and whether she was aware of Gloria's and my struggle for control over the interview. I was not surprised when she replied that she had hardly noticed what was happening around her.

In retrospect, the struggle that occurred between Gloria and me makes a lot of sense. Though I had assumed Gloria would be an observer that afternoon, this was not her definition of the situation. Instead, she was directing a scene of her film in which Helen played the lead. By steering and probing, Gloria was doing what any director must do: instructing an actor how to deliver her lines.

If Gloria appeared as an interviewer in her own film, this would detract from the story she wanted to tell. Thus she needed me to fill the supporting role of interviewer. As an "other"—a professional interviewer and "detached" witness—I legitimated the scene. In actuality, though, Gloria could have interviewed Helen by herself.

As I reflect on the means of production of Helen's life history, I am somewhat chagrined. I realize just how tightly I held onto control during the interview, even as I "allowed" Helen to determine the content and set the pace of her story. I am confident that Gloria's presence helped to make the interview comfortable for Helen, and this matters a great deal. Indeed, Gloria's leading and probing may, at times, have stimulated the stream of Helen's memories, as my nondirective approach could not.[14] Who can say for sure?

As you already may have anticipated, the point of this story is that survivors need not depend on outsiders whose business is remembering to bear witness. They have each other, and that, too, matters a great deal.

Indeed, it matters more than I had originally understood. Gloria responded to the story you have just read by offering a counterinterpretation, from which I quote at length.

> I respect your comments about the way the interview with Helen came about as well as your understanding of the role you were to play at the filming session. However, . . . my recollection differs somewhat from yours. . . . I feel the record must be set straight, so as to reflect my point of view as well as yours.
>
> Here is the way I remember it. I was much looking forward to Helen Chalef's Mother's Day weekend with us, particularly because she came from the same area where I was born. I did not learn until the night she arrived that her town was only nine kilometers away from my birthplace, Nagy Bereg, and that we were in the same ghetto in Beregszasz. Imagine our excitement! We were up till the wee hours of the morning discussing in great detail our respective pasts. Helen did most of the talking and I asked her questions. Helen wanted to hear how her experiences corresponded with mine here and there, and we cried in joy as our memories spilled over faster than words could follow. It was as if

we opened the locks in each other's memory bank. Such was the excitement for both of us that it can never be duplicated.

Before Helen's arrival, Jameson C. Goldner, our film director, had made plans to film our conversation for our documentary film. He was shooting on 16mm film, a much more expensive process than videotape. . . . Because of the expense involved . . . the filming had to be curtailed. This meant that we had to limit ourselves to important recollections and get to the point quickly. Obviously, the filming session could not be done at the leisurely pace of the usual oral history interview.

As I said, Jim prearranged to film our conversation the following day. Having worked . . . with you in Washington, D.C., I thought of you as a friend and as someone with whom I wanted to share this precious experience. I felt it would make the film sequence more interesting if you were present and we could tell our stories to you. So I called you on the spur of the moment and asked you to come over. But basically it was still to be a conversation between Helen and me, not an interview in the usual sense. I do not believe I ever asked you to "interview" Helen. I may have said that if you have any questions, feel free to ask. . . .

I told Helen about your work and asked if she minded if I invited you for the filming session, and that you might ask some questions. Basically, I told Helen that "you and I will have a conversation much like we are having now," referring to the night before. I also explained that Jim might enter the conversation by asking questions. Helen agreed. . . . She looked forward to the filming session and told me to remind her about this and that, for she has not thought about many points she told me since the Holocaust. She said that I helped her to remember much. I believed her, for she played the same role for me. Although I had given many talks about my experiences, memories surfaced that were too painful to remember before. In fact, some I could not recall again even the following day for the filming session. The same happened to Helen. Before the filming session she complained that she could not remember some of the things we had talked about the night before, and she asked me to remind her during the filming. I told her to relax and ignore the camera and we would help each other remember. This was the reason that during the filming session I sometimes broke in to jog Helen's memory. I realized that she had forgotten details she had told me the night before. I also knew that our tight film budget allowed us only a brief filming session, and that we had to cover a lot of territory in a short time.[15]

CODA

Surviving the Holocaust was a social process; it could not be done alone. So, too, constructing memories and narratives about surviving

cannot be done in isolation. Stories about surviving ought to be polyvo-
cal—collectively woven braids in which individual lives and memories
are intertwined.

Fieldwork practices are rooted in assumptions about how knowledge
is and ought to be constructed. By exploring Gloria's and my interaction
during Helen's interview, I have exposed my own expectations about
how knowledge is produced in life histories. Conducting interviews in
individual rather than group settings determines the kinds of experiences, thoughts, and feelings that are remembered and expressed as
memories. This approach needs closer examination.

Earlier in this chapter, you may have been disturbed by my use of the
terms *manipulate* and *use*. This, too, was deliberate, for I wanted to
displace the view that interviews are passive encounters devoid of
strategic maneuverings and power struggles.

Ethnomethodologists have shown how conversation is purposive and
tactical—hence, political. Gloria's and my stories about interviewing
Helen suggest that we both used talk to accomplish desired outcomes. I
take it for granted that manipulations as such are part and parcel of
discourse.

Manipulations of the Holocaust can have widely disparate meanings.
For instance, meanings of "historical revisionism," whose proponents
claim the Holocaust is a "hoax," are different in kind from benign
interview probings.[16] Yet interviews necessarily manipulate memories,
for memories are always constructed in light of the present.

8

THE PHENOMENOLOGY
OF SURVIVING
Toward a Sociology of the Holocaust

A survivor is one who must bear witness for those who foundered; try to tell how and why it was that they, also worthy of life, did not survive. And pass on ways of surviving; and tell our chancy luck, our special circumstances.

Tillie Olsen, *Silences*

Since the liberation of the Nazi death camps in 1945, American sociology has maintained a daunting silence about the Holocaust. In 1979 two books momentarily broke this silence: *Accounting for Genocide*, by Helen Fein; and *Values and Violence in Auschwitz*, by Anna Pawelczynska. Along with Everett C. Hughes's 1964 essay, "Good People and Dirty Work," these are our discipline's best-known contributions to Holocaust studies in English and English translation.[1]

Especially in recent years, Holocaust scholarship has proliferated across the humanities and social sciences, in history, philosophy, religion, and psychology. My review of the literature suggests that sociology's virtual silence is unique among the disciplines.[2] Like the *sho'ah* itself, this silence must be accounted for.

Why is there virtually no discussion of the Holocaust in sociology? How might sociologists begin exploring this area? What methods should be used, what problems examined?

TOWARD A SOCIOLOGY OF THE HOLOCAUST

A crucial aspect of the Holocaust which sociologists could investigate is the range of Jewish responses to the Final Solution, including Jewish resistances. This subject has caused more confusion than practically any other issue in Holocaust studies. Scholars now recognize that there was, indeed, significant Jewish resistance inside and outside the concentration and death camps.[3] Yet an oversimplified, idealized view of Jews as "victims" on the one hand, or self-conscious resistance fighters on the other, has obscured our understanding of everyday Jewish life during the Holocaust.

Millions of Jews were murdered by the *Einsatzgruppen* and marched to the gas chambers. Still, even as they met their deaths, the Jews defied Nazi stereotypes of a people "cringing, acquiescent, and easily manipulated by crude appeals to individual self-interest."[4] At the same time, the vast majority of Jews never engaged in armed struggle or anything resembling it. The icon of resistance—a partisan fighter throwing a Molotov cocktail—is as unfaithful to the experiences of most Holocaust victims and survivors as the Nazis' own depictions of Jewish complicity.

To begin exploring a sociology of the Holocaust, I propose a change in terminology—hence, a shift in our thinking. I suggest the phrase "phenomenology of surviving" to describe the broad scope of actions taken by Jews during the Holocaust. By introducing new language, I intend to sidestep ongoing debates among historians and philosophers about how to define resistances. I assume, however, that as a rule people acted to protect their families and communities, and to stay alive.

The phenomenology of surviving would be a central concern of a sociology of the Holocaust. I share historian Konnilyn G. Feig's view, which emphasizes "the critical importance of the theme of struggling and surviving as a positive, strong, and unique element running through the Holocaust. The survivor, the struggler . . . is the most important story of the Holocaust, one of the most astonishing, strongest, and unusual human actions in modern times."[5] A sociology of the Holocaust would be empirically based and sensitive to problems of constructing and interpreting personal and historical narratives. It would be aimed at exploring broad theoretical issues, such as how human agency is exercised under genocide and other conditions of extreme repression and terror. Sociologists could refine the concept of phenomenology of surviving by collecting and analyzing survivors' personal narratives; clarify problems of "knowing" and complicity by gathering and analyzing personal narratives of Germans, Poles, and citizens of other countries occupied or annexed by Germany;* and conduct comparative analyses of genocide.[6]

---

*"Knowing" refers to how information about the Final Solution was revealed to, believed (and in many instances, not believed), and acted upon by persons in Germany and the occupied countries, and the Allies.

Dates . . . laws . . . military occupations . . . hundreds of transit, concentration, labor, and satellite camps . . . millions of deportations and deaths. Scholars have constructed detailed historical narratives out of these fragments. As a concept, "Holocaust" permits us to recognize patterns amid the variations, similarities alongside uniqueness, and continuities among statistics of lives and communities destroyed. But the Holocaust was not a discrete event fixed in time with a beginning and an end. It is an analytic construct abstracted from lived experiences. Feminist philosopher Joan Miriam Ringelheim explains that:

> The Holocaust . . . is a term that seems written in stone and which can't be changed (and perhaps one doesn't want to). However, I would like to suggest that there is no such thing as "The Holocaust." What men, women and children experienced was not one event, but a myriad of events which we've tied into an analytic knot so we can speak about it with ease and with single breaths. The Holocaust is made up of individual experiences. They may have been momentous experiences for some, but it seems to me that the momentousness often occurs after we've identified what the event is. There was no such language for those experiences when people were going through them.[7]

The Holocaust was not a uniform experience either for those who were killed or those who survived. Jews living under the Nazi occupation did not have a static, unified understanding of what was happening to them, their families, and communities. They made sense of their lives through a mixture of concrete events, feelings, rumors, and hunches: a sense of looming danger, loss of their jobs, restrictive curfews, deportation orders, constant hunger, sick children, imprisoned friends.

No one survived the Holocaust per se. They survived ghettos, deportations, and concentration camps. They hid. They passed on the Aryan side. They resisted. These experiences are more mundane than the terms *Holocaust* or *genocide* suggest.

Annihilation of the Jews was overdetermined. A sociology of the Holocaust must reconcile this fact with the Jews' steadfast refusal to die—as a people in the biological sense, and as a culture thousands of years old. Struggles to stay alive in the ghettos and death camps cannot be taken for granted. Neither can survival be dismissed as mere luck, although luck surely was a factor in surviving.

Inside and outside the camps, the Jews of Nazi-occupied Europe must be viewed as interacting, knowing subjects, reasoning and strategizing their way from one day to the next. Sometimes they negotiated or manipulated complex interactions with SS guards, *kapos* (prisoners who oversaw other prisoners), Gestapo, Jewish police, Jewish Council members, and Dr. Mengele himself. Even in the extermination camps, where death was *inescapable* for millions of Jews, no single fate was *inevitable*. With this apparent paradox in mind, we can now pose a crucial question: How did perhaps one-half million Jews manage to survive the Holocaust?[8] I return to this question later in the chapter.

WHO ARE HOLOCAUST SURVIVORS?

My research is confined to Jews, although other groups also were singled out for death by the Nazis. Jews and Gypsies (Sinti and Roma)* were the principal targets of the Final Solution.[9] In addition, homosexual men and Jehovah's Witnesses were incarcerated and sometimes killed, along with other people deemed politically or socially undesirable, or biologically or racially inferior, including Communists, Hutterites, criminals, and Slavs. Children and adults labeled mentally and physically ill were murdered by various means, including gas, in chambers installed inside German psychiatric hospitals.[10]

Holocaust "survivor," like Holocaust itself, is a problematic concept. "Survivor" is a socially constructed identity, yet the term tends to reify Jews' experiences under the Nazi occupation.

Many survivors were deported to concentration camps. Others went into hiding, passed as gentiles on the Aryan side, and/or joined resistance groups. The experiences of camp survivors are diverse. In part, this reflects significant variations among the camps themselves.

The Nazis made clear distinctions between the killing centers and other concentration camps.[11] There were four exclusive-function death camps, all located in Poland: Chelmno/Kulmhof, Belzec, Sobibor, and Treblinka. Auschwitz/Birkenau and Majdanek, also located in Poland, were the two labor-extermination complexes. In Germany, Bergen-Belsen was created as a model repatriation and transit center, and a camp for privileged prisoners. Eleven concentration camps were given official status by Himmler, such as Dachau, Buchenwald, and Ravensbrück. The fortress town of Terezin/Theresienstadt, located near Prague, was classified as a ghetto for Protectorate Jews, along with prominent Jews and members of other special categories. There were also transit camps

---

*Sinti are the German Gypsies; Roma, the Gypsies of Eastern Europe, are a distinct cultural and linguistic group.

in each of the occupied countries, such as Drancy, outside of Paris, and Westerbork and Vught in Holland. Finally, hundreds of labor and satellite camps were concentrated in Poland and Germany.

The implementation of the Final Solution was experimental, incremental, and chaotic. Indeed, circumstances varied tremendously from ghetto to ghetto, country to country, camp to camp, and year to year. Even in a single camp, such as Birkenau, over the course of a few months, or between different work *kommandos* ("groups") or blocks (barracks), significantly different conditions often prevailed. Inmates manipulated the dynamic social structure of the camps in order to stay alive.

Prisoners were frequently moved from one camp to another. Sometimes transfers occurred because slave labor was needed at a new site, but often they were motivated by no apparent reason. Toward the end of the war, populations of entire camps shifted dramatically and conditions in the camps rapidly changed.

What do Holocaust survivors have in common as a group? A definition frequently mentioned in the literature is the shared experience of persecution under the Nazi regime. But this definition demands that we probe how identities are forged from experiences of persecution. In other words, how does a Holocaust "victim" become a "survivor"? To explore this question, we must first recognize that Nazi persecution was local, multidimensional, and ever-changing. Meanings of persecution, in turn, are shaped by a person's experiences before, during, and after the Holocaust. They are interpreted and reinterpreted over the course of a lifetime.

Fully 25 percent of the Jews deported to concentration camps did not actually consider themselves Jewish.[12] Indeed, they held a range of religious identities and maintained various practices. Still, the Nazis defined who was a Jew based on criteria defined in the Nuremberg Laws. In Poland, for instance, the "Regulation for the Definition of the Term 'Jew' in the Government-General, July 24, 1940" was passed. This decreed that "A Jew is a person descended from at least three fully Jewish grandparents by race."[13] If a person had only two grandparents who were "full Jews by race," then they were considered a Jew if they also were a member of the Jewish community on or after September 1, 1939; if they were married to a Jew on or after August 1, 1940; or if they were "the product of extra-marital intercourse with a Jew . . . born after May 31, 1941."[14]

The women and men I interviewed have constructed diverse identities as Holocaust survivors. Their commonalities cannot be severed from their differences. Both need to be explored empirically.

METHODOLOGY

The respondents in my study have survived even more than genocide. Many also endured decades of silence imposed by a world decidedly ambivalent about coming to terms with the Holocaust. Some of the survivors in my sample had never before talked with another person about their experiences during the war. Others are accomplished speakers, writers, and Holocaust educators.

A victim is one who is acted upon; a survivor is an active subject. The respondents in my sample are survivors. In the years following the war, they immigrated to a new land and made their way in a country that didn't always welcome them. As survivors, they are oriented toward the present and the future. Yet they remember the past and share their memories, an immense accomplishment for people who have known such extreme suffering and loss.

However, for several reasons, my sample is probably not representative of Holocaust survivors as a group. First, an unknown number of survivors, about whom we know practically nothing, has died since 1945. Second, the survivors who attended the meetings where my respondents were interviewed are a self-selected group. My respondents are a self-selected subpopulation of this group.

Those who are excluded from my sample may tell different kinds of stories about surviving the Holocaust, or perhaps they tell no stories at all. We know little about these people. Some do not want to share their memories with strangers. Some have debilitating chronic illnesses directly traceable to their experiences during the war. Others may be plagued by emotional problems. Still others may be socially isolated, poor, or otherwise unable or unwilling to travel to survivors' gatherings. Some "survivors" have reconstructed their pasts, for instance, their dates of emigration from Europe. They depend on silences to mitigate their haunting nightmares.

We have much to learn about Holocaust survivors as a group, especially about their lives before and after the war. My analysis of the phenomenology of surviving is exploratory. Technically, it is not representative of my sample, nor can it be generalized beyond my sample.

My interviews with Holocaust survivors are life-history narratives. Sociologist Gareth Williams describes narrative as "a process of continuous accounting whereby the mundane incidents and events of daily life are given some kind of plausible order."[15] Narratives emerge from the continuous flow of lived experience. They are reconstructions of the past in light of the present.

Lived experiences are fleeting. They last only a moment, then disappear, leaving only traces—stories. Narratives are stories. They change over time because they are anchored in time. Selective remembering, reinterpreting and resequencing the past, and idealizing people and events routinely occur as narratives are produced.

Survivors' narratives reconstruct the Holocaust in light of the present. They privilege the self as an active, knowing subject. They represent the Holocaust as lived experience.

My analysis is informed by symbolic interaction and grounded theory.[16] Grounded theory is a comparative method for coding and analyzing qualitative data. However, I did not sample comparative cases for this study; hence, my analysis is not fully "grounded."

The analysis presented in the next two sections of this chapter emerged from the interview I refer to as n90. My description of the basic social process of surviving was produced with data from this respondent and interviews with eleven other survivors.

Conditions for Surviving: Certainties and Uncertainties in the Camps

Certainties   Concentration camp inmates faced similar constraints from camp to camp. Starvation and dehydration during the dry months, when no snow was on the ground, were serious problems. As one survivor remembered:

> The only thing you thought about was food. [We had] . . . an absolute obsession with talking about recipes. . . . I never cooked so well as I did with my mouth in Auschwitz. Because at the time, I mean I had never cooked in my life. I didn't know from anything. I just remembered. That was your conversation. (n90/#92A, p. 7)*

Infectious diseases were rampant due to inadequate or nonexistent sanitation and contaminated drinking water. Intestinal bugs were epidemic; and lice, which carry the salmonella bacteria associated with

---

*Throughout this chapter, except where noted, quotations from survivors are indicated as follows: the first number, an "n" number (e.g., n90) identifies the respondent in my data set; a second number (e.g., #92A) indicates the tape on which the interview was recorded; and a third number (e.g., p. 7) corresponds to the page of the interview transcript where the quoted passage appears. "1981" appears in citations of interviews conducted in 1981, at the World Gathering of Jewish Holocaust Survivors in Jerusalem.

typhoid fever, flourished. "Everybody had to have [typhoid fever]. I mean everyone who survived will tell you they all had typhoid fever," remembered the respondent quoted above, who was imprisoned for two years at Birkenau (ibid.). "With having diarrhea continuously, it was a godsend that the menses stopped," she added (#92B, p. 21).

It was impossible to maintain normal hygiene. Inmates couldn't keep themselves clean because they often went for months at a time without an opportunity to bathe or change their clothes. Slave labor on twelve-hour shifts, often at a backbreaking pace, was routine and injuries were not uncommon. The climate of Eastern Europe is harsh, and inmates were fully exposed to the elements: relentless heat in the summer and bitter cold in the winter. These were the baseline conditions at any concentration camp. "I think it was those of us who accepted that fact immediately, that is what you had to do, [those were] the parameters of your life, you couldn't look back and you couldn't look forward . . . were the ones that had a chance of survival" (n90/#92A, p. 6).

Uncertainties   The unpredictable circumstances—what could not be anticipated—must have been at least as hard to bear as the constant privation. "The fear is the worst thing, to be afraid," according to one survivor of Auschwitz and Mauthausen (n6/#123B, p. 4). Punishment for individual deeds often was meted out to the group. The same respondent recalled the following incident:

> There was a terrible thing [that] happened. . . . I didn't even know what it was. Only later did I learn what it was. They called us in the middle of the night, they had to stand in no shoes or anything in the muck (that was November or December). . . . There were 250 girls [in the camp]. There was a rumor that one German [guard and one in-mate had run] away and that was the German punishment. They take every tenth person out . . . to shoot them, and I was the ninth one. (n6/#123B, p. 2)

Being singled out for extra punishment for deeds you might or might not have committed was a condition of daily life. Punishments were arbitrary and random. Camp inmates often learned the hard way what the consequences were of asking for extra soup if they spilled their bowl or of trying to get another slice of bread if someone happened to grab their ration. They could be beaten into unconsciousness or shot for bending down to scoop up a handful of snow while marching back to camp for roll call at the end of the day. But there was also the chance of not being noticed. How to calculate the odds, when hunger, thirst, and exhaustion are paramount?

In nine concentration camps officially sanctioned medical experiments were conducted: Auschwitz/Birkenau, Buchenwald, Dachau, Majdanek, Mauthausen, Natzweiler, Neuengamme, Ravensbrück, and Sachsenhausen.[17] Inmates in these camps were at risk of being selected for the experiments, which the Nazis kept secret from them. Most people who were experimented on either died or were killed.[18]

In survivors' accounts of medical care in the camps, it is often difficult to differentiate "treatment" from "torture." A respondent named Eva described a harrowing confrontation at the Auschwitz hospital block. She was assigned to an outdoor *kommando* that carried stones from one place to another. She injured her leg while working and the wound became infected. But Eva was afraid to go to the hospital, where she thought she would be killed. As Pawelczynska explains, "The right to be 'cured' in the camp hospital was a prisoner's 'privilege.'" To be sure, the privilege was an ambiguous one, for camp officials regularly ordered prisoner-doctors to "clean out the hospital by means of selection for the gas chamber."[19]

Meanwhile, Eva's wound began to fester and she was in constant, excruciating pain. One day an SS guard dragged her to the hospital and told her they intended to amputate the lower half of her leg. She grabbed the guard's gun and screamed, "Kill me now!" The guard grew alarmed and sent a nurse to dress the wound.

Eventually, Eva was allowed to leave the hospital. She was even permitted to return periodically for the wound to be cleaned (n79/#136A).

Perhaps the greatest uncertainty existed in Auschwitz/Birkenau and Majdanek, the labor-extermination camps. In the exclusive-function killing centers (Chelmno, Belzec, Sobibor, and Treblinka) most inmates died within several days of arrival. But in these two camps, inmates who were not immediately ordered to the gas chambers were sent to forced labor. Then, at regular intervals, they were subjected to selections. One survivor described the arbitrariness of the selections:

I was there [in Auschwitz] for three days when they took us out. Again, they stripped us naked. A German was standing in front of us, looking us over. He was making a second selection. The German . . . looked at my chest. And he looked at me, and he looked at me, and he looked. I couldn't understand why he looked at me. Finally, he decided to make a signal with his finger that I should live.

I looked over my chest [because] I wanted to see what he sees there. I saw a little pimple, like a head from a pin. He was thinking if I should go to the gas chamber or if I should go to work. Finally, he decided that I should live. Can you imagine? A little pimple [was] what a human being's life was worth! (GS, 1981, pp. 1–2)

The unpredictability of selections forced every survivor to confront the unanswerable question of why she or he was allowed to live:

I went through selections where people next to me were taken out while I had the typhoid fever, and people next to me were yanked out that had survived already three months, four months, and they didn't take me. . . . There was no rhyme or reason for the selections, never. It was the face, the nose, something. Or a quota to fill. . . . [The Jews who went] directly into the gas from the ramp . . . were the lucky ones. Not until the doors clanged shut of those gas chambers did they know what hit them. The ones that were taken out . . . at a selection after a roll call in the morning, they had to wait all day knowing . . . what was waiting for them. It was [the Nazis'] typical thoroughness. Those who were put into Block 27, which was the collection block for the daily trip, why waste food on them, why waste water on them? They were there all day long. Sometimes you would see a hand stretching out for water, water, out the barbed windows on Block 27. They would give them nothing. And these were the really . . . horrible, tragic things. (n90/#92B, pp. 15–16)

The *Appell* was the twice-daily ritual of roll call. Allegedly, its purpose was to account for all inmates, even those who had died during the night. But "roll call in the camp served as an additional means of biologically destroying the prisoners by forcing them to endure hours of standing, in their thin rags, unprotected from rain and snow."[20] There were no excuses for not standing in line: "Look, I marched out for . . . six or seven days with 103 or 104° temperature. . . . I had at that time a support group of German-Jewish women who shlepped me out through the gate every morning after the roll call, who held me up during the roll call" (n90/#92A, p. 7).

But the uncertainties of daily life in the camps neither began nor ended with roll calls and selections. Jews in the occupied countries were constantly being deported to unknown destinations: from urban ghettos or transit camps to labor or death camps, then from one camp to the next. The same respondent, a survivor of Theresienstadt ghetto and Auschwitz, explained that

> Theresienstadt was a sort of passing-through distribution camp, but nobody knew where the transports went to from Theresienstadt. They were going east. Nobody knew anything. . . . In 1943 I was sent on a transport. By that time we had an inkling that there was a place like Auschwitz, but nobody expected what Auschwitz was.

[You didn't know about the gassings?]

> Nobody knew. You knew quick enough after you arrived. . . . The first thing that assailed your nostrils was the absolutely indescribable smell. I pray to God nobody ever in his life has to smell that again. But you didn't know what it was. (n90/#92A, p. 2)

For most of the survivors I interviewed, being transferred from camp to camp was a confusing and frightening experience. A Czech woman (GHL), who was deported to Auschwitz in April 1944, was shuffled among seven camps in the course of a single year. The shock of being wrenched from loved ones and banished to unfamiliar surroundings was agonizing. Separations and dislocations created uncertainties that had to be dealt with.

In addition, as the Allied bombings increased, there was constant uncertainty about when the war would end.

> Again, they shipped us out to—I didn't know it at the time but it was to Mauthausen. It took about two or three weeks we were en route. . . . We didn't know it but the railroads were bombed. We sometimes stood for days and nights in one spot in the railroad without no food or anything. . . . We got to Mauthausen and we didn't know it, but the Nazis weren't there anymore, but we didn't know it. What they did, they dressed some of the *kapos* in Nazi uniforms. You see, all the Nazis ran away. You see, the war was coming to an end. (n6, pp. 8–9)

These conditions—certain and unpredictable—assured death for millions of concentration and death camp inmates. But if you weren't selected for the gas chamber, what could you do to survive? What negotiation and manipulation strategies were possible within the changing parameters of camp life? This question lies at the core of the phenomenology of surviving.

THE PHENOMENOLOGY OF SURVIVING

In the preceding section of this chapter, I described conditions in the concentration camps under which millions of people were murdered. Although death was overdetermined for Jews in the camps, perhaps as many as seventy-five thousand people managed to survive.[21] How was survival possible?

To a great extent, survival was a matter of chance, of fortuitous circumstances beyond a person's control. Luck is among the reasons most frequently given by the survivors I interviewed to explain how they survived. Luck is beyond intentions—beyond actions and consequences, cause and effect. In a sense, luck is the final cause, the cause of all causes.

> Survival . . . was so much a matter of luck, a matter of where you were, the luck, the chance. There was no manipulating, yes manipulating in the sense you knew somebody, getting in somewhere, because then, only then, could you have a chance. So those that survived here [Auschwitz/Birkenau], any one of them will tell you that they had to have some kind of break, chance, coincidence, that helped them at one point. (n90/#92B, pp. 14–15)

Indeed, it was necessary to have luck on your side. Still, luck alone was an insufficient condition for surviving. Concentration camp inmates—those who were killed and those who survived—engaged in an active struggle *not to die*, to stay alive. Esther, a survivor of Majdanek, recalled why "fighting back," in the literal sense of the term, was discouraged by camp inmates. "I saw young people picking up stones and throwing them at the SS guards and fighting. The next second they were dead. I saw it. Everyone would say, 'Don't get crazy. Don't give them a chance to kill us. Let's live!'" (ED, 1981, p. 3).

However, when death was certain, some chose to die as martyrs. This was the situation of the resistance fighters during the final days of the Warsaw Ghetto uprising. The *Sonderkommando* ("special work crew"), which revolted in Auschwitz on 7 October 1944, faced similar circumstances. As a last resort, fighting back was a strategy for defining the conditions of death.[22]

Jews mobilized multiple resources in order to survive inside and outside the camps. People were remarkably ingenious in situations that might have appeared choiceless, hopeless, or doomed. Four classes of resources emerged from my analysis of concentration-camp survivors' narratives: knowledge and information, practical skills, affiliations, and attitude. In practice, each of these categories is inseparable from the others. My distinctions, then, are strictly analytic.

Knowledge and Information   For prisoners, local conditions in the camps were "the parameters of your life" (n90, p. 6). Knowing what dangers to try to avoid was a crucial link to survival. Other inmates and even SS guards could be vital sources of information. Lee described how she lied about her age during the initial selection at the Auschwitz train platform. She didn't know at the time that by saying she was eighteen years old, she had saved her life.

> A man came over, one of the inmates, and said, "How old is your daughter?" He told us to tell the Germans that I was eighteen. But my mother and I didn't want to do this because I was younger and we didn't want to lie. He came over to us again and repeated his thought: "Tell them that your daughter is eighteen."
>
> And my mother, who was very young, she was in her thirties, she could have survived if she hadn't had children. But this man saw that my mother was doomed because she had the two little girls. He knew that because of the children, they wouldn't let her go into the other line where she could have survived, so he was trying to at least get me away from her. Yet he couldn't tell her why he wanted me away from her. (1981, p. 4)

Susan, also an Auschwitz survivor, recalled how she and the other women who worked at "Kanada" were prepared for evacuation of the camp by the commandant himself. Kanada was the warehouse area at Birkenau, where clothing and food confiscated from incoming inmates was sorted, repaired, and stored.

> That we survived [the death march], I mean my group and I, was again only due to the fact that we were where we were working, because the night before we were evacuated, the commandant went to the barracks and he said, "Listen, we are going to evacuate. Go into the barracks," he said. "Never mind, we are going to burn everything here anyway. . . . Get solid shoes, get socks, get all the warm clothes that you can. Be ready for a very rough march." (n90/#92B, pp. 14–15)

Regine's mother saved her from deportation to Auschwitz by acting on her knowledge that native-born and immigrant Jews had different status under French law. On 16–17 July 1942, nearly thirteen thousand non-French Jews living in Paris were rounded up. Along with her parents, who were Polish nationals, Regine was sent to Drancy, the transit camp outside of Paris.

But Regine was a French citizen. Technically, she was exempt from deportation. In mid-1942, most French Jews were still relatively safe. However, Jewish emigrés and refugees living in occupied France were in grave danger.

Although Regine's mother could not save herself, she recognized this as an opportunity to try to save Regine and pressured the camp authorities into releasing her. She acted strategically to accomplish what may have been her most agonizing deed before she died: separating from Regine in order to save her life.

Regine was held in Drancy for two weeks. Then, along with three other young women, she was permitted to leave the camp. Shortly thereafter, Regine's parents were deported to Auschwitz and immediately sent to the gas chambers. Regine hid in the countryside until the end of the war (n1 / #5a).

Lee, Susan, and Regine each faced situations with uncertain outcomes, where they might well have died or been killed. However, they were forewarned of specific dangers and how to avoid or prepare for them. They heeded warnings and took risks to stay alive. For these women, information about danger was a life-saving resource.

Practical Skills   Inmates provided the slave labor necessary for running the camps. There were numerous jobs in each camp and competition was fierce for the "better" ones. These were few in number. "You must manage to get work, work that was needed by the SS," explained one survivor (EK, 1981, p. 6). Sometimes inmates with special skills would be kept alive by the Nazis, as long as they could serve the Reich. For instance, the noted bacteriologist Ludwick Fleck:

> was forced to divulge to several German doctors the procedure for obtaining the new vaccine [for typhoid fever, and] he and his staff were deported to the Nazi concentration camp in Auschwitz. In 1943, after recovering from a serious illness, Fleck was attached to the camp's hospital and, under duress, continued to produce his vaccine for the German armed forces. In 1944, Fleck was transferred to the concentration camp in Buchenwald and again ordered to prepare typhus vaccine.[23]

In Auschwitz inside work was preferable to outside work. Usually it was less physically taxing, and workers on inside *kommandos* had access to additional food and information networks. They were also permitted to bathe and change their clothes. Susan recalled that after she had been imprisoned in Auschwitz for about a year, she got a job working as a typist.

> Dear Katya [another inmate] found a job in the so-called building *kommando* for me as a typist, because I told her that I could type. . . . Thank God for my mother who insisted that I learn typing before we went in Prague, 'cause that's how I earned a living in Prague. I couldn't go to school anymore, so I did typing. . . . (n90/#92A, p. 10)

Susan's account of meeting Katya, who helped her get the typing job, illustrates another practical skill that served her well: speaking Czech.

> I was in that block [where] there were mostly German women, and I was one of the few that spoke Czech, *and so I could speak with Ilka* [the *kapo*]. . . . I think Ilka must have been the one who mentioned this to one of the runners between the administration and the Germans, that there was a Czech girl in her block from Prague. And so this little girl, I think her name was Katya, came to the block and asked me, "Did I know this and this and this person in Prague?" because most of the people in Prague at the time, of our age, were in certain movements, certain circles. I mentioned some names and one was, I think, the boyfriend of her sister, and so she just said, "I'm gonna help you." . . . She got me into the so-called *Schreibstube*, the camp administration. (Pp. 8–9)

But a scientist or typist didn't necessarily have a better chance of surviving in the camps than an "unskilled" person. Practical skills, such as typing, producing vaccine, or language fluency, could be resources only to the extent that they were used strategically. In this sense the term "strategic" refers to opportunities that inmates recognized and seized upon to direct or change the course of their lives. Through their relationships with each other, inmates often created such opportunities.

Affiliations

That was the thing in camp. It wasn't what you knew [but] who you knew. (n90/#92A, p. 9)

You must have friends. Without friends you were almost dead. You needed friends to help you, not only physically but to inspire you, to give you courage. (EK, 1981, p. 6)

I have already described how prisoners alerted each other in order to avoid dangers, encouraged one another to take potentially life-saving risks, and discouraged impetuous ones. Concentration-camp inmates were interdependent in the most fundamental ways. Surviving was a social process. It could not be done alone.

Camp inmates also shared food and friendship networks. They helped each other get better jobs and gave each other reasons to carry on. Susan remembered how her friends helped her recover from typhoid fever, her first illness in Auschwitz.

> You had to have your support group. I had at that time a support group of German-Jewish women who shlepped me out through the gate every morning after the roll call, who held me up during the roll call, who would lay me down behind a piece of ruin or something (we were at that time on a *kommando* that was breaking up bombed-out houses), watched me, looked after me. Every few hours, somebody would come look at me, bring me maybe a live frog that they had caught to give me to eat, or some greenery, 'cause, of course, you needed some food and you couldn't keep anything down. The only thing I really kept down at that time was some raw frog legs or some green stuff. (P. 7)

Susan's second illness occurred about a year later, in February 1944. This time, she was taken to the Auschwitz hospital. Although periodically, the hospital was a selection point for the gas chambers, Susan was treated there for strep throat.

> By that time . . . the Germans [had] sort of loosened up the arrangements. Jews were allowed to go to the large German hospital, about twenty blocks. . . . Interestingly enough, the person that supplied me that time with sulfa, . . . the guy that smuggled the sulfa for me was a Polish electrician who had befriended me when I worked in the building *kommando*. He brought the sulfa in and they would inject it everyday, and so I got out of there. (P. 11)

Tonia recalled an incident that happened in a slave-labor camp close to the end of the war. She was working in an airplane factory beside a civilian German, whom she was required to address as "Master." One day, without permission, she went to get a drink of water. When she returned to her work station, she was severely beaten by an SS guard.

> When I was hit by the *Unterscharführer* ("guard"), my master was standing there, facing the wall. And when the *Unterscharführer* left, my

master turned around and he had one artificial eye, and I saw from the
other eye there were tears coming down his face. And I realized that he
was really human. I wish I knew his name. Then I realized he was also
being punished. He couldn't talk to me because he was not allowed. He
would be shot.

He told me that he comes from a northern city and his family was
there because he didn't join the Nazis. I don't know if I imagined this or
if he really told me, but I had this feeling. [Then, he gave me some
food.] His food wasn't fantastic. I mean, to me it was like a feast, but he
had just black bread and some salami and black coffee. And then he
scolded me. . . . "Why didn't you tell me you're going for water? . . .
You stupid?" And then he would watch out for me.

We became very close without talking. Before Christmas, he told
me he was going home. I made him little toys for his children from the
aluminum, the scraps. It's hard to explain, but they're soft nails that you
squeeze together for the airplanes. I made a little cone that goes into a
little case with a nail. . . . Anyway, I made some things and he took
them; and when he came back, he brought me zwieback. (n6, pp. 4, 6)

Making human connections was a basic survival strategy. Inmates
formed alliances to ease the desolation and regimentation of camp life.
Sometimes, too, friendships turned out to be lifesaving.

In Auschwitz protective bonds were institutionalized between the
more privileged women in the Kanada *kommando* and the SS guards.
Susan described these relationships as "symbiotic" and "patriarchal"
(pp. 12, 18).

The guards looked a lot the other way when it came to food. All the
food [that incoming inmates brought with them] went to the prisoners
[who worked in Kanada] because prisoners in the Kanada commando
looked the other way when the SS helped themselves to stolen property,
which they were strictly forbidden to do. Therefore, [there was a] tacit
agreement. (P 12; and pers. comm., 31 January 1991)

Inmates' relationships with others reflected their attitudes toward
surviving. One's attitude, in turn, was shaped by one's relationships
with other inmates.

Attitude   Many survivors described how a determined attitude
fostered day-to-day survival in the camps. This meant not giving up,
holding on, hoping. Those who lost the will to live were known as
muselmännen. Susan explained that a *muselmänn* was "any prisoner who

you could see in their eyes, in their behavior, in their movement, they weren't going to live. They were on the verge of giving up. And I was practically a *muselmänn* but somehow or other, I must have had some kind of . . . I didn't want to give up" (p. 10). Later in the interview, she thought more about her attitude: "I don't know. Maybe I had such a . . . dead head grin but I never let anybody see fear. . . . That was the one preeminent thought. Don't let them see that you're afraid" (p. 15).

Some women survivors recalled the importance of caring for their bodies. Picking lice out of your hair (if you were lucky enough to have hair), "brushing" your teeth with a piece of fabric torn from your skirt, and washing your face in the morning's ersatz coffee all were life-affirming acts. Livia, who was deported to Auschwitz in the spring of 1944, remembered "women immediately tearing off pieces of their dresses and putting them on their heads to look prettier because they were so ashamed to look so terrible. Their heads were shaved, but they tied this material to their heads. These are the first signs of vitality, this urge to survive" (LB-J, 1981, p. 8).★

Others found strength by looking away from the past, toward the future. Another survivor recounted:

> Not once in the camps did I feel sorry or sad that my family was gone. I thought if I were beaten less often than the day before—this was good. I'd live for the days when they split the bread three ways instead of five. Or if the soup was a little thicker, or if I had a chance to get a top bunk instead of a bottom one because when it collapses, it doesn't collapse on you. (MOB, 1981, p. 3)

An optimistic attitude could make a world of difference:

> I always thought I'd survive. I knew that Hitler would be conquered and I kept thinking, "I'm going to live in a better world." I had that feeling. And when I came to the concentration camp, you could just feel that there was no hope. My girlfriend said, "Here is the end of us." I said, "Not of me. I'm going to see a better world." (SL, 1981, p. 3)

★Susan Cernyak-Spatz offered the following comment when she reviewed this passage: "Kerchiefs were issued [to Auschwitz inmates] at the processing in upon arrival and had to be tied one certain way" (pers. comm., 31 January 1991). According to her, only after regulations had slackened, during the final three months before the camp was evacuated, could inmates have had an opportunity to make their own kerchiefs.

The time frame of LB-J's observations is not clear from her interview. Nor is it possible for me to determine whether she was referring to inmates in Auschwitz-Birkenau or another concentration camp.

There is a great deal we can understand about how concentration-camp inmates managed to carry on — what they did to survive. Yet, in the end, surviving the Holocaust remains ineffable. What, if anything, did survivors do differently from those who were killed? Historical evidence and our own good sense tell us this is where luck came into play.

We will never know for sure whether those who survived took greater risks, had tougher bodies and spirits, or held onto life with a tighter grip. Still, it is certain that those who died in the camps fought as long and as hard as they could to stay alive. Given the overriding odds of being gassed, or dying from starvation or illness, we need not ask why so many people died. Rather, the question is how so many managed to survive.

Earlier in the chapter I suggested one answer to this question: concentration-camp inmates stayed alive by actively struggling not to die. They responded to the constraints of camp life by mobilizing and manipulating material and interpersonal resources. They depended on each other for life itself.

Many survivors believe that luck enabled them to survive. Yet luck is a different order of explanation than the resources and strategies described in this chapter. Luck is not an expression of human agency. Rather, it is an artifact of survivors' narratives, which supplants or codetermines all other explanations.

I close this chapter on a cautionary note. My analysis may go too far in the direction of constructing concentration-camp inmates as rational strategists. Emphasizing Holocaust survivors' agency rather than their victimization may run the risk of construing motives and intentions where, in any given instance, there may have been none. In George Herbert Mead's words, "consciousness leaves and consciousness returns, but the organism itself runs on."[24]

In a related way, my representations of the phenomenology of surviving are more fragmented and mechanical than many survivors' accounts of their lived experiences. Indeed, the ineffability of the Holocaust renders any narrative with scientific aims wanting. Mine is no exception. This is the predicament of writing a sociology of the Holocaust, which I explore in the next chapters of the book.

9

REFLECTIONS ON "THE PHENOMENOLOGY OF SURVIVING"

What I had not been taught was that there are circumstances when ethics call for identification rather than disguise.

Barbara Myerhoff, in *Between Two Worlds*

With "The Phenomenology of Surviving: Toward a Sociology of the Holocaust," I redefined my work with Holocaust survivors as ethnography. I recorded the transition from my role as director of the Holocaust Media Project in a research memo for "Phenomenology":

> My multiple roles are entangled. The role of interviewer-observer is clouded by my struggle to sort out my identity as a Jew; my professional identities as a sociologist and writer are complicated by my personal relationships with survivors and people I've worked with on the Holocaust Media Project. The blurry boundaries between "work" and "life" must be carefully examined.[1]

It is not unusual to define an experience as fieldwork after the fact. According to John Van Maanen, "occasionally ethnographic reports appear as retrospective accounts of a distinct period in a researcher's life not marked off at the time as fieldwork."[2] The process of redefining my work with survivors as ethnography involved reconstructing and reinterpreting dozens of relationships and experiences. Above all, it required making a significant identity transition[3] in order to explore the impress of the Holocaust on my own life.

I wrote "The Phenomenology of Surviving" in 1985, two years after I attended the American Gathering of Jewish Holocaust Survivors. My use of the grounded-theory method reflected my commitment to doing antipositivist field research. In contrast with logicodeductive approaches, grounded theory is an inductive method of data collection, analysis, and theory building. *The Discovery of Grounded Theory* (1967) introduced this approach, reconceptualizing the prevailing link between theory and methodology in the social sciences.[4] In an era still dominated by the functionalism of Merton, Parsons, and their intellectual kin, grounded theory offered a generation of sociological fieldworkers an alternative.

After twenty-five years, *The Discovery of Grounded Theory* still marshals a forceful case against the reductionism that has dominated sociology since the Second World War. Yet the discipline has changed considerably since this book was published. In Marcus and Fischer's words, a "crisis of representation"[5] has dissolved the hegemony of functionalism. They explain that "Parsonian social theory has not vanished; too many generations of students, now prominent scholars, were trained in terms of it for that to happen. But the theoretical edifice of Parsons has been thoroughly delegitimated."[6]

An interest in hermeneutics, narratives, and epistemology is revitalizing sociology and the human sciences generally. Yet grounded-theory studies seem ill equipped to address these issues because they are unreflexive about fieldwork practices, ethnographic writing, and the kinds of knowledge they produce. It is no coincidence, then, that these concerns are absent from "The Phenomenology of Surviving."

When I wrote "The Phenomenology of Surviving" I was reluctant to inscribe myself in the text. I used dialogue as a representational strategy in only one instance, when discussing how concentration-camp inmates lived with uncertainty:

> By that time we had an inkling that there was a place like Auschwitz, but nobody expected what Auschwitz was.

[You didn't know about the gassings?]

> Nobody knew. You knew quick enough after you arrived. . . . The first thing that assailed your nostrils was the absolutely indescribable smell. I pray to God nobody ever in his life has to smell that again. But you didn't know what it was. (n90/#92A, p. 2)

In the only portion of text represented as conversation, I neglected to identify myself as the interviewer. However, it seems I was at least as ambivalent about exposing the respondent's identity as I was about revealing my own. Thus, immediately preceding the excerpt quoted above, I had identified her, not by her name, which is Susan E. Cernyak-Spatz, but instead only as "a survivor of Theresienstadt ghetto and Auschwitz" (p. 93).

Susan is cited in "The Phenomenology of Surviving" a total of nineteen times (see Table 9.1). Yet it was not until the tenth time I quoted her that I actually identified her by name. I guarded her anonymity by obliquely referring to her as "one survivor" (p. 90), "the respondent quoted above" (p. 91), and "the same respondent, a survivor of Theresienstadt ghetto and Auschwitz" (p. 93). On page 93 I identified her synecdochically as "every survivor." Sometimes I even quoted her without identifying her in the narrative (pp. 91, 93, 95, 96, 98, 100). If you paid close attention to the string of characters following each citation, then perhaps you noticed that "Susan," who is mentioned by name or other direct reference nine times, and the anonymous "survivor of Theresienstadt ghetto and Auschwitz" are indeed the same person. You might also happen to recall my statement in the previous chapter that "the analysis presented in the next two sections of the chapter emerged from the interview I refer to as n90" (p. 90). Indeed, the text is deliberately structured in order to fragment Susan's life story. Interestingly, the twelfth time that Susan is mentioned in the chapter, I deleted "n" and tape numbers from the parenthetical citation. This was the third time I had referred to her as Susan. Looking back on "The Phenomenology of Surviving," it seems as though Susan's subjectivity literally broke through the text simply by virtue of my inscribing her by name.

In the next (thirteenth) inscription, an epigraph to a subsection of the chapter, Susan is again identified by numbers only. However, with only one exception, the final six times Susan is quoted in the text she is identified by her name or by reference to a prior quote attributed to her. Henceforth, I abandoned my numerical notation system.

There is a peculiar irony to my choice of numbers as an inscription device for Susan, as opposed to a pseudonym or initial. Like virtually all Auschwitz inmates who were not immediately sent to the gas chambers or transferred to other camps, she had been tattooed with a number. When I interviewed Susan, she had pushed the long sleeves of her sweater up above her elbows, and the tattoo on her forearm was prominent. Having never before seen a survivor's tattoo up close, I felt a mixture of horror and curiosity. I asked her if I could touch it. "Go ahead," she nodded. "But it's not raised so there's nothing to feel." I ran my fingers over her left arm, making continuous circles with my thumb. She was right, of course. I felt only her firm flesh beneath my fingers.

It is difficult to describe just what this experience meant to me at the time. Children and animals, of course, are inclined to touch a "strange" person or object, perhaps first asking for permission or simply proceed-

TABLE 9.1

Inscriptions of Susan E. Cernyak-Spatz
in Text of "The Phenomenology of Surviving"

Citation Number	Page Number	Inscription in Text	Parenthetical Citation
1	p. 90	One survivor	(n90/#92A, p. 7)
2	p. 91	The respondent quoted above	(ibid.)
3	p. 91	She (continuity is established in the text between this inscription and the previous one)	(#92B, p. 21)
4	p. 91	—	(n90/#92A, p. 6)
5	p. 93	Every survivor	(n90/#92B, pp. 15–16)
6	p. 93	—	(n90/#92A, p. 7)
7	p. 93	The same respondent, a survivor of Theresienstadt ghetto and Auschwitz	(n90/#92A, p. 2)
8	p. 95	—	(n90/#92B, pp. 14–15)
9	p. 96	—	(n90, p. 6)
10	p. 96	Susan	(n90/#92B, pp. 14–15)
11	p. 98	Susan	(n90/#92A, p. 10)
12	p. 98	Susan	(pp. 8–9)
13	p. 98	—	(n90/#92A, p. 9)
14	p. 99	Susan	(p. 7)
15	p. 99	Susan	(p. 11)
16	p. 100	Susan	(pp. 12, 18)
17	p. 100	—	(p. 12; and pers. comm. 31 January 1991)
18	pp. 100–101	Susan	(p. 10)
19	p. 101	She (continuity is established in the text between this inscription and the previous one)	(p. 15)

ing unselfconsciously. Touching can make someone who appears to be "different"—even frightening—seem familiar.* We adults, however, usually have learned to repress or ignore our spontaneous urges for tactile contact with strangers because we don't want to be rude or violate other people's body space. Indeed, this felt like a forbidden exchange three times over: first, simply wanting to touch her tattoo; second, expressing the urge; and third, acting upon it.

For the SS guards in Auschwitz/Birkenau, tattooing a number on a concentration-camp inmate was an integral step in the process of degradation and dehumanization. Once inmates were tattooed, numbers became their official identities. Guards referred to them by their numbers and forbade them to address each other by their given names. Social scientists, however, are not in the business of degradation and dehumanization. Yet we too "protect" our respondents by expunging their names and replacing them with numbers. (The legal term used by the Nazis for arresting Jews and deporting them to labor and death camps was *Schutzhaft*—"protective custody.") But from what, exactly, are we protecting our research subjects?

The American Sociological Association's "Code of Ethics" describes anonymity and confidentiality as "rights" belonging to our research subjects and as "*prima facie* obligations that may admit of exceptions but which should generally stand as principles for guiding [researchers'] conduct":[7]

> Subjects of research are entitled to rights of biographical anonymity.[8]

> To the extent possible in a given study sociologists should anticipate potential threats to confidentiality. Such means as the removal of identifiers, the use of randomized responses and other statistical solutions to problems of privacy should be used where appropriate.[9]

Generally, social scientists define anonymity as an ethical issue. But I find this view problematic, for it masks the fact that anonymity is a representational strategy with political, historical, as well as psychological consequences for our respondents and us alike.

By definition, anonymity effaces the subjectivity of both ethnographers and ethnographic subjects. Ethnographic representations may be

---

*Rebecca D. King has suggested to me that "touching the subject is equivalent to touching one's own subjectivity [while] 'protection' of the subject is equivalent to protection of the researcher's subjectivity" (pers. comm., September 1988).

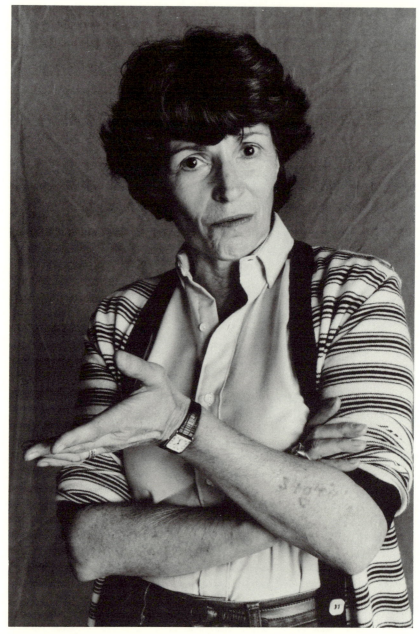

Susan Cernyak-Spatz at the American Gathering of Jewish Holocaust Survivors, Washington, D.C., 1983. Photo copyright 1990 by Carol Bernson and Stephen Shames.

assimilated (albeit with ambivalence) by our subjects as they read texts or view documentary films about their lives and cultures.[10] This is the reason Barbara Myerhoff came to believe "that the worst thing we had done to the center people [elders at the Israel Levin Senior Center] was to exclude them from the film [when editing decisions were made to cut entire interviews], to change their names in the book."[11]

Reflecting on her fieldwork with Jewish elders living in Venice, California, Myerhoff explained why she decided to stop "protecting" her informants' anonymity:

> After much deliberation I decided to use real names in this paper, for the Center, the community, and the pertinent individuals. This is not consonant with general anthropological practice, which seeks to preserve the anonymity of the populations it studies. In this case, however, the groups' [*sic*] urgent desire to be recorded suggests that it is appropriate to name names; it is also consistent with the approach that they have pressed me to take and that I have agreed is suitable. In view of the wide distribution of the film about them, anonymity is not genuinely possible, in any case. Since I live in close proximity to these people and continue to be in contact with them, I regularly submit my writings and photographs to them for comment. There is usually some disagreement about my interpretations; sometimes I amend the original statements, sometimes I merely note that our views do not concur.[12]

Shortly before her death, Barbara Myerhoff reconsidered the themes of anonymity and visibility in the lives of her informants. She recounted the following story about Rebekkah Goldman's reluctance to sign a new release form and her struggle to persuade Rebekkah to change her mind. (Rebekkah is the widow of Shmuel, Barbara's key informant in *Number Our Days*.) Rebekkah resisted signing the form because she realized that *Number Our Days* was an "ethno-reality" more obdurate than the actual lives on which it was based, including her own. For Rebekkah the irony of the situation verged on being unbearable.

A play adapted from the book was being produced at the Mark Taper Forum in Los Angeles, and Rebekkah,

> the only living, identifiable person in the piece, had to sign a new release form giving permission for her portrayal. The release form would allow the theater to portray her "fictionally, anonymously, without any claims." I was uneasy from the start. For so many of the elderly, their very lives depended on making claims, on not releasing their identity. I sensed trouble. . . . [Rebekkah] wouldn't sign. . . .

I go over the release [with her] word by word. There will be a
character based on her, fictionalized, an actress portraying her who may
or may not look like her. No claims. Everything is all right until we get
to the part about changing her name. "You mean you wouldn't use my
real name? How would anybody know it was me? My children, my
grandchildren. It will all be lost. You and I know Shmuel's greatness.
Without your book, it would have remained hidden. By your work,
you put it out to the world. Now, you take that away if you change the
name. Why couldn't you use our real names? . . ."

"Rebekkah, if you don't sign this, there will not even be a play. Or
there will be a play with you left out altogether. . . ."

"Will this be a good play? Will it be correct? How can you be sure it
will be true, if they make it a fiction?"

"I'm working very closely with the writer and director, Rebekkah.
They love the material. They love you and Shmuel and are making it
very carefully, full of respect and understanding. Art has its own truth.
Trust me, Rebekkah. Sign. . . ."

"But the name you will use in the play — it must be my real name. It
should say 'Rebekkah and Shmuel Goldman.'"

"But those are the names in the book that I substituted for yours."

"That's right. That's where the story is. My own name, no one
knows. What difference would it make? In the book I am known. I can
show that's me. Let them use those in the play."

"I don't know if they will. Let's try. I'll put down that this is your
request, that we use Rebekkah and Shmuel Goldman, not your actual
names or any others. I can't promise, but we'll try."

"How should I sign this paper? I'm also known as Regina, it was my
name when I lived in Paris."
At noon she signs. . . .[13]

Like the center people with whom Barbara Myerhoff worked, the
Holocaust survivors we interviewed relied on our promise to remember
and retell their stories. "Protecting" their anonymity would have been
gratuitous, because they had signed releases authorizing us to publish
and broadcast their names, voices, and photographs. Indeed, anonymity
would have contravened their wish to be known as survivors. If we are to
fulfill our commitment to keep their stories alive, then genuine anonymity
will be impossible.

Masking respondents' identities may be necessary in research that
generates abstract principles about aggregates of people. However, in
research designed to explore lived experiences and life worlds, this
practice ought to be questioned. A wish to be anonymous expresses

secrets and silences that lie at the core of what it means to have—or be—a self. Researchers' *and* respondents' desires for anonymity reflect cultural constructions of privacy and power. As such, they can be examined and probed. They can be grist for the ethnographic mill.

As an alternative to the conventional view of confidentiality and anonymity as "rights," "*prima facie* obligations," and "principles,"[14] together with our respondents, we can explore the meanings and consequences of revealing or masking their identities. To strive to honor our respondents' wishes by negotiating the terms of inscription with them would introduce an unprecedented level of accountability into ethnographic writing.

"The Phenomenology of Surviving" reads like a veiled life history, for I took great pains to obscure Susan's identity as my key respondent. Even so, it is evident that her story is central to the analysis. As I explained in the methodology section:

> The analysis presented in the next two sections of this chapter emerged from the interview I refer to as n90. [Although grounded theory is a comparative method,] . . . I did not sample comparative cases for this study; hence, my analysis is not fully "grounded." . . . My description of the basic social process of surviving was produced with data from this respondent and interviews with eleven other survivors.

When I wrote "Phenomenology," I was in a methodological bind. It seemed to me that grounded theory was incompatible with a life-history approach. Yet at this point in my research, I was reluctant to place the weight of my analysis on a single subject.

My reservations about grounded theory remain implicit in "Phenomenology." In retrospect, I recognize my ambivalence about the unit of analysis I had selected—the basic social process of surviving as against my key respondent's life history. Ironically, hedging my analysis of Susan's life history with data from an additional eleven respondents further ruptured her narrative. In the end, it seems I was determined *not* to present her story as being all of a piece.

In writing "Phenomenology," I performed textual maneuvers that severed, splintered, and truncated Susan's narrative. I repudiated my own subjectivity along with hers. Readers will scarcely recognize Susan's commanding presence as a storyteller, or her position as a key informant in my research, but for the traces inscribed in these reflections.

CODA

I wrote "The Phenomenology of Surviving" toward the end of my first year of living in New England, 1984–85. In San Francisco, where I spent the summer of 1985, I circulated drafts of the chapter to my friends. Gloria Lyon was among those who read the piece.

I vividly recall sitting with her and Karl at their dining-room table, while Gloria pored over the manuscript with laser-like concentration. Karl and I sat side by side as he guided me through a scrapbook of photographs from their recent trip to Israel. In less than an hour, we visited several different archaeological ruins, Mount Kinneret, and the Old City.

Gloria sat across the table from Karl and me, oblivious to our conversation. About two-thirds of the way through the chapter, she stopped abruptly and gasped. Placing the manuscript face down, she began to cry. My reference to Eva's experiences at the Auschwitz hospital block had triggered, for Gloria, a long-forgotten memory of being sent there herself.

Eventually, Gloria was calm enough to tell us what she could remember about the Auschwitz hospital. I did not record her story at the time, and by now I have forgotten the details. What I do recall is how her voice halted and broke as she constructed these experiences, for the first time, as memories.

As I record my own memories of Gloria's remembering, I am struck once again by survivors' interdependence for stimulating the process of recall. For Gloria, remembering will be a lifelong project. As new memories surface, she will revise her account of being deported and imprisoned. And each new memory may take her by surprise.

Memories are fashioned in continuous, weaving motions between "past" and "present" selves. Back and forth, as the shuttle of a loom passes the thread of the woof between the strands of the warp, memories are the greatest achievements of Holocaust survivors.

"IN THE NAME OF THE HOUSE OF ORANGE"
A Life History of Leesha Rose during the Holocaust

In the beginning we grasp whatever we can to survive.

Adrienne Rich, *Sources*

I feel we can call every Jew a survivor. Hitler didn't mean only me and my family and the six million. He meant every one of us.

Leesha Rose, Jerusalem, 1981

O n 10 May 1940 Germany invaded Holland. After three days of fighting, Dutch resistance forces were devastated. By day four of the invasion the Dutch had capitulated. The Nazis targeted the Jewish community for immediate destruction.

Midway through the occupation, which lasted for five years, Leesha Rose, a twenty-year-old Dutch Jew, made contact with the resistance and began to help other Jews go into hiding. My account of Leesha's life is based on her interview with Lani Silver, my collaborator on the Holocaust Media Project,[1] and her memoir.[2]

THE OCCUPATION (1940–MID-1943)

Leesha had just graduated from high school when the German occupation began. She remembered the invasion vividly: "It was a gorgeous Friday morning. . . . In the early morning hours, we heard shooting and a lot of noise, and ran outside. I heard all the neighbors in their gardens. Everyone was talking and shouting and looking up. There we saw the most horrible sight. The Germans parachuted right into Holland like a plague of locusts" (p. 1).

One hundred forty thousand Jews were living in Holland when the occupation began. Leesha lived with her family in one of the largest Jewish communities, The Hague, the de facto capital of the country. Prior to the occupation, Dutch Jewry had enjoyed full civil rights.[3] As

---

113

Leesha explained, "The Dutch Jews were considered equal. You could rise to any position on your own merit. There was absolutely no discrimination" (p. 2).

Six weeks after the capitulation agreement was signed, the Germans enacted the first anti-Jewish decree, expelling Jews from the civil defense service, the Dutch ARP.[4] By the end of October 1940, Jews owning businesses were ordered to register them. More anti-Jewish edicts were passed during fall and winter of the first year of the occupation, and on 10 January 1941, all Jews were ordered to register with the Census Office.[5]

> It started with the registration. They registered everybody and the Jews had to sign that they were Jews. . . . And from that time on, they had us marked. So started a gradual social isolation, where it was forbidden for Jews to mix in the professions, to teach in non-Jewish schools. [Jewish] children were not allowed to go to gentile schools. . . . All the Jews were fired from the civil service. (P. 2)

The "Final Solution" of Dutch Jewry was implemented in stages.[6] For more than two years before mass deportations began, economic and civil restrictions gradually disenfranchised the Jewish community. The Nazis intended to wreak confusion with each new decree. For how much longer could the Jewish community remain intact? When would the repression end? What would happen next?

Implementation of the Final Solution by increments significantly determined how the Jews made sense of events happening around and to them. In each country occupied or annexed by the Third Reich, a veil of deception or "closed awareness context" was imposed.[7] By preventing Jewish communities from knowing the scope of the Final Solution beyond their borders, the Nazis intended to quell fear and manipulate the Jewish leadership.[8] This was a ruse and, for the most part, it succeeded.

The Jewish community responded to the mounting restrictions with combined relief and horror. Many people believed that they were safe because they had not yet been ordered to appear for "relocation" or deportation. Yet the repression was frightening and humiliating, and day-to-day survival became progressively difficult. Leesha recalled that during the first years of the occupation her mother remained steadfastly optimistic, encouraging her family to look on the brighter side. "So we won't go to the museum, so we won't go to a concert. At least we will be together" (p. 3).

But where was the line between hope and delusion? The Jewish community and its leaders wanted to believe the Nazis would keep their word to treat Dutch Jews as ordinary citizens. Yet with each new decree the duplicity and danger increased. Under the occupation, Jews were forced to accept the fundamentally changed conditions of their lives. As the repression escalated, the Jews accommodated—personally, politically, socially, and economically. "Look," Leesha explained, "in wartime years and in emergency, you go through it, you live with it, you learn how to adjust yourself to misfortunes" (p. 4).

In April 1941, Jews were ordered to forfeit all wireless radios—their access to news from the Allies and the Dutch Government-in-Exile. Broadcasts from London connected them to the world beyond Nazi propaganda and the German war machine. For those who dared to risk death or deportation, it was possible to disobey (p. 3). Leesha's family took the risk.

> We had a cupboard, and my father made sliding doors that you couldn't see were there—they looked like the wall—and behind that was our radio. . . . We listened to the BBC and to the . . . broadcast from the Dutch Government-in-Exile. . . . I still remember, my brother sat in the hallway to listen for somebody trying the door. . . . I was there in the little room with the cupboard, where many of my father's friends came. After the news was over, I translated it and they had an armchair "war cabinet," where they discussed and decided everything. (P. 5)

Full-scale deportation of the Dutch Jews began in July 1942.[9] However, since as early as February 1941 the Jewish quarter in Amsterdam had been subjected to raids; periodically, the Nazis would round up Jews and cart them off to Buchenwald and Mauthausen.[10] Leesha remembered 1942 as a period of interminable waiting. By now, the fate of Dutch Jewry was more certain and more horrible than anyone had imagined. No one doubted *whether* they would be called up for "labor service." Only *when* remained uncertain.

> That whole year, we were waiting to be deported. At that time, it was as if the whole world was sinking from under you. . . . You didn't know from one day to the next if you were going to live or die. It was a time that felt like the whole world was just disintegrating. You didn't know where to get even a moment's peace, a moment's relaxation. (Pp. 9–10)

After high school Leesha applied to study medicine at university. However, by early 1941 no new Jewish students were being admitted to Dutch universities. Still, Leesha's desire to become a physician remained strong. As a compromise, she applied for nurse's training at the Jewish Invalid Hospital in Amsterdam, and in April 1942 she was accepted (p. 9).

Leesha lived in the hospital quarters for student nurses. She was deeply caring, committed to patients, and got on well with other students and her supervisors (*Tulips*, p. 73). Working at the hospital made her indispensable to the Jewish community and temporarily exempted her from deportation. Indeed, she was fortunate to hold this position. According to Jacob Presser:

> The inviolability of [the Jewish Invalid Hospital] . . . had become almost legendary among the Jews, so much so that many people offered their services as voluntary staff or even paid for the privilege of working there. Someone even called the place a human safe; at the end of February [1942] it held 416 patients, 197 full-time staff and 158 part-time staff.[11]

During her first year away from home, Leesha missed her family terribly. But the demands of her job and the solidarity and community that developed among the student nurses helped to mitigate the pain of separation.

Throughout 1942 the hospital provided a margin of safety from nightly raids and roundups. But by the end of February 1943 the hospital director could no longer stave off the Nazis. On the last day of the month, the day before the Gestapo planned to raid the hospital, the Jewish Council★ "leaked" word that deportation was imminent.[12]

> So, what would you do if somebody announced today that tomorrow you are going to be caught and you are going to be sent to a concentration camp? Naturally, everybody started running away. Everybody. The staff, even the patients who could walk, left. Anyone who had a place to go [left]. (P. 10)

FIRST ESCAPE (MARCH 1943)

Along with a few of her coworkers, Leesha decided *not* to leave the hospital. She had been assigned to night watch that week and, she

★The Jewish Council (*Joodse Raad*) was the committee of Jewish leaders that mediated between Nazi officials and the Jewish community at large. It was responsible for implementing local anti-Jewish edicts, and ultimately, for selecting Jews for deportation. During the occupation the Jewish Council also provided housing, food, and other vital community services.

explained, "I just couldn't get it over [*sic*] my conscience. I just couldn't reconcile myself to running away" (p. 10).

Half a dozen other staff also stayed on at the hospital. The night before the raid, Leesha was responsible for one hundred patients, most of whom had chronic conditions. Although the patients on the wards were too ill to leave, they "knew exactly what was going on" (p. 11). Leesha remembered the deep satisfaction she derived from caring for her patients that night.

> If I ever got any kind of reward for the little bit I did during the war, it was during that night, seeing the gratefulness and the love shining for me through the eyes of those unfortunate people. I mean, what did I do for them? I gave them some medicine, I brought them some food, something to drink. I helped them go to the bathroom. (P. 11)

Leesha wanted to stay with her patients for as long as she could. But she and her friends had no intention of being rounded up. Instead, they made an escape plan.

Early the next morning, a nurse would be stationed on the hospital roof as a lookout. His job would be to alert the other staff when the Nazis began to surround the hospital. After the nurse on lookout gave the sign, Leesha and her comrades would leave the hospital building via the roof, jump to the roof of the adjacent building, and enter it through a trap door. This was how they would make their way down the block until they were clear of the SS.

If the roof route proved unfeasible, their alternate plan was to hide in a crawl space in the hospital sanctuary. They prepared for the possibility of a long stay while the Nazis occupied the hospital by storing away mattresses, candles, water, and bread.

At six o'clock the next morning, the first shift was due to arrive, but no one dared to enter the hospital. At 8:30 A.M., when the Nazis were expected to come, the Jewish Council telephoned the hospital director to say that yesterday's warning had been a false alarm. No raid was planned after all. However, by the time the hospital director had hung up the telephone, the nurse standing guard on the roof had given the signal that the hospital was surrounded by SS.

Leesha and her coworkers fled to the hospital roof, but it was too late to escape. An entire city block was covered with armed SS guards and deportation vans. Nor could the alternate plan be implemented, because when Leesha and her comrades approached the sanctuary, a German soldier sent them away to prepare patients for deportation. There was no safe place to hide in the hospital. The only way out seemed to be with the patients in the deportation vans.

> And then it happened. Something. It was as if somebody or something was pushing me. I don't know where I got this from. It was like an instinct. I put down my satchel. I took out only my ID card and change purse and I folded my white nurse's apron under my coat and I went to the door.
>
> Then I saw another nurse coming and she said, "Where are you going to?" I said, "I don't know but I'm not going to the right to the wagons. I'm going to try to get away." She said, "Can I come with you?" I said, "Look, it's all on our own risk. They can shoot us down right now in cold blood."
>
> She said she wanted to come with me, so instead of going to the wagons, we went to the left. We were walking and I said just to walk very calmly. You know, every yard there was another black shirt standing there surrounding that whole block.
>
> Then, all of a sudden, I heard someone yell, "Where are you going?" One of the black shirts was yelling after us and this other nurse started to whimper, and I tell you, my knees turned to jelly. But I said to her, "Let's just go very calmly, as if we are going for a walk. Just make believe you are going for a walk." This is how we came to the next main street.
>
> I jumped right into traffic, crossed the road and then we turned the corner and we started running for a whole hour. We ran until we came to another neighborhood where it was already safe, and we came to a certain address where we rested up.
>
> So now what was I to do? I had a stamp of being exempt from deportation as long as I was useful to the Germans (being a nurse in the hospital), but now the hospital was deported. So I didn't know what to do. I went to my mother [in The Hague]. (Pp. 12–13)

The train trip between Amsterdam and The Hague took Leesha about an hour. By 1943 Jews were prohibited from using public transit (train or tram) or private vehicles (bicycle or motor car) without special permits. These were infrequently granted.[13] Leesha didn't want to call attention to herself by requesting a travel permit from the Gestapo, so she simply removed her yellow star, walked to the station, and boarded a train to The Hague. (For the past ten months, Dutch Jews had been required to wear a yellow star on their clothing, which publicly marked them.)[14]

Leesha's visit home was brief. Her father had already been deported and her mother was waiting for orders of her own. Yet, there was still a glimmer of hope because the family had registered to go to Palestine (*Tulips*, p. 99). Until they could emigrate, her mother expected to remain with her husband and two sons, Leesha's brothers, in Wester-bork, a Dutch transit camp. She was confident that her family was safe from being deported to a death camp.

Over BBC broadcasts while Leesha was home, she and her mother heard rumors of gassings in the camps (*Tulips*, p. 99). Before parting, they discussed what she should do next. They agreed that Leesha would be safest in Amsterdam, where she was legally registered. She would try to join the staff of the Netherlands Israelite Hospital (NIZ) (*Tulips*, p. 99).

SECOND ESCAPE (JUNE 1943)

The following day, Leesha applied for work at the NIZ. She was readily granted a position on the nursing staff because of her escape from the Jewish Invalid Hospital. It wasn't long before she was assigned to care for a patient named Peter under special police guard. Peter was a member of the Dutch resistance. The Nazis wanted to keep him alive in order to interrogate him.

Peter told Leesha about his resistance work. He had heard about her escape from the Jewish Invalid Hospital and praised her courage and wits. He asked Leesha to consider doing rescue work at the hospital — helping Jews to go into hiding with gentiles — and gave her a contact address and the underground password "the tulips are red" (p. 15).

Leesha was conflicted about joining the resistance. She was concerned about what her mother would say, yet she realized that to talk with any-one would endanger both the underground and herself. She also worried about the personal risks, especially getting caught (*Tulips*, p. 102).

Still, Leesha recognized that she was hardly safe at the NIZ, where the most she could hope for was to buy time while waiting to be deported. "Why should I submit meekly to this slaughter without offering resis-tance? I did not want to go on living in fear," she remembered thinking (ibid.).

Leesha was deliberating whether to join the resistance when her brother Paul telephoned the hospital to report that their mother and younger brother, Jackie, had been picked up in a raid. This call inten-sified her feelings of vulnerability and impelled her to act. She requested permission to leave the hospital and travel home to The Hague.

With no time to apply for a travel permit, Leesha removed her yellow star once again to avoid being harassed on the train (*Tulips*, p. 103). As a hospital nurse she had an exemption, indicated on her identity card, that enabled her to visit her mother and brother at the deportation assembly place. Her hesitancy about joining the resistance was resolved during this trip home, when she saw her mother for the last time. She decided to take the risk (*Tulips*, pp. 105, 107).

> Whenever I heard [about] someone who wanted to go into hiding, I would speak to him in secret. During visiting hours someone from the resistance would come, ostensibly to visit a certain patient. Then at the conclusion of the visit, they would walk out together, unnoticed among the crowd of visitors. Sometimes I brought children to an appointed place and they would be met there by an underground contact and taken into hiding. (*Tulips*, p. 108)

Toward the end of June 1943, the NIZ was raided. Half the staff was rounded up and taken to the *Borneokade*, a secluded and well-patrolled quay. Leesha was among them. After a day of waiting on the heavily guarded platform, the deportees were loaded on trains (*Tulips*, p. 113).

> Then, sitting on the train, I heard a German walking alongside the train calling out four names. I saw two nurses jumping down with their satchels and they went to the Aus der Fünten [Chief of Transports, SS Haupt Sturmführer Ferdinand Aus der Fünten, who was responsible for the day-to-day administration of the Central Office for Jewish Emigration], and he talked with them, and then he made a motion for them to stand to the side. The German was still going around calling two names and one was Lilly Bromet, but Lilly didn't jump down. Nobody jumped down. Then I realized what the four names were. They were the names of four nurses that were working on the communicable disease board. . . .
>
> All of a sudden I felt as if something else was telling me to do something. I didn't know what. I just took a chance and at that time I didn't even realize I was taking a chance at all.
>
> I took my satchel and jumped down and went to the Aus der Fünten and said, "I'm Lilly Bromet." Well, that man was already so impatient he started screaming at me, and I could feel the breath right on my cheek as he was yelling at me. I thought in the next minute he is going to beat me or shoot me down. Not only that, in my pocket was my ID card and that is the first thing that Germans ask for. *The first thing*. It was your passport to life or death, mostly death.
>
> It was right there in my pocket with my Jewish name, not Lilly Bromet. My Jewish name was Hava Bornstein. And he didn't ask me for it.
>
> It was like a miracle that he didn't ask me for my ID card. He started yelling at me again and asked me why I didn't leave the train, why I didn't come down before. So I said I hadn't heard him. Anyhow, finally

he stretched out his arm and motioned for me to stand aside. The other nurses and I didn't look at each other. We were just scared. Nobody even motioned anything with their eyes. Not even a sign of recognition.

Subsequently, the train left and this whole row of black shirts left with the motorcycles and then the three of us were brought back on the same big wagon with the Gestapo, back to the hospital. This was my second escape. (Pp. 17–18)

When Leesha returned to the NIZ, she was greeted by the Jewish Council's liaison to the hospital, a man named Mr. Wolf. In April, shortly after Leesha's mother and Jackie were deported, her brother Paul had been picked up in a raid. Wolf had offered to use his influence to try to rescue Paul, but in exchange for his trouble he had tried to seduce her.[15] Leesha slapped him across the face, making it clear that his behavior was way out of line.

This time, Wolf was enraged that Leesha had interrupted the deportation process by taking Lilly Bromet's place. Lilly was an exempted nurse who, most likely, had "disappeared" from the hospital before the raid. Wolf was not interested in Leesha's escape, which had saved her own life without endangering anyone else. (In the place of nurses who hid instead of reporting for deportation, the Gestapo took veteran nurses as hostages [*Tulips*, p. 113].)

Wolf and other *Joodse Raad* functionaries helped to transform Dutch Jewry into mere bodies that filled deportation quotas. Like many Council members, Wolf may have believed that he could save himself and his family by delivering up the required number of Jews. Perhaps he cooperated out of fear of Nazi reprisal if deportation orders were not followed exactly. It is even possible that he might have reacted more favorably to Leesha's report of her escape had she not previously resisted his sexual advances. Ironically, Leesha might have been turned over to the SS by this member of the *Joodse Raad* if the hospital director-general had not intervened on her behalf (*Tulips*, p. 116).

After her second escape, Leesha seriously considered going into hiding. But she remained above ground for two reasons. First, along with her mother, she hoped that her family would soon be permitted to emigrate to Palestine and avoid deportation to the east. Since her parents and brothers were interned at Westerbork, Leesha needed to be at large in order to deliver money to the Palestine exchange agent and sign documents.* The second reason Leesha decided against going into hiding

* Between 1943 and 1945 hundreds of letters were distributed to Jews living in Nazi-occupied countries stating that their bearers were candidates for exchange to Palestine. The

was her commitment to helping other Jews "disappear" through the underground. Only by staying at the hospital could she continue doing rescue work (*Tulips*, pp. 116–17).

Leesha's motives for staying above ground were complex. They cannot be reduced to self-sacrifice, martyrdom, or altruism, on the one hand, or to blind faith or naiveté, on the other. These were not the values or attitudes that shaped her thinking and actions. Instead, we must imagine what it might have meant to Leesha to protect herself at the expense of honoring commitments to her family. What might she have thought and felt had she stopped doing rescue work with the resistance?

Genocide can reframe life's meanings. For Leesha, the Final Solution rendered her own survival wanting as an end in itself. Instead, she found purpose in the struggle to help preserve other lives—through commitments and responsibilities to other people.

Yet resisting was extremely risky. Historian Michael R. Marrus notes that three-quarters of all Jewish resisters were deported, only one-third of whom survived.[17] If Leesha had gone into hiding after her second escape from the SS, it is likely she would have faced less danger and increased her chances of survival. However, such a choice surely would have brought her great moral anguish.

Rescue work afforded Leesha opportunities for meaningful action in the face of enormous losses and an extremely uncertain future. Her concern for other people's safety helped to mitigate her sense of vulnerability as a Jew and an underground worker. Her relationships with people who shared her commitments and situation—comrades in the resistance and *onderduikers*, Jews who had gone into hiding—buffered the terror and isolation of surviving mass deportations. In spite of the risks of being arrested, tortured, and killed, Leesha's decision to remain above ground served her well, in addition to benefiting the Jews she helped to hide.

---

counterparts of Jews slated for exchange were Germans living in Palestine, the British Empire, and South America. The exchange document that Leesha held was probably issued in Geneva by the Jewish Agency's Palestine Office. However, her family's certificate and others like it did not guarantee that exchange would actually occur, nor even that the Germans would approve exchange. Yet bearing these papers often served to postpone and sometimes prevent deportation to the death camps, especially for Jews in the Netherlands and Belgium.

Altogether, as a result of exchange negotiations, only 550 Jews actually arrived safely in Palestine. Indeed, thousands of Jews who held passports and other identity documents— both authorized and forged, including exchange certificates—were deported and murdered by the Nazis.[16]

THIRD ESCAPE (JULY 1943)

Deportation of patients and staff at the NIZ continued during the second week of July.[18] Deportees were taken to the *Hollandse Schouwburg*, the Jewish theater in Amsterdam being used as a concentration center. They were held in the overcrowded theater for five days, without adequate food, air, medicine, or sanitation, or sufficient staff to care for the sick. On day six of the ordeal, word spread that trains to Westerbork would leave the following day (*Tulips*, p. 123).

Virtually all the deportees were on their way to a death of one sort or another. Transports left Westerbork weekly for "points east": principally Auschwitz/Birkenau, but also Bergen-Belsen, Sobibor, and Theresienstadt.[19] The deportees' uncertainty about their final destination must have made their last night at the *Hollandse Schouwburg* interminable.

Leesha remembered that "it became almost impossible to calm the people" (*Tulips*, p. 123). By mid-1943, "places with the names of Theresienstadt, Bergen-Belsen, Dachau, Auschwitz, and Buchenwald did not sound strange to us anymore" (*Tulips*, p. 99). As early as March 1943, rumors had begun to circulate about people being gassed in death camps (ibid.); yet no one believed this could happen to them until they actually confronted the smoke and stench from the crematoria. Those deportees who survived the journey east probably died in the gas chambers at Birkenau in the summer or autumn of 1943.

The night before the transport left for Westerbork, the unexpected happened once again.

> It was ten o'clock at night and all of a sudden, a young man came over to me and he introduced himself as Ron, and said that he was working for the Jewish Council. Actually, he was working for the Dutch resistance. And the Dutch resistance had decided to rescue me. He told me to come at six o'clock to the rooftop of that very tall building and not to tell anyone anything.
>
> Well, that whole week I didn't sleep at all. I mean, how could you sleep under these circumstances? That night I was just so excited and so frayed and so apprehensive as to what was going to happen. Finally, six o'clock came around and I made my way up. It was dark and I thought, "Oh no! I fell into a trap. This is a trap."
>
> Then I saw a flashlight and saw a couple of my friends there also, and Ron was there. He put his fingers on his lips and we were quiet. That whole city block was surrounded by Germans, and in between the buildings there were Germans patrolling. It was very difficult to get from building to building because there was a distance bigger than a person could jump, actually.

Well, I must tell you, I am terribly scared of heights, and especially to walk on the edge of a Dutch building is no pleasure. Very often, I just blacked out with fear. This escape took from the morning until the afternoon, making our way from rooftop to rooftop, down fire escapes; and making our way through the spaces where the Germans were patrolling, waiting until finally they moved away for a second; and then we would jump onto the next building, through a door and then up onto that building, again on the rooftop. That's how we were jumping.

Some people twisted their ankles and tore their clothes, but it didn't matter. Finally, there I was in the afternoon sun, coming through the last garden, and Ron told me, "You just go through this garden and then you are free. You have to go to the Jewish Invalid Hospital. They are waiting for you there. Ring the side door and they will be waiting for you."

Well, I had to control my inclination to just run into freedom, but I controlled it, and I walked over to the hospital and there was Alan Hartog. He was the engineer of the building. He opened the door and it was like an angel [appeared], like an angel. Finally, he showed me to a little room in the old part of the hospital, to a small room where I was hidden for five weeks, because I was already on the black list of the Gestapo, and they were after me.

The Dutch resistance said that I had to wait there in the meantime. Nobody knew about it, nobody knew about my existence except two people. (Pp. 19–20)

RESISTANCE (JULY 1943–APRIL 1945)

During the summer of 1943, the Nazis used the Jewish Invalid Hospital as a warehouse for stolen medical equipment and supplies. A handful of hospital staff, including Leesha's friends Alan Hartog and Jules Godefroi, were responsible for maintaining the building and keeping the inventory in order. They brought her food while she was *onderduike*, in hiding. For five weeks her sole human contact was with them (p. 21; *Tulips*, p. 127).

Several times weekly, Dr. Mayer, the German director of the hospital, inspected the building where Leesha was hiding. Whenever he arrived, an alarm buzzer warned Leesha to leave her room and hide in the shaft of a service elevator that had been disabled in order to serve as a temporary refuge. She would hang between floors in the immobilized elevator until Dr. Mayer left, sometimes waiting for an hour or two or even longer. At first she hid in the shaft by herself. Eventually, though, others hiding in the hospital waited together.

Leesha had been in hiding for nearly a month when Jules was warned that the Germans suspected members of the skeletal hospital staff of engaging in illegal activities. To ensure Leesha's safety he temporarily moved her to quarters outside the Jewish Invalid Hospital. Sure enough, the Nazis raided the hospital. After two days, when she returned "home," Jules reported that "'they checked every inch from top to bottom.'" It wasn't long before Leesha received an ID card, stolen from the City Registry, and a gentile name (*Tulips*, pp. 130–31).

> The day I got it, . . . I put down my fingerprints and became Elisabeth Bos, a gentile, a nurse. I entered the Dutch resistance.
> From Elisabeth came Leesha for short and that's why my name, Leesha, continued—for sentimental reasons, actually. The name Leesha gave me life at that time. That ID card was supplied to me by a Christian minister, Dominee Ader and also, Jan Meilof Yver, another very active member of the Dutch resistance. (Pp. 21–22)

Leesha/Hava left the hospital with her new identity papers. As a safeguard against questions that might expose her as a Jew, she began reconstructing her life story as a gentile. A gentile member of the Dutch resistance named Denencamp escorted her from the hospital out of Amsterdam, by now a far too dangerous place where she could have been recognized. For a short time Leesha stayed in Utrecht with the Denencamp family and their crowd of "guests"—other Jews in hiding and in transit.

Leesha and Denencamp traveled together the rest of the way to Leiden, her destination. Staying hidden indoors had made Leesha feel like a prisoner and she told Denencamp she wanted to continue doing rescue work. Denencamp, a kind and fatherly man, feared the danger Leesha would face as an active member of the resistance. Still, he agreed to "propose your request at our next cell meeting" (*Tulips*, p. 134). Indeed, he kept his promise to recommend Leesha to the underground movement in Leiden, and soon she became a courier (*Tulips*, p. 144).

By this time Leesha was safer than she had been since the deportations had begun a year earlier. Yet now her mind was free to worry about her family. She remembered thinking, "I wanted to be involved body and soul in the activities of the Resistance movement, in order to blot out the steady flow of agonizing images about my parents, brothers, and friends that kept plaguing me without rest" (*Tulips*, p. 155).

Leesha clung to the hope that her family would soon be safe. She believed their emigration to Palestine was assured by diamonds and cash

Leesha Rose [Hava Bornstein], 1941.

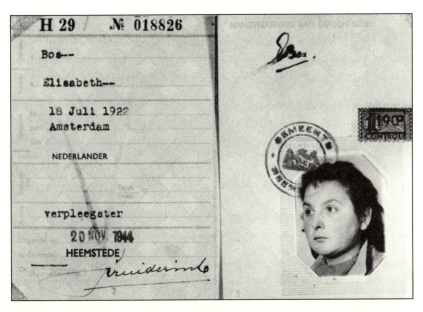

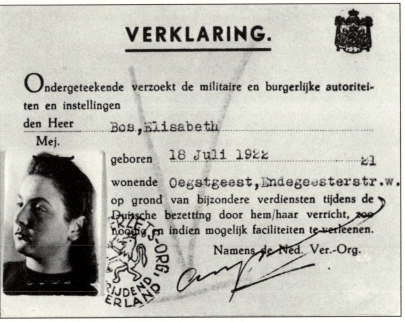

Leesha's illegal identity card and resistance ID card.

she had delivered to the exchange agent and an affidavit from relatives living there, which the International Red Cross had confirmed (*Tulips*, p. 143). Although her brother Paul had been gassed at Sobibor that May, it wasn't until the war had ended that she learned of his death (*Tulips*, p. 271).

During Leesha's early months *onderduiken*, she was hidden by two different families. When the Gestapo raided the first house, they found her ID in order. Still, as a hedge against future danger, the underground arranged for her to hide elsewhere. After Leiden, she moved to Heemstede, a suburb of Haarlem, where she lived and worked at *Het Marishuis*, a convalescent home. In Heemstede she resumed her work as an underground courier (*Tulips*, pp. 158–64).

Leesha turned twenty-two shortly after D-Day — 6 June 1944, when the Allies landed at Normandy (*Tulips*, pp. 168–70). By this time she had been underground for nearly a year. Her friends in the resistance were a great comfort to her, especially her contact, "Uncle Fritz," Fritz van Dongen, né Reinier van Kampenhout (*Tulips*, p. 164). A married man some years older than Leesha, Fritz fell deeply in love with her. But Leesha could not return his romantic feelings (*Tulips*, p. 172). Leesha recalled what their relationship and his love had meant to her.

> I could neither deny nor end our relationship. It was an unbreakable bond of pure friendship in which the one filled certain specific needs of the other. Those needs were not necessarily similar. Fritz accepted the fact that I did not love him the way he would have wanted it to be.
>
> In a world of war and hatred, in a time of killings and raids, insecurity, hunger, and loneliness he was the only human being who cared about me, who restored my ties with humanity, and who unreservedly offered me warmth and love on my terms.
>
> I loved him as a close friend, as a generous benefactor, and above all, as my mentor. He understood me so well. (*Tulips*, p. 175)

As the fifth year of the occupation began, Leesha was inconsolably lonely. She yearned for her mother's "caring eyes, [her] words so sweet and tender" and her father's "open hands" (*Tulips*, p. 161). She did not yet know that her mother and brother Jackie had been gassed at Birkenau in November 1943, or that her father had been killed just that spring.

After D-Day the tide began to turn in the Allies' favor. But as Germany's losses mounted, the Nazis stepped up their terrorizing of the Dutch people. Males between the ages of seventeen and fifty were deported to work in Germany. Gentiles were arrested at random, shipped to concentration camps, and sentenced to death on trumped-up charges. Hostages were publicly executed (*Tulips*, p. 172). Food became increasingly scarce. As men disappeared into hiding or were deported to forced labor, women's work in the resistance assumed new importance.[20]

> Nothing was too much or too dangerous for me. We did all kinds of actions against the Germans. We made raids on offices where we confiscated booklets of ration cards and illegal ID cards that were actually legal. Later on, it became a very efficient kind of working unit.
>
> We also made raids on Dutch farmers who were Nazi sympathizers. . . . The leader of that action group used to come in and say, "In the name of the House of Orange, we are taking possession of everything you own." That was not stealing, but that was [the] supply that we had to have for all the people that were hidden. . . .
>
> I was carrying all kinds of incriminating paper and ammunition from place to place because I was a girl. I was very often in danger. . . . But I felt during that time, I cannot sit still. I had to fight. Fight the injustice, and the deportation, and the loneliness that I felt in my heart—the injustice and the butchery that I saw everyday, no matter what the consequences of my own life. I thought, "I will fight until my last drop of blood [is gone]." (Pp. 22–23)

Antwerp, Belgium, was liberated on 4 September 1944. This was just 114 kilometers from Heemstede, where Leesha was living. By the next day, schools, shops, restaurants, and cafés were closed, and the occupying police had mysteriously left. It was even rumored that Rotterdam had been liberated! Spirits soared and tensions mounted in anticipation of the arrival of the Allies (*Tulips*, p. 177). But they were slow in coming. The Green Police soon returned and the Nazis resumed their reign of terror. The end of the war was still eight months away.

Over the BBC Dutch Government-in-Exile broadcasts announced the liberation of Maastricht, located in the south province of Limburg (*Tulips*, p. 184). Meanwhile, in armed and unarmed actions, the underground moved aggressively against the Nazis. One of the most spectacular acts of defiance was a railway strike, ordered by the Government-in-Exile and supported by the resistance, that aimed to hinder the advancing German army (*Tulips*, pp. 184–85). In retaliation the Germans placed an embargo on food transports in an east-west direction, and began bombing the Amsterdam and Rotterdam harbors (*Tulips*, p. 185). Meanwhile, the Dutch people were starving.

For some, food became an obsession. In July 1944, as part of a birthday package from Fritz, Leesha received an extra bread coupon. Instead of spending it immediately, she tucked it away.

Several months later, Leesha went on a shopping trip with Nora, a young Jewish girl she had taken into hiding at *Het Marishuis*. Leesha remembered the extra coupon and bought a small loaf of bread to share with her companion. They devoured it eagerly, but after it was gone Nora was still hungry. Although there had been only one coupon, she wanted a second loaf.

The two continued on their way, Leesha hauling a sack of potatoes for the convalescent-home pantry and Nora carrying their pocketbooks. But Leesha could hardly keep up with Nora. The young girl ran ahead and searched inside Leesha's purse for additional ration coupons. She found none. However, when she came upon Leesha's *persoonsbewijs* ("identity card") she held onto it.

Nora began joking that she would destroy Leesha's *persoonsbewijs* if she didn't get more bread. Leesha became furious and implored her to stop. The teasing grew serious, and moments later Nora shredded the card and threw it into the gutter (*Tulips*, pp. 185–87).

A valid ID was Leesha's only protection against deportation. Once again, she was in grave danger. Yet she was able to get word to Fritz explaining what had happened and he quickly mobilized the under- ground connections necessary to issue a new card.

First, Fritz sent Leesha to the local police to report the loss of her card. He instructed her to arrive at a designated hour and to speak with a specific person—a resistance infiltrator. Then, she had to be re- photographed. This was another vulnerable point at which she could have been discovered or betrayed. But to Leesha's surprise, the whole process went smoothly, and soon she was instructed to pick up her new card at the local municipality office (*Tulips*, pp. 187–88).

> This was almost unbelievable! It meant that the Underground Resis- tance movement had penetrated into the official government offices and that their workers were performing their illegal activities under the very eyes of the N.S.B.-Nazis [the Dutch Nazi party] and the Germans. I marveled at the daring and ingenuity of the Resistance, and I was eternally grateful to Fritz for his swift action, his reliability, and above all, his loving care. (*Tulips*, p. 188)

By the turn of the year, conditions in Holland were desperate. The Germans' retaliatory campaign against the railway strike had been effective. There was virtually no food in the western part of the country, nor electricity or coal for light and heat. Street raids were a constant threat. Public transportation stopped; since few people had bicycles, they had to walk great distances (*Tulips*, pp. 195, 202).

In January 1945 *Het Marishuis* shut its doors. By this time, food and heat had become impossibly scarce. However, the decisive factor in closing down was the great danger to the residents posed by German rockets, which were now being launched from Heemstede (*Tulips*, pp. 195–96).

Leesha relocated once again. From *Het Marishuis* she moved into the home of the Kruizinga family, righteous gentiles who lived near Leiden.

Shortly after New Year's, Fritz's home was raided by the Nazis, and he and his wife were taken away. Stolen ration cards, underground newspapers, shortwave radios, and guns were discovered in his possession. Leesha was asked to take over his duties — caring for over two hundred Jews and gentiles in hiding. Fritz had not recorded the names or hiding places of the *onderduikers* in his care, for the risk of this information falling into the Nazis' hands was too great. From just six names, Leesha reconstructed the identities and locations of the people in hiding for whom she would provide food, ration cards, fuel, money, identity cards, and news about the events of the war during the next five months.

> My main task was to keep alive . . . close to two hundred Jewish people. . . . I took care of them. I supplied them with a safe home and if it wasn't safe, I had to go and look for some other home with Christian people. I supplied them with an ID card and later on, we even legalized the illegal ID card on the assumed name. It was a bit complicated, but we had an entry into the offices of the city hall.
>
> We supplied our people with food. I got the money from a certain fund that was supplied by the Dutch Government-in-Exile. It was nothing too much. (Pp. 22–23)

> I found solace in attending to the needs of the people who were now in my charge. It was a source of deep pride and satisfaction to make a difficult decision and then to execute the daring deed that the situation required. Above all I loved to visit my *onderduikers*, the hidden people, to talk to them, to advise them, to bring them ration cards, extra food, financial aid, and even coal for heating. (*Tulips*, p. 220)

By April the end of the war was near. Every day, Allied bombers flew east over Holland to Germany. It was no longer a question of when the war would end, but rather "would we make it to the end?" (*Tulips*, p. 247). The Allies began making food drops to Dutch provinces in a "state of starvation." Thousands of tons of food were flown in from England and delivered by car from the liberated zones (*Tulips*, p. 250). Toward the end of April an unofficial truce was in effect.

The German surrender was days away from being signed when Leesha set out to discover what had happened to Reinier/Fritz five months earlier when the Nazis had arrested him (*Tulips*, p. 252). Along the way, she managed to obtain the assistance of a former German collaborator who was anxious to cover his tracks. This man hoped to protect himself from retribution on the part of the underground by providing Leesha with his car and being her driver. Still, Leesha faced the problem of finding gasoline for the trip. Ironically, now that the war was over, the German occupying forces were willing to cooperate with the resistance by providing her with fuel.

Leesha sought information about Reinier at three different prisons before she learned that he had been tortured and shot (*Tulips*, p. 257). After months of hoping against hope, the long wait was over. Reinier's death was devastating news, the first of many losses that would be confirmed once the occupation ended.

LIBERATION

May 8, 1945, was declared Victory (VE) Day. Leesha celebrated the defeat of Germany with a group of her friends, *onderduikers* she had taken care of. Her work continued as the occupation forces withdrew, for Jews who had been in hiding now needed help resettling (*Tulips*, p. 269).

Everyone was searching for news about family and friends who had been deported. Lists of survivors were published each day; the International Red Cross office kept a registry of the dead. As the full horror of the death camps began to unfold, the anxiety and restlessness of waiting settled over the Jewish community. Eventually, the fate of Leesha's family was reported (*Tulips*, pp. 270–71).

> I want to tell you, when I read this [list from the International Red Cross telling me what had happened to my family], it was as if a fire consumed me. I wasn't aware of anything. I must have blacked out. I only knew that somebody was pulling me away from the wall by my shoulders, where I was beating with my fists until the blood came out.
>
> From that time on, whatever I had experienced, whatever I went through, was just locked in my heart. *I didn't talk about it for twenty-five years.* (Pp. 26–27)

Leesha was now a young woman — twenty-three years old, alone, and on her own. Her hopes of being united with her family and her dear friend Reinier were shattered. The devastation wreaked by the occupation and the Final Solution was gradually coming into focus. Leesha described the period following liberation as "a throbbing cameo of excruciating torment" (*Tulips*, p. 272).

Still, Leesha found the resolve to begin medical studies at the University of Amsterdam, as she had wanted to do before the occupation. A committed Zionist, she also worked in the international underground movement that smuggled displaced Jews bound for Palestine across the Dutch-Belgian border. In 1946 she supervised a pioneer training center that prepared young people to make *aliyah*. "My energy knew no bounds," she recalled (*Tulips*, p. 273).

Leesha studied medicine and worked in the Zionist movement for two years. Then she left university and Holland to be married. Isaac Rose had been a Jewish chaplain in the Canadian Armed Forces. He and Leesha had met during the last days of the occupation. Isaac was the first person to whom Leesha had admitted she was Jewish since 1943 (p. 24). Their friendship became her lifeline. "I don't think I would have been able to survive that period [after the war without him]" (p. 25).

Leesha and Isaac Rose raised their family in Long Island, New York. She recalled wanting to protect her children from bearing the stigma of having a parent who was "different" (p. 27).

> They never knew anything. I brought them up only with the knowledge that their mother had been a fighter in the Dutch resistance. Otherwise, I didn't tell them anything. . . . I see how wrong I was then but . . . at that time, I thought the best thing for them would be to grow up like normal American children. (P. 27)

During the 1950s and 1960s, many survivors felt that it was virtually taboo to speak about the Holocaust. The view of America as a "melting pot" encouraged survivor-refugees to put the past behind them and assimilate quickly. The child-rearing ideology of the day defined children's sense of being "different" as a source of insecurity and a threat to their well-being. This affected both how survivor-parents shared their experiences with their children and what information was actually communicated between generations. Acknowledging the realities of genocide was well beyond the picture-book life-style to which many Jewish *and* gentile, middle-class American families aspired.

Yet, after decades of silence, it was Leesha's college-age son who impelled her to begin to reckon openly with her past.

> "Hey Mom, you actually never told me anything about the time you went through in Holland. What happened during the war? How did you feel as a young person under the Nazi regime? How could you stand it? What happened to your family? Where is our family?" . . .
>
> It was as if that whole world that was clogged up gradually opened up and everything came tumbling out. . . . I thought, if my son, the future generation, is interested in what happened, then all the other generations [will] want to know and must know. I owe it to them. (P. 28)

Eventually, Leesha began to speak about the Holocaust publicly and to organize community commemorations. She wrote and directed plays about Jewish heroism during the Nazi era and studied the period intensively. She also wrote a memoir, *The Tulips Are Red* (1978). For Leesha, as for many Holocaust survivors, the reckoning process consists of remembering and retelling: recounting the destruction of her family and community while affirming Jewish survival and resistance.

Leesha Rose, 1981.

REFLECTIONS ON "'IN THE NAME OF THE HOUSE OF ORANGE'"

I wanted to know what it meant to understand just one other person. For me, that was a question of basic sanity that I needed to explore and answer for myself. One of the things I did, part of my method, was to examine why I would choose such a topic. . . . I was able to talk about, make myself visible to myself, some of the painful experiences of my own life—material I had to deal with or die. I needed to exist, to be. At that point, how could I go to a New Guinea or Swaziland? For what possible reason? With what sense of myself? And with what illusion of helping whom?

Gelya Frank, "Barbara, May She Rest in Peace,
But Her Spirit Be with Us Always"

"'In the Name of the House of Orange'" is free of the fractured subjectivity embedded in "The Phenomenology of Surviving." I made no effort to mask Leesha's identity in my account of her life, although as a fugitive from the Nazis hers is the story of a masked and reconstructed self. I took great pains to inscribe Leesha's subjectivity in the text, instead of focusing on abstract sociological concepts, such as social structure, basic social process, or an ideal-type path through the Holocaust. "'In the Name of the House of Orange'" is written and presented as Leesha's story. It is told, presumably, from her point of view.

But a life cannot speak for itself a priori, nor only about itself. Meanings of lived experiences emerge and change over time, for reading and writing a life are fundamentally social acts. Life-history subjects are not the magical tracings left by an ethnographer's pen or computer; they are actively inscribed by means of narrative strategies. In Riv-Ellen Prell's words, "two lives [the life-history subject's and the ethnographer's] together produce one."

A hearer and listener ask, respond, present, and edit a life. The recorder, especially one who casts herself as student, is taking that life in, perhaps assimilating it to her own great story. So that as the life history takes shape, it is inevitable that the recorder will enact what Paul Rabinow, borrowing from Paul Ricoeur, thought constituted the essence of participant-observation fieldwork: "Comprehension of the self by detour of the comprehension of the other" (cited in Rabinow 1977). One must know oneself through and in light of the other.[1]

Clifford Geertz describes these representational concerns as "the question of signature, the establishment of an authorial presence within a text."[2] He suggests that ethnographers have disguised and confused the textual problem of "how best to get an honest story honestly told" with a straw epistemological problem—"how to prevent subjective views from coloring objective facts."[3]

> A number of unfortunate results have arisen from this burial of the question of how ethnographical texts are "author-ized" beneath anxieties (to my mind, rather exaggerated anxieties) about subjectivity. Among them is an empiricism extreme even for the social sciences; but one of the more mischievous has been that although the ambiguities implicit in that question [of signature] have been deeply and continuously felt, it has been extremely difficult to address them directly. Anthropologists are possessed of the idea that the central methodological issues involved in ethnographic description have to do with the mechanics of knowledge—the legitimacy of "empathy," "insight," and the like as forms of cognition; the verifiability of internalist accounts of other peoples' thoughts and feelings; the ontological status of culture. Accordingly, they have traced their difficulties in constructing such descriptions to the problematics of field work rather than to those of discourse. If the relation between observer and observed (rapport) can be managed, the relation between author and text (signature) will follow—it is thought—of itself.
>
> It is not merely that this is untrue, that no matter how delicate a matter facing the other might be it is not the same sort of thing as facing the page. The difficulty is that *the oddity of constructing texts ostensibly scientific out of experiences broadly biographical, which is after all what ethnographers do, is thoroughly obscured.*[4]

How did I construct Leesha Rose in the preceding life history? And how did I construct myself in the text—as a hearer, listener, asker of questions, recorder, interpreter, and editor? By what "rhetorical machinery"[5] did I achieve the appearance of representing "the native's point of view"? As author of the life-history text, I positioned the two of us in a dialogue across time, geography, generations, and, most significantly, across decades of silences and myths about the Holocaust. How I accomplished these textual maneuvers is the subject of this chapter.

Let me begin by calling your attention to three factors that shaped the writing of "'In the Name of the House of Orange.'" First, I did not personally interview Leesha. In fact, I have never met her. Lani Silver interviewed Leesha in 1981 at the World Gathering of Jewish Holocaust Survivors in Jerusalem, two years before we began our collaboration.

The second point I want you to notice is that "'In the Name of the House of Orange'" relies on two primary sources—*The Tulips Are Red* (Leesha's memoir) and the life-history interview that Lani conducted.[6] However, when I wrote Leesha's story, the interpretive consequences of merging an oral and a written text into a single narrative eluded me. Although my account distinguishes between these two sources with parenthetical citations, I made no substantive distinctions between them. My method of tacking back and forth between the two documents was grounded in my belief in a high degree of intertextuality. Toward the end of this chapter, I discuss how my assumption that Leesha was telling the "same" story in both texts proved to be problematic.

The third issue I want to address is my primary narrative strategy in "'In the Name of the House of Orange'": representing the "native's point of view."[7] In line with this injunction from feminist oral history and interpretive anthropology, I tried faithfully to represent Leesha's experiences in the resistance as she had come to understand and recount them. Yet in striving to tell Leesha's story as I believed she would, I overlooked my own positivist assumptions about the nature of life histories. Among these assumptions, I took for granted the verisimilitude between Leesha's experiences and her stories about her experiences.

Anthropologist Vincent Crapanzano suggests that the presumption of a correspondence between lives as they are lived and stories about lives lies at the heart of the personal narrative.[8] He contends that this is a distinctly modern, Western view, which has become conventionalized in the genres of biography and ethnography. Following Foucault, Crapanzano problematizes the idea of personal history as something "possessed" by every self. Instead, he claims it is a construct that rests on three culture-bound notions: *memory*, an active force or agent mediating between the past and present; *linear time*, the clear demarcation between past, present, and future; and *personality*, a stable (but flexible) entity that endures from birth until death, linked in some way to our physical bodies. Crapanzano makes a distinction between "the reality of personal history and the truth of autobiography."

> The former rests on the presumption of a correspondence between a text, or structure of words, and a body of human actions; the latter

resides within the text itself without regard to any external criteria save, perhaps, the I of the narrator.[9]

My understanding of life histories has changed considerably since I wrote "'In the Name of the House of Orange.'" I no longer view them as freestanding objects akin to shards of pottery or weavings, or as testimony that lies dormant inside a person until an interviewer comes along and asks the "right" questions. Rather, it seems to me that life histories represent moments—sometimes crucial, sometimes not—when people remember and reinterpret themselves. They may be told spontaneously or during formally enacted, ritual-like performances, such as ethnographic interviews. Because remembering is an active, self-fashioning process, the context in which stories are recounted is as significant for their overall interpretation as any single detail revealed in an unfolding narrative. As Barbara Myerhoff explained:

> Victor Turner has used the term "Re-membering," bracketing it by the hyphen to distinguish it from ordinary recollection. Re-membering, he offers, is the reaggregation of one's members, the figures who properly belong to one's life story, one's own prior selves, the significant others without which the story cannot be completed. Re-membering, then, is a purposive, significant unification, different from the passive, continuous, fragmentary flickerings of images and feelings that accompany other activities in the normal flow of consciousness. The focused unification provided by Re-membering is requisite to sense and order. Through it, a life is given shape that extends back in the past and forward into the future, a simplified, edited tale where completeness may be sacrificed for moral and aesthetic purposes. Then history approaches art, myth, and ritual. Perhaps this is why Mnemosyne, the goddess of memory, is the mother of the Muses. Without Re-membering, we lose our history and ourselves.[10]

Yet, conventionally, life histories are interpreted independently of their means of production, as though context and content and form and content were neatly separable. On the whole, ethnographers have assumed that valid and reliable representations and interpretations, told from a "native's point of view," can be achieved only by effacing their own subjectivities. Exposing the means of textual production by writing myself into this study is one device I have used to challenge the false duality between "subjective" and "objective" knowledge, between "self" and "other." By reinscribing myself in this chapter, as a partner in dialogue or an active commentator on Leesha's narrative, I aim to push against the fiction of self-provoked accounts, suspended in the timeless, ethnographic present.

The two tables that follow visualize the self/other dialectic (Table 11.1) and shifts in authorship and subjectivity (Table 11.2) in four versions of Leesha Rose's life story. Leesha is the author of one of these texts, her memoir. Together with Lani Silver, she is the coauthor of her life-history interview. I am author of both "'In the Name of the House of Orange'" and "Reflections on '"In the Name of the House of Orange,"'" which you are now reading.

Authors are always inscribed in our texts, for we leave traces of ourselves with every word we write. As a move against the duality between "subjective" and "objective" knowledge, I identify Leesha and me as cosubjects of "'In the Name of the House of Orange'" (Table 11.2). Yet when I wrote Leesha's life history I considered myself absent from the text; I merely intended to be a "transparent mouthpiece" for her story. I assumed that my understanding of her as a subject—particularly, the meanings of her decision to join the resistance—was sufficient for me to speak for her when I chose to do so. Indeed, on occasion I did speak for Leesha, but not as an outside observer. Consider the following three paragraphs, whose authoritative tone suggests that I am a privileged insider.

> Leesha's motives for staying above ground were complex. They cannot be reduced to self-sacrifice, martyrdom, or altruism, on the one hand, or to blind faith or naiveté, on the other. These were not the values or attitudes that shaped her thinking and actions. Instead, we must imagine what it might have meant to Leesha to protect herself at the expense of honoring commitments to her family. What might she have thought and felt had she stopped doing rescue work with the resistance?
>
> Genocide can reframe life's meanings. For Leesha the Final Solution rendered her own survival wanting as an end in itself. Instead, she found purpose in the struggle to help preserve other lives—through commitments and responsibilities to other people.
>
> . . . If Leesha had gone into hiding after her second escape from the SS, it is likely she would have faced less danger and increased her chances of survival. However, such a choice surely would have brought her great moral anguish.

As I reflect on this passage, I am troubled by the transparent veil in which I have cloaked myself. In the absence of negotiation and dialogue between Leesha and me, I assumed that it was appropriate for me to conjecture what she might have thought and felt. Such presumption,

TABLE 11.1

Self/Other Dialectic in Four Life-History Texts

#1	*The Tulips Are Red* (memoir)	Self-reflexive encounter for Leesha, as both subject and recorder
#2	Transcript of life-history interview	Self/other encounter between Leesha and Lani
#3	"'In the Name of the House of Orange'"	Self/other encounter between Ruth and Leesha's texts (mirrors #2)
#4	"Reflections on '"In the Name of the House of Orange"'"	Self-reflexive encounter for Ruth, as both subject and recorder (mirrors #1)

TABLE 11.2

Shifts in Authorship and Subjectivity
in Four Life-History Texts

Text	Author/s	Subject/s
#1	Leesha	Leesha
#2	Leesha/Lani	Leesha/Lani
#3	Ruth	Leesha/Ruth
#4	Ruth	Ruth

however, is routine among biographers, life historians, and ethnographers generally. Like novelists who employ an omniscient narrator to accomplish difficult textual feats, we also use narrative strategies that suggest we can and do know our "informants" as they know themselves—perhaps even better than they know themselves. As James Clifford remarked, "We need not ask how Flaubert knows what Emma Bovary is thinking, but the ability of the fieldworker to inhabit indigenous minds is always in doubt."[11]

The Final Solution rendered her own survival wanting as an end in itself. Instead, she found purpose in the struggle to help preserve other lives. . . . However, such a choice surely would have brought her great moral anguish.

These statements, phrased in no uncertain terms, express *my struggle* to understand what joining the resistance meant to Leesha, just as they may explain why—or how—she actually made up her mind. In my effort to grasp something of Leesha's consciousness and conscience as a resister, I have substituted my own words and values for hers (individual lives, as such, had lost their meaning; the demands of conscience conflicted with going into hiding to save her own life; subjecting herself to extreme personal danger was the most honorable stance Leesha could take).

Consider now the following exchange between Lani and Leesha, which occurred approximately three-quarters of the way through their interview.

LEESHA: But I felt during that time I cannot sit still. I had to fight. Fight the injustice, and the deportation, and the loneliness that I felt in my heart—the injustice and the butchery that I saw everyday, no matter what the consequences of my own life. I thought, "I will fight until my last drop of blood [is gone]."

LANI: Did you think, "I am being brave"? Or did you just think, "I have no choice and must fight"?

LEESHA: I don't think that I thought in terms of bravery or no choice. I just knew this had to be done. Who else was going to do it? I must do it, that's all. I mean, nobody else. . . . Whatever had to be done had to be done. We tried to get as many people as possible.[12]

"I cannot sit still. . . . I just knew. . . . Who else was going to do it? . . . I must do it, that's all." These phrases suggest the ineffability of Leesha's consciousness and conscience as a resister. Like a blurred frame of film that begs to be refocused, something in these words unsettles, even disturbs, me. But as I approach the projector, I discover that the lens actually is in focus. This is as clear as it gets, so to speak. No mechanical adjustments or probes can sharpen the image—that is, clarify the urgency that propelled Leesha to act.

To the best of her ability, Leesha communicated to Lani what it was that she "just knew." But language alone cannot evoke or "focus" an understanding of her words; lived experience is also necessary. Grammar tends to impose its own causal order—a fabricated correspondence between thought and action—in accordance with rules for producing syntax. These rules—hypostatized relations of grammar—comprise the foundation of scientific methods and discourses.

Social scientists have cast our professional lot with the belief that human conduct is ultimately explicable. Presumably, motives are knowable, although at any given moment, an actor's intentions or definitions of a situation may be "unconscious" to her or opaque to others. Conduct, then, can be rationalized, except when an actor is duly labeled "insane." (Yet even when a person is declared "insane," many would contend that her behavior and thinking can be interpreted, even explained. Psychiatric diagnoses are one sort of explanation of "mental illness"; biochemical etiologies provide another sort of explanation.)

Scientific explanations are a means of establishing and maintaining control over what may be unknown, threatening, "other." In Western cultures, scientists and nonscientists alike are reluctant to concede that everything cannot always be accounted for. Throwing up one's hands, figuratively speaking, and taking the position that all things cannot be understood once and for all, leads to an alternative conception of meanings as open-ended, polyphonic, and indeterminate.[13]

Interpreting a text puts a reader in tension with it.[14] Indeed, I have experienced the tension between trying to isolate in a single passage of Leesha's life history what joining the resistance meant to her and facing the indeterminacy of the phrase "I just knew this had to be done." As Leesha explained to Lani, it was not a matter of choice or even of "no choice." In Leesha's life history, she does not mention *making a decision* to join the resistance. Thus, in this account, joining the resistance cannot be located in a discrete moment privileged above all others.

Six years have passed since I wrote "'In the Name of the House of Orange.'" I now realize that Leesha's words eluded me when I wrote her life history. Then, I didn't understand that I didn't understand the force of her narrative. Now, as I reread my interpretation of what joining the underground meant to her, my narrow grasp of resistance is reflected back to me. I feel as though I am staring into a mirror at my own image.

My recognition that I had not understood (and perhaps do not now fully understand) what joining the resistance meant to Leesha became apparent to me when I read Renato Rosaldo's extraordinary essay "Grief and a Headhunter's Rage: On the Cultural Force of Emotions." Rosaldo recounts how, for fourteen years, he struggled to comprehend Ilongot males' explanations of why they cut off (or long to cut off) human heads. Then, in 1981 Rosaldo's wife, anthropologist Michelle Rosaldo, was killed in an accident in the field. The rage he experienced in his bereavement "repositioned" him to understand the meanings of rage for an Ilongot male—rage so overpowering that it begs to be vented by severing and tossing away a victim's head. Rosaldo's discussion of the concept of emotional force is particularly helpful for understanding actions and desires that seem to defy explanation—the ineffable:

> The vocabulary for symbolic analysis . . . can expand by adding the term *force* to more familiar concepts, such as *thick description, multivocality, polysemy, richness,* and *texture.* The notion of force, among other things, opens to question the common assumption that the greatest human import always resides in the densest forest of symbols and that cultural depth always equals cultural elaboration. Do people always, in fact, describe most thickly what to them matters most?[15]

When Leesha reviewed an earlier draft of this chapter, she took me to task for glossing significant differences between *The Tulips Are Red* and her life history. Leesha was concerned about how I had constructed her agency in my interpretations of the two accounts. She directed my attention to two passages from *The Tulips Are Red* that suggest my assumption of a high degree of intertextuality is problematic. The first passage reads as follows: "My mind was resolute now. I was going to join the Underground Resistance movement. I was determined that I would not permit myself to be destroyed and I would fight to the bitter end" (*Tulips*, p. 107). In the second passage, Leesha describes her last meeting with Peter, the Dutch resister who became her initial underground contact. Peter had been captured and shot by the Germans. Close to death, he was under police guard at the NIZ. "As soon as I returned to the NIZ hospital in Amsterdam I hurried to Peter's room. . . . I tried to catch his eye. He saw me and I nodded. The look of relief on his face told me that he understood that I had agreed to join the Underground Resistance movement" (*Tulips*, p. 108).

These two passages signal a turning point in *Tulips* that is submerged in the life-history interview. They bifurcate time, demarcating the narrative into "before" and "after" Leesha made up her mind to join the resistance. In addition to signifying a temporal divide, they mark a transformation in Leesha's identity: her emergence as a resister.

When I first encountered Leesha's accounts of joining the resistance, I didn't know how to read them. I had expected that each time Leesha recounted her story she told it the same way. Thus, I assumed that she was telling the identical story in both texts. I had concluded that by the time Lani interviewed Leesha her story had already reached the point of saturation. However, I eventually discovered that this view was in error on two counts.

First, the appearance of a stable, complete narrative is a rhetorical accomplishment. It is not—and cannot be—an intrinsic property of stories themselves, because remembering is an ongoing process throughout one's life. Second, retellings of stories can never be "the same" because their meanings are situated in the "past-present relation."[16] By necessity, the frame of the present is obdurate. It refuses to be stripped away, for the here and now is the vantage point required for a story to be told, registered, and remembered.

In *The Tulips Are Red*, Leesha's account of joining the resistance is thicker and denser than the story told in her life history. Yet the difference between the two narratives is not simply that specific and sometimes significant details included in *Tulips* are omitted from the life history. Rather, it seems to me the crucial distinction is that Lani's interview with Leesha is a conversation, a collaboration between two situated subjects. Thus, the knowledge produced in and through the life history is shaped, not only by Leesha's position in the conversation, but by Lani's as well.

Lani's struggle to understand what joining the resistance meant to Leesha—in effect, to comprehend Leesha's agency—and Leesha's responses to Lani's questions constitute the knowledge they produced together. But at the moment in the narrative when Leesha reflected on becoming a resister, the membrane separating her experiences from Lani's became impassable. A chasm formed between teller and listener, prompting Lani to ask, "Did you think, 'I am being brave'? Or did you just think, 'I have no choice and must fight'?"

Desire is a powerful incentive for both knowledge and conversation. I entered the conversation between Leesha and Lani because, in Gelya Frank's words at the head of this chapter, "I wanted to know what it meant to understand just one other person." I entered their conversation wanting to discover patterns in my method of knowing, as well as the limits of what I could know. I wanted to explore how knowledge is created in and through conversation and introspection—knowledge that consists of moments of identification and understanding, as well as impassable chasms and ruptures.

An ethnographer/author is positioned—historically, culturally, politically, and morally. Our locations are inscribed in our interpretations of others, even as we strive to anchor our texts in "native points of view." Ethnography "from the native's point of view" is actually an oxymoron, for the relational—indeed, reflexive—character of fieldwork and writing requires at least two situated, experiencing subjects. To follow this injunction to the letter would restrict us to writing autobiography, a genre that locates the two subjectivities of teller and recorder in a single subject/author.

Life histories bring the life historian close to, and sometimes inside of, a previously unknown world—physically, culturally, and morally. While bridging distances between lives and cultures is the task of social analysis, intersubjective and intercultural knowledge is necessarily circumscribed. Translations of lives and cultures are always "provisional; they are made by positioned subjects who are prepared to know certain things and not others."[17] Few of us who are not survivors of genocide may recognize what, for Leesha, was self-evident about joining the underground. But we can deepen our understanding of Holocaust resistance by repositioning ourselves to reckon with the meanings of genocide throughout history and in our own time.

EPILOGUE

GENOCIDE/CONSEQUENCES

It is only our monographs that end. The lives of our subjects persist after we have stopped looking and listening.

Barbara Myerhoff, in *Between Two Worlds*

All I want is to take you with me through my experience of writing about the Holocaust, and to leave with you some of the problems I have encountered along the way.

Lore Segal, in *Writing and the Holocaust*

It is August of 1991, more than eight years since Lani Silver and I wrote the first chapter of this book—which, it turns out—has become Chapter 6. As I finish making final revisions on the manuscript, I am closing down the apartment in central Connecticut I have lived in this past academic year. In a few days, I will return to Boston to teach at Brandeis, where I completed an earlier version of this book as my doctoral dissertation. This will be the third time in three years that I have changed jobs and moved. For me, as for many itinerant academics, displacement and wandering have become familiar ways of life.

In 1983, I began the project from which this book evolved—interviewing Holocaust survivors—without a plan in mind. Then, I had no idea how I would be changed over a period of years by working with survivors and their texts, nor that, in the process, my own Jewish identity would be refigured. I did not expect to write a book that would represent my own life alongside the stories of Holocaust survivors. Nor did I expect I would discover that "self" and "other" are inseparably fused in a dialectic of situated knowing. Feminist theorist Donna Haraway explains that

> situated knowledges require that the object of knowledge be pictured as an actor and agent, not as a screen or a ground or a resource, never finally as slave to the master that closes off the dialectic in his unique agency and his authorship of "objective" knowledge. The point is paradigmatically clear in critical approaches to the social and human sciences, where the agency of people studied itself transforms the entire project of producing social theory. Indeed, coming to terms with the

agency of the "objects" studied is the only way to avoid gross error and false knowledge of many kinds in these sciences.[1]

In and through my struggle to write about the Holocaust, I have learned and relearned that genocide is ineffable. (Why do I seem to forget this lesson, then remember it later, then forget, only to remember it again?) The illusions of comprehension and control that a written text can confer seem, in moments, more obdurate than "reality," with its attendant ambiguities and indeterminacies. Even so—perhaps *because* the Holocaust is ineffable—we must juxtapose an understanding of the limits on our knowing with a commitment to producing better, more complex accounts, what Haraway calls "faithful knowledge."[2] This is a contradiction to be sure, but a necessary one, for it seems to me that what is at stake in comprehending genocide are the possibilities of life for our own and future generations.

The annihilation of European Jewry was not an event outside of history, a "unique" or momentary aberration from Western humanistic traditions.[3] Indeed, only when the Holocaust is contextualized historically does the true banality of genocide come into focus.

The first recorded genocides occurred in antiquity; however, their motives and meanings in different societies and eras varied widely.[4] During the Middle Ages nine million women were burned as witches in the Inquisition; and with the dawn of modernity, European imperial powers began the centuries-long project of colonizing and destroying the native peoples and cultures of Asia, Africa, Australia, the Pacific, and the Americas. In our own century genocide has been a constant: to wit—the massacre of nearly one-and-a-half million Armenians by the Turks between 1915 and 1923; Stalin's Great Purge, resulting in the death of twenty million Soviets, according to one conservative estimate; the Final Solution of between five and six million Jews and one-half million Sinti and Roma during World War II; the murder of about one-half million Indonesians and Chinese nationals living in Indonesia during 1965–66; and the slaughter of between one and three million Bangladeshi by the (West) Pakistani military in 1971, and between one and two million Kampucheans (Cambodians) by Pol Pot's regime during a three-year period beginning in 1975.[5]

This list is selective, not comprehensive. Although numbers of dead are careful approximations, it will never be possible to calculate exact figures for victims of genocide on a world scale. Indeed, statistics—the barest "facts"—sanitize the slaughter, perpetuating the illusion that genocide is fathomable. Do actual numbers really make a difference in our ability to comprehend the reality of genocide?

Epilogue

According to Frank Chalk and Kurt Jonassohn,

> The most painful question about genocide is, How is it possible for people to kill other people on such a massive scale? The answer seems to be that it is not possible, at least not as long as the potential victims are perceived as people. We have no evidence that a genocide was ever performed on a group of equals. The victims must not only not be equals, but also clearly defined as something less than fully human.[6]

As I reflect on this passage, my thoughts drift to what has become, for me, a self-evident connection between the reality of genocide in our own and past eras, and the decimation and extinction of thousands of other species by direct human action. It is not only that massacres of human groups are rationalized by some of the same psychological and political processes as destruction of nonhuman species, including "defin[ing] . . . victims [as] . . . not . . . equals, as something less than fully human."[7] While true, the linkages are more complex than this statement suggests.

My reflections on the persistence of genocide have led me to believe that all lives—human and nonhuman alike—exist as part of an interconnected totality. Thus, the consequences of destruction of one part of the whole will reverberate throughout the whole, affecting every other part. "Self" and "other" *are* inseparably fused, for Homo narrans, the storytelling species, constructs itself through coreflection and interaction with others. We act on the world through and in light of others.

The fusion of self and other crosscuts the human/nonhuman divide. Yet in recent centuries in the West, we have exercised a penchant for telling stories that constitute our species as an amalgam of separate, autonomous selves. From Genesis to Darwin, our origin stories have located Homo sapiens at the crown of creation, the center of the universe. But there are other tellings, alternative versions of who we are and our places on the planet. The possibilities of life for our own and future generations may hinge on dissolving dualities at the heart of Western constructions of reality—binary oppositions such as mind/body, self/other, and human/nonhuman.

I propose that we begin to explore interconnections between the destruction of human lives in the Holocaust and the devastation of other species that accompanied the killing of human beings. This move implicitly refigures the Holocaust not as a crisis of God or Western civilization or the modern, rational-bureaucratic state, but as a crisis of ecology. Ecology is "the science of interrelations and interdependence between organisms and between organisms and their environments."[8] But the boundary "between organisms and their environments" is often spurious, blurry—somewhere other than where we might expect it to be. I use the term *ecology* with three intentions that oppose conventional Western thought: to decenter narrowly anthropocentric views of the consequences of human destruction; to underscore the physical, material, and biological embeddedness of all human (and nonhuman) actions; and to problematize the animal/human divide itself.

We might begin to understand the Holocaust from an ecological standpoint by asking the following questions. What has been the impact on the ecosystems of lakes and rivers, forests and woods, of Eastern Europe, where so many millions of lives were destroyed? What are the remaining traces of acts that occurred a half-century ago: crematoria expelling oily, dark smoke, burning twenty-four hours a day, day in and day out, for months at a time; thousands of pounds of human ash dumped into lakes and rivers; millions of decomposing bodies hastily buried in mass graves? Consider Konnilyn Feig's description of the problem of disposing of corpses at Auschwitz during the camp's early years of operation.

> The gassing process generated enormous piles of corpses, and the number grew daily. The small crematorium could not cope, so the squads buried the corpses in mass graves in the Birkenau woods. Although the corpses were covered with chlorine, lime, and earth, after a few months the inevitable decomposition began to poison the air, causing an intolerable stench throughout the entire neighborhood. Doctors found deadly bacteria in springs and wells, and predicted serious epidemics. Experts at the fisheries began to complain that the fish in the ponds in the vicinity were dying, which they attributed to the pollution of the ground water through cadaveric poison. The bodies, rotting under the summer sun, swelled up and a brownish red mass began to seep through the cracks to the surface. Quick action had to be taken.[9]

Quick indeed. Feig reports that during the summer and autumn months of 1942, Auschwitz inmates, working in two shifts, were forced to exhume and burn some fifty thousand decaying corpses.[10]

Yet it is not only Jews who bear the burden of the Holocaust, nor only Nazis and former Nazis. Nor only those citizens of more than twenty European nations who actively collaborated with the Nazis; nor even the thousands, perhaps millions, of citizens of the Allied countries who stood by in full knowledge of the genocide. True, Jews were slaughtered, asphyxiated, and burned before the eyes of the entire world—at least the Western world. But it was not only Jews who died in the camps, although Jews and Gypsies were the targets of the Final Solution. Among those who were murdered by various other, hideous means—for instance, in the "euthanasia" program and in the slave-labor camps—were communists, socialists, homosexual men, Jehovah's Witnesses, Hutterites, the mentally ill and retarded, Poles, persons convicted of breaking laws of one sort or another, and resisters—in short, "non-Aryans," "asocials," "deviants." However, these human casualties are only part of the story.

On *Yom Kippur*, the Day of Atonement, Jewish communities around the world recite a litany of sins and ask for God's forgiveness. This act of contrition is always spoken in the first-person plural, for the identity of a person who has committed a particular sin is not considered important. Rather, traditional Jewish wisdom teaches that the entire community shares responsibility for its members' wrongdoings. When Jewish ethics is widened to include the whole human group—and then ever-extended to embrace all life-forms—it expresses what Buddhists call interbeing. Interbeing is the principle that nothing can exist by itself—that, in Barbara Deming's words, "we are all part of one another," literally, concretely.[11]

The consequences of the Holocaust are imprinted on our planet itself and on all lives that draw breath. For, in the aftermath of the Holocaust and in the continuing face of genocide, the earth is utterly and forever changed.

> We say you cannot divert the river from the riverbed. We say that everything is moving, and we are a part of this motion. That the soil is moving. That the water is moving. We say that the earth draws water to her from the clouds. We say the rainfall parts on each side of the mountain, like the parting of our hair, and that the shape of the mountain tells where the water has passed. We say this water washes the soil from the hillsides, that the rivers carry sediment, that rain when it splashes carries small particles, that the soil itself flows with water in streams underground. We say that water is taken up into roots of plants, into stems, that it washes down hills into rivers, that these rivers flow to the sea, that from the sea, in the sunlight, this water rises to the sky, that this water is carried in clouds, and comes back as rain, comes back as fog, back as dew, as wetness in the air.
>
> We say everything comes back. And you cannot divert the river from the riverbed. We say every act has its consequences. That this place has

been shaped by the river, and that the shape of this place tells the river where to go. . . .

We say look how the water flows from this place and returns as rainfall, everything returns, we say, and one thing follows another, there are limits, we say, on what can be done and everything moves. We are all a part of this motion, we say, and the way of the river is sacred, and this grove of trees is sacred, and we ourselves, we tell you, are sacred.[12]

NOTES

PREFACE

1. Wittig, *Les Guérillères*, p. 89.
2. Myerhoff, *Number Our Days*, p. 272.

PROLOGUE

1. On the emplotment of historical narratives and, by extension, other kinds of accounts, see White, *Metahistory*, pp. 7 and 8; emphasis in original.

2. See James Clifford and George E. Marcus, eds., *Writing Culture: The Poetics and Politics of Ethnography* (Berkeley: University of California Press, 1986).

3. Marcus, "Rhetoric and the Ethnographic Genre in Anthropological Research," p. 510.

4. Ricoeur, "The Model of the Text," pp. 91–117.

5. See Mills, *The Sociological Imagination*; Glaser and Strauss, *The Discovery of Grounded Theory*; Gouldner, *The Coming Crisis of Western Sociology*; and Reinharz, *On Becoming a Social Scientist*.

6. Geertz, *Works and Lives*, p. 9.

7. For a survey of experimental ethnographies and the "literary turn" in anthropology, see Marcus and Fischer, *Anthropology as Cultural Critique*. For a sampling of experimental ethnographies, see Bruner and Plattner, eds., *Text, Play, and Story*; Clifford and Marcus, eds., *Writing Culture*; and Turner and Bruner, eds., *The Anthropology of Experience*. For an interesting discussion of how some critics have misapplied the term *postmodern* to experimental ethnographies, see Robert Pool, "Postmodern Ethnography?" (*Critique of Anthropology* 11 [1991]: 309–31). Current research and debates may be followed in the journal *Cultural Anthropology*.

8. On debates about feminist ethnography, see *Inscriptions*, nos. 3/4 (1988); Judith Stacey, "Can There Be a Feminist Ethnography?" *Women's Studies International Forum* 11 (1988): 21–27; Frances E. Mascia-Lees, Patricia Sharpe, and Colleen Ballerino Cohen, "The Postmodernist Turn in Anthropology: Cautions from a Feminist Perspective," *Signs* 15 (1989): 7–33; Marjorie L. DeVault, "What Counts as Feminist Ethnography?" Paper

presented at "Exploring New Frontiers: Qualitative Research Conference," York University, Toronto, 13–16 May 1990; and Laurel Richardson, "Postmodern Social Theory: Representational Practices," *Sociological Theory* 9 (1991): 173–79.

Recent ethnographies by feminists explore diverse issues, including problems of constructing representations and texts, power, and authority. See, for example: Margaret Trawick, *Notes on Love in a Tamil Family*; Judith Stacey, *Brave New Families*; Dorinne K. Kondo, *Crafting Selves*; Susan Krieger, *Social Science and the Self*; and Ruth Behar, *Translated Woman*.

9. On underreporting and falsifying of failures in research, see Reinharz, pp. 25–29.

10. Paul Rabinow, *Reflections on Fieldwork in Morocco*, p. 6.

11. Van Maanen, *Tales of the Field*, p. xv.

12. Benjamin, a German Jew, was reluctant to emigrate from Europe to America along with other members of the Frankfurt School. Thus he remained in Paris until 1940. Following internment in the concentration camp at Nevers, he attempted to reach the Spanish border via an escape route over the Pyrenees. Although Benjamin could not obtain an exit visa in France, colleagues at the Institute of Social Research (the Frankfurt School in exile in New York) obtained an emergency American visa for him. But just before the party arrived in Spain, authorities sealed the border. That night, Benjamin committed suicide. The next day the border was reopened and the rest of the group entered Spain safely. (See Jay, *The Dialectical Imagination*, pp. 197–98.)

13. Hannah Arendt, Introduction to *Illuminations*, by Walter Benjamin, p. 47.

14. Ibid., p. 39, citing *Schriften*, intro. and ed. Theodor W. Adorno (Frankfurt am Main: Suhrkamp Verlag, 1955), 2:192.

15. Clifford and Marcus, *Writing Culture*.

16. Reinharz, *On Becoming a Social Scientst*, pp. 124–25; emphasis in original.

17. Cesara, *Reflections of a Woman Anthropologist*, p. 9. On the conjunction of ethnographers' lived experience and interpretations, see Bateson, *With a Daughter's Eye;* Frank, "'Becoming the Other'"; Heilman, *The Gate Behind the Wall*; Kondo, "Dissolution and Reconstitution of Self", pp. 74–88; Myerhoff, *Number Our Days*; Rosaldo, "Grief and a Headhunter's Rage"; Zola, *Missing Pieces*, and "When Getting into the Field Means Getting into Oneself," pp. 193–200.

18. Van Maanen, *Tales of the Field*.

19. Turner, "Foreword," in Myerhoff, *Number Our Days*, pp. ix–x.

20. Cesara, *Reflections of a Woman Anthropologist*, p. 9.

21. On the confessional genre of ethnographic writing, see Van Maanen, *Tales of the Field*; esp. pp. 73–100. Unlike realist narratives, confessional accounts are written in the first person; they are told from the fieldworker's point of view. However, they tend to be naive about their own means of production.

22. Rich and varied traditions of cultural critique were practiced during the interwar years by cultural anthropologists, the Frankfurt School, French surrealists, and American documentary critics. See Marcus and Fischer, *Anthropology as Cultural Critique*, esp. pp. 111–64.

23. See Herrigel, *Zen in the Art of Archery*.

24. See, for instance, Frank, "'Becoming the Other'"; and Agar, "Toward an Ethnographic Language."

25. Myerhoff and Metzger, "The Journal as Activity and Genre," p. 103.

26. I have borrowed the image of "intellectual perpetual motion" from Geertz, "From the Native's Point of View," p. 69.

CHAPTER 1

1. The *Passagen-Werk*, edited and annotated by Rolf Tiedemann, was posthumously published in 1982. Susan Buck-Morss explains that "the *Passagen-Werk* itself [as Benjamin conceived it] does not exist—not even a first page, let alone a draft of the whole." This "nonexistent text" is the subject of her study. See Walter Benjamin, *Gesammelte Schriften*, ed. Rolf Tiedemann and Hermann Schweppenhauser, with the collaboration of Theodor W. Adorno and Gershom Scholem, 6 vols. (Frankfurt am Main: Suhrkamp Verlag, 1972–), vol. 5: *Das Passagen-Werk*, ed. Rolf Tiedemann (1982); and Susan Buck-Morss, *The Dialectics of Seeing: Walter Benjamin and the Arcades Project* (Cambridge, Mass.: MIT Press, 1989), p. 6.

2. Jay, *The Dialectical Imagination*, p. 200. See also Scholem, "Walter Benjamin," in *On Jews and Judaism in Crisis*, pp. 189–90.

3. Hannah Arendt, Introduction to Benjamin, *Illuminations*, p. 47.

4. Walter Benjamin, *Briefe* (Frankfurt am Main, 1966), 2:695, quoted in Arendt, Introduction, p. 11; Walter Benjamin, *Schriften* (Frankfurt am Main: Suhrkamp Verlag, 1955), 2:192, quoted in Arendt, Introduction, p. 39.

5. Arendt, Introduction, p. 13.

6. Benjamin, quoted in Jay, p. 203; Arendt, Introduction, p. 12; Benjamin, *Schriften*, 1:349 (quoted in ibid., p. 12).

7. Benjamin, *Briefe*, 1:193, quoted in Arendt, Introduction, p. 39.

8. See Walter Benjamin, "Unpacking My Library: A Talk about Book Collecting" [1931], in *Illuminations*, pp. 59–60.

9. Walter Benjamin, "The Storyteller: Reflections on the Works of Nikolai Leskov" [1936], in *Illuminations*, pp. 83, 84, and 87.

10. Ibid., pp. 100, 109, and 87.

11. Ibid., p. 98; emphasis in original.

12. On nostalgia, Benjamin wrote: "In the ruin history has physically merged into the setting. And in this guise history does not assume the form of the process of an eternal life so much as that of irresistible decay . . . the events of history shrivel up and become absorbed in the setting." Walter Benjamin, *The Origins of German Tragic Drama*, trans. J. Osborne (London: New Left Books, 1977), pp. 177 and 179, quoted in Kathleen Stewart, "Nostalgia—A Polemic," *Cultural Anthropology* 3 (August 1988): 238.

13. Arendt, Introduction, p. 47.

14. Benjamin, *Briefe,* 1:329; Arendt, Introduction, p. 48.

15. Ibid., p. 49.

16. Benjamin, *Briefe*, 1:330, quoted in ibid., p. 48.

17. Arendt, "Isak Dinesen," p. 104.

18. Myerhoff, *Number Our Days*, p. 272.

CHAPTER 2

1. R. Ruth Linden, "Tribute to Marion Hozenpud Berry: 18 June 1886–24 November 1983," San Francisco, 1983 (typescript).

2. Stanley et al., "The Transformation of Silence into Language and Action," p. 18; emphasis in original.

3. "Affidavit of Leah Hosenpud," 9 November 1940.

4. "Herman I. Levine, 57, Dies Suddenly," from an unidentified newspaper, possibly published in Binghamton or Hancock, New York.

5. Letter to author, 20 September 1990, p. 3.

6. My reconstruction of Herman Levine's life is based on his obituary (n. 4 above).

7. Lola Curiel to author (n. 5 above), p. 4.

8. My reconstruction of Annie Kraemer's life is based on the memories of Lola Curiel (letter to author [n. 5 above], pp. 1–2, 6). My father's cousin, Martin Gersh, of Ann Arbor, Michigan, helped me reconstruct the Kraemers' passage to America (telephone conversation with author, 18 August 1990). On the Jewish-Anarchist movement in East London, see Fishman, *East End Jewish Radicals, 1875–1914*; and Oliver, *The International Anarchist Movement in Late Victorian London*.

9. Letter to author (n. 5 above), pp. 5–6.

CHAPTER 3

1. On stock images of the Holocaust, see Linden, "Speaking Gently of Genocide."

2. Silver and Linden, "Santa Rita Jail Diary," pp. 21–23 (typescript).

3. Durkheim, *The Elementary Forms of the Religious Life*, trans. J. W. Swain (1951; reprint, New York: Collier Books, 1961).

4. *A Vanished World* is the title of Roman Vishniac's photographic study of Eastern European Jewry on the eve of the Holocaust (New York: Farrar, Straus and Giroux, 1983).

CHAPTER 4

1. See Traweek, *Beamtimes and Lifetimes*, pp. 51–52.

2. Mannheim, *Ideology and Utopia*, p. 259 and passim.

3. "Working Collectively," University of California, Santa Cruz, 1975, p. 1 (typescript). Laurie Garrett distributed this handout to students in "Female Physiology and Gynecology" (Kresge 183, Spring 1975) and probably wrote it as well.

4. Jill Sabina, "The Myth of Student as Consumer: A Manifesto for Student Liberation," and Ründa Elnasdätter, "To Whom It May Concern," both in *Thornside* 1 (30 January 1976).

5. "Student Union?" *Student Union News*, April 1976, p. 4.

6. Lyons, *Constructive Criticism*, p. 12.

7. Myerhoff, *Number Our Days*, p. 32.

8. On secular ritual, see Moore and Myerhoff, "Introduction: Secular Ritual," pp. 3–24.

9. On evaluating the outcomes of rituals, see Moore and Myerhoff, "Introduction: Secular Ritual," pp. 13–17. On liminality, see Victor Turner, "Variations on a Theme of Liminality," in Moore and Myerhoff, pp. 36–52. According to Turner (after van Gennep), rites of passage are marked by three phases: separation, margin (or *limen*), and reaggregation. The first and last phases "detach ritual subjects from their old places in society and return them, inwardly transformed and outwardly changed, to new places" (p. 36). The

middle phase, the *limen*, is a threshold. It is neither here nor there, and those undergoing it are neither this nor that.

> The most characteristic midliminal symbolism is that of paradox, or being *both* this *and* that. Novices are portrayed and act as androgynous, or as both living *and* dead, at once ghosts and babes, both cultural and natural creatures, human *and* animal. They may be said to be in a process of being ground down into a sort of homogeneous social matter, in which possibilities of differentiation may still be glimpsed, then later positively refashioned into specific shapes compatible with their new postliminal duties and rights as incumbents of a new status and state. (P. 37; emphasis in original)

10. On metaphoric uses of the Holocaust, see Young, *Writing and Rewriting the Holocaust*, pp. 81–146.

11. Philip Levine, "For the Poets of Chile," in his *The Names of the Lost*, pp. 41–43.

12. Journal of Robin Ruth Linden, Spring 1978.

13. Journal of Kirsten Greer, 24 May 1977, pp. 2–3 (typescript).

14. Three significant early works are: The Combahee River Collective, "A Black Feminist Statement" (April 1977), reprinted in *Capitalist Patriarchy and the Case for Socialist Feminism*, ed. Zillah R. Eisenstein (New York: Monthly Review Press, 1979), pp. 362–72; *Conditions* 5, "The Black Women's Issue," ed. Lorraine Bethel and Barbara Smith (1979); and *This Bridge Called My Back: Writings by Radical Women of Color*, ed. Cherríe Moraga and Gloria Anzaldúa (New York: Kitchen Table Press, 1981). See also Colbert (a.k.a. Sarahgold), "The 'All Women's Interests Are the Same' Line," pp. 49–60; and Lorde, *Sister Outsider*.

15. My understandings of segmentation in the women's movement have developed over many years through conversations with Susan Leigh Star.

16. For a description of global feminism, see Debbie Dover, "Women Plan a Convoy to U.S. and Central America," *Central America Reporter* February 1989, p. 2. The following passage, from the "Statement of Purpose" of the Women's Convoy to Central America, is quoted by Dover:

> We are women of urban neighborhoods and the countryside, from farms, small towns and villages. Our languages vary; our cultures are diverse. We come from different communities in Central and North America. In our efforts to create a secure and enriching life for ourselves and our communities, we encounter common obstacles. While we strive to better our lives, our survival is in jeopardy. Jobs are hard to find and too often underpaid, unsafe and demeaning. Public services are absent or inadequate. The policies of most of our national governments attend to the wants of the few while being hostile to the needs and aspirations of the many. Those who seek to change are treated as the enemy. In the face of this, women are extending hands of friendship and support to one another inside and outside their communities and countries. Between women, there are no boundaries.

CHAPTER 5

1. Linden and Star, "Survived by Her Silence: For the Memory of Fay Abrahams Stender (1932–1980)," 1980 (typescript).

2. See Russell, "Fay Stender and the Politics of Murder."

3. Collier and Horowitz, "Requiem for a Radical," pp. 64–71 passim, 133–47 passim. In response to the article, letters to the editor were published in *Mediafile*, May 1981, pp. 5 and 12, and July–August 1981, pp. 4–5 and 10. This quote is from "The Great Debate: Covering and Uncovering the Left," *Mediafile*, May 1981, p. 5.

4. Evelyn Torton Beck, ed., *Nice Jewish Girls: A Lesbian Anthology* (Watertown, Mass.: Persephone Press, 1982).

5. Robin Ruth Linden to Evelyn Torton Beck, 8 January 1982.

6. Robin Ruth Linden et al., eds., *Against Sadomasochism: A Radical Feminist Analysis* (East Palo Alto, Calif.: Frog in the Well, 1982).

7. Audre Lorde with Susan Leigh Star, "Interview with Audre Lorde," in *Against Sadomasochism*, p. 69.

8. Friedrich, "The Kingdom of Auschwitz," pp. 30–60.

9. Arendt, *Eichmann in Jerusalem*.

10. Bernstein, "Personal History (The Bernstein Family)," *New Yorker*, pt. 1, 22 March 1982, pp. 53–127, and pt. 2, 29 March 1982, pp. 58–121.

11. Anne Roiphe, *Generation Without Memory: A Jewish Journey in Christian America* (Boston: Beacon Press, 1981).

12. On reflexivity and film, see Jay Ruby, "Exposing Yourself: Reflexivity, Anthropology, and Film," *Semiotica* 30, nos. 1–2 (1980): pp. 153–79.

13. Letter to author, 20 September 1990, pp. 2–3.

14. On the concept of positioned subjects, see Rosaldo, "Grief and a Headhunter's Rage," pp. 178–95; reprinted.

15. Starhawk (Miriam Simos), a witch and a Jew, defines magic as "*the art of changing consciousness at will.*" See Starhawk, *Dreaming the Dark*, p. 13; emphasis in original.

16. Myerhoff and Metzger, "The Journal as Activity and Genre," p. 99.

CHAPTER 7

1. "Bearing Witness" has the same narrative structure as "Survived by Her Silence," the essay Leigh Star and I wrote about Fay Stender. Both works experiment with collaborative autobiographical writing; however, the blurring of voices and subjectivities discussed in this chapter did not occur when we wrote the Fay Stender piece. See Linden and Leigh Star, "Survived by Her Silence."

2. Gertrude Stein, *The Autobiography of Alice B. Toklas* (1933; reprint, New York: Vintage Books, 1960).

3. Clifford Geertz uses the term "author-ized" to signify the double meaning of the word: both written, i.e., authored, and legitimated. See Geertz, *Works and Lives*, p. 9.

4. See Rabinow, "Representations are Social Facts," in Clifford and Marcus, eds., *Writing Culture*, pp. 234–61.

5. James E. Young poses the question, "What are the consequences for our current lives in light of the ways our past is memorialized?" See Young, "The Biography of a Memorial Icon," pp. 101–2.

6. On community responses to the San Francisco memorial, see Coffelt, "'The Holocaust' and the Art of War"; Smith, "Panel Accepts Holocaust Sculpture"; Gluck, "Controversy Shadows Dedication," and "So We'll Never Forget."

7. "Steve Ross Sparks Plans for Hub Holocaust Memorial," *Jewish Advocate*, 2 July 1987.

8. Larrabee, "How to Remember."

9. Regine Barshak, untitled presentation at meeting of Freedom Memorial Inc., Parkman House, Boston, 15 December 1987, p. 1; emphasis in original.

10. Joan Bond Sax, letter to William Carmen, 15 December 1987.

11. Antonelli, "Holocaust Memorial Group Revamps."

12. "Memorials 'Distort' Holocaust, Says Scholar," *Houston Post*, 30 October 1988, E4.

13. This phrasing is Riv-Ellen Prell's. See her essay, "The Double Frame of Life History in the Work of Barbara Myerhoff," in *Interpreting Women's Lives: Feminist Theory and Personal Narratives*, ed. Personal Narratives Group (Bloomington: Indiana University Press, 1989), p. 254.

14. In "Living History" classes with Jewish elders, Barbara Myerhoff observed that class "members stimulated each other's memories and collectively were able to re-evoke long buried early experiences." See Myerhoff and Tufte, "Life History as Integration," pp. 543.

15. Letter to author, 2 October 1990, pp. 1–3.

16. Thanks to Karl D. Lyon for challenging my thinking about how manipulations of the Holocaust differ in kind.

CHAPTER 8

1. Fein, *Accounting for Genocide*; Pawelczynska, *Values and Violence in Auschwitz*, and Hughes, "Good People and Dirty Work," in Becker, ed., *The Other Side*, pp. 23–36. See also Horowitz, "Bodies and Souls" (review of *Accounting for Genocide*), and Fein, "The Holocaust and Auschwitz," pp. 489–92 and 495–98. Fein and Horowitz's exchange about "Bodies and Souls" is published in "Commentary," *Contemporary Sociology* 10 (March 1981): 167–71.

After this manuscript had gone to press, *Modernity and the Holocaust*, a significant and provocative book by Polish sociologist Zygmunt Bauman (Ithaca, NY: Cornell University Press, 1989) came to my attention. Rather than developing a sociology of the Holocaust, Bauman suggests that "*the Holocaust has more to say about the state of sociology than sociology in its present shape is able to add to our knowledge of the Holocaust*" (p. 3; emphasis in original). He rejects conventional frameworks for conceptualizing the Holocaust—both particularizing tendencies, which define the Holocaust "as an event in *Jewish* history," and universalizing tendencies, which define the Holocaust either as an exemplar of the ubiquity of human conflict and prejudice; of oppression and persecution between ethnic, cultural, or social groups; or of "the most awesome and sinister—yet still theoretically assimilable category—of genocide" (p. 2; emphasis in original). Instead, *Modernity and the Holocaust* seeks to de-marginalize the specialized area of Holocaust studies by linking it with classical, European sociology. Thus, tensions arising from processes of modernization and modernity—including the "social-engineering ambitions [of modern nation-states], the emergence of the racist form of communal antagonism, and the association between racism and genocidal projects"—are at the center of this study (p. xii).

2. Holocaust studies is a huge and expanding area. A bibliography compiled by Vera Laska in 1985 lists nearly two thousand books. See Laska, *Nazism, Resistance, and the Holocaust in World War II: A Bibliography*, and Marrus, "The History of the Holocaust: A Survey of Recent Literature," pp. 114–60. My thanks to Michael N. Dobkowski for suggesting that I read Marrus's work and for talking with me about these issues. Current

Holocaust scholarship may be followed through the *Simon Wiesenthal Annual* and *Holocaust and Genocide Studies*.

3. On resistance, see Bennett, "Annotated Bibliography," which includes eighty-seven items. See also Bauer, "Forms of Jewish Resistance during the Holocaust," in *The Jewish Emergence from Powerlessness*, pp. 26–40; Laska, *Women in the Resistance and in the Holocaust*; and Marrus, "History of the Holocaust," pp. 153–59, and *The Holocaust in History*, pp. 133–55. For an excellent analysis of the German-Jewish resistance literature, see Kwiet, "Problems of Jewish Resistance Historiography."

4. Marrus, "History of the Holocaust," p. 151.

5. Feig, *Hitler's Death Camps*, p. 501, n. 56.

6. On the problem of knowing, see Bauer, *The Holocaust in Historical Perspective*; Laqueur, *The First News of the Holocaust*; Brownstein, "The *New York Times* on Nazism (1933–39)"; Wyman, *The Abandonment of the Jews: America and the Holocaust 1941–1945*; and Marrus, *Holocaust in History*, pp. 157–64. For an excellent comparative study of genocide, see Chalk and Jonassohn, *The History and Sociology of Genocide*.

7. Katz and Ringelheim, eds., *Women Surviving the Holocaust*, pp. 23–24.

8. Like other Holocaust statistics, the number of Jewish survivors can only be estimated. Historian Raul Hilberg suggests that the final count of Jewish displaced persons was 250,000, 72,000 of whom eventually emigrated to America (Hilberg, *The Destruction of the European Jews*, def. rev. ed. [New York: Holmes and Meier, 1985], 3:1150–51). On problems of collecting and interpreting Holocaust statistics, see Hilberg, 3:1201–20. The figure of 400,000 to 500,000 survivors is cited by journalist Helen Epstein in *Children of the Holocaust* (New York: Bantam Books, 1979), p. 4.

9. On the "Final Solution to the Gypsy problem," see Tyrnauer, "'Mastering the Past,'" in Porter, ed., "'Mastering the Past,'" in Chalk and Jonassohn, and *Gypsies and the Holocaust*.

10. On Germany's "euthanasia" program, see Proctor, *Racial Hygiene*, pp. 177–222; and Lifton, *The Nazi Doctors*, pp. 45–79.

11. All information on the taxonomy of the concentration camp system is from Feig, *Hitler's Death Camps*.

12. Konnilyn G. Feig, lecture at San Francisco State University, Department of History, 17 October 1983.

13. Arad, Gutman, and Margaliot, eds., *Documents on the Holocaust*, p. 214.

14. Ibid.

15. Williams, "The Genesis of Chronic Illness," p. 178.

16. On symbolic interaction, see Blumer, *Symbolic Interactionism*. On grounded theory, see Glaser and Strauss, *The Discovery of Grounded Theory*; Glaser, *Theoretical Sensitivity*; Strauss, *Qualitative Analysis for Social Scientists*; and Charmaz, "The Grounded Theory Method," in Emerson, ed., *Contemporary Field Research*, pp. 109–26.

17. See Feig, *Hitler's Death Camps*; Proctor, *Racial Hygiene*, pp. 217–21; and Mitscherlich and Mielke, *Doctors of Infamy*.

18. Meanings of the Nazi medical experiments are currently being examined and contested by American scientists and scholars. According to historian of science Robert Proctor, "the experiments were undertaken not out of sadism, but to gain knowledge about certain conditions faced by German military men" (Proctor, *Racial Hygiene*, p. 217). Should clinical researchers and physicians in our own era use the findings of experiments conducted in the camps? If so, then how? But if not, then on what grounds? "The Meaning of the Holocaust for Bioethics," a 1989 conference sponsored by the Center for Biomedical Ethics at the University of Minnesota, explored these and other questions raised by the Nazi data. See Arthur Caplan, "'Legacy of the Holocaust': A 1989 Center Conference," p. 1.

19. Pawelczynska, *Values and Violence in Auschwitz*, pp. 72–73.

20. Ibid., p. 147.

21. This figure is cited by Helen Epstein in *Children of the Holocaust*, p. 4.

22. On martyrdom in the Warsaw Ghetto uprising, see Krall, *Shielding the Flame*; and Todorov, "On Heroic Narrative." See also Lubetkin, *In the Days of Destruction and Revolt*. On the Auschwitz revolt, see Buszko, "Auschwitz," pp. 115–16; and Gutman, "Roza Robota," pp. 1286–87, in Gutman, ed., *Encyclopedia of the Holocaust*. Roza Robota was the Jewish underground activist who helped smuggle in minute quantities of explosives used in the *Sonderkommando* mutiny.

23. Fleck, *Genesis and Development of a Scientific Fact*, p. 151.

24. Mead, *Mind, Self, and Society from the Standpoint of a Social Behaviorist*, 1:27–28.

CHAPTER 9

1. R. Ruth Linden, "Methodological Memo," Cambridge, Mass., 29 January 1985 (typescript).

2. See Van Maanen, *Tales of the Field*, p. 9.

3. On identity transitions, see Strauss, *Mirrors and Masks*, pp. 89–131.

4. See Glaser and Strauss, *The Discovery of Grounded Theory*.

5. Marcus and Fischer, *Anthropology as Cultural Critique*, pp. 7–16.

6. Ibid., p. 11.

7. American Sociological Association, "Code of Ethics," rev. 28 January 1989, p. 1 (typescript).

8. Ibid., p. 4.

9. Ibid.

10. Texts find their way into our subjects' hands by various means. Marcus and Fischer mention:

> apocryphal stories . . . in professional folklore about the American Indian informant who, in response to the ethnographer's question, consults the work of Alfred Kroeber, or the African villager in the same situation who reaches for his copy of Meyer Fortes.

They also recount a story about a Toda woman who visited Houston.

> A trained nurse among her people as well as a culture broker, she was on tour in the United States, giving talks about the Todas [of India], of the sort that anthropologists might have given in past decades. By chance, she was visiting the home of a colleague of ours just as a BBC documentary about the Todas appeared on the television, in which the visitor was featured prominently as the filmmaker's prime informant. Her comments as she watched the program along with our colleague did not much concern the details of Toda culture, but rather dealt with the ironies of the multiple representations of her people — by herself, by anthropologists, and by the BBC. (Marcus and Fischer, *Anthropology as Cultural Critique*, pp. 36–37)

Western ethnographic subjects may be even more likely than non-Western informants to read our texts and view films about themselves. As a matter of course, in the United States ethnographies of domestic cultures and social worlds reverberate well beyond professional audiences.

11. Myerhoff, "Surviving Stories," p. 273.
12. Myerhoff, "'Life Not Death in Venice,'" p. 285.
13. Myerhoff, "Surviving Stories," pp. 272 and 274–75.
14. American Sociological Association, "Code of Ethics," p. 1.

CHAPTER 10

1. Leesha Rose, life history conducted with Lani Silver, World Gathering of Jewish Holocaust Survivors, Jerusalem, Israel, June 1981. References to this interview will be indicated parenthetically in the text by page numbers only.
2. Leesha Rose, *The Tulips Are Red* (New York: A. S. Barnes, 1978). References to this book will be indicated in the text as *Tulips*, with page numbers.
3. Dawidowicz, *The War Against the Jews*, p. 367.
4. Jacob Presser, *Ashes in the Wind*, p. 12.
5. Dawidowicz, *War Against the Jews*, p. 367.
6. See Presser, *Ashes in the Wind*, for a detailed account of the Final Solution in Holland. Fur summary accounts, see Hilberg, *The Destruction of the European Jews*, 2:570–97; and Dawidowicz, pp. 366–68.
7. The concept of awareness contexts is developed in Glaser and Strauss, *Awareness of Dying*, pp. 29ff.
8. See Feig, *Hitler's Death Camps*, pp. 242–43.
9. Presser, *Ashes in the Wind*, p. 135.
10. Ibid., p. 51.
11. Ibid., p. 188.
12. Ibid., pp. 45–57ff.; and Isaiah Trunk's *Judenrat*, a study of the Eastern European Jewish Councils that applies, as well, to the structure and organization of the Jewish Council in Amsterdam.
13. Presser, *Ashes in the Wind*, pp. 131, 133.
14. Ibid., pp. 118–20.
15. *Tulips*, pp. 109–10; and letter to author, 12 April 1989, p. 5.
16. On diplomatic plans to exchange Germans for Jews, see Zaris, "Exchange: Jews and Germans," in Gutman, ed., *Encyclopedia of the Holocaust*, 2:457–59; and Wasserstein, *Britain and the Jews of Europe*, esp. pp. 223–35.
17. Marrus, *The Holocaust in History*, p. 155.
18. Final deportation of the NIZ took place on 13 August 1943. A few staff members managed to escape, and somewhere between 130 and 153 patients with infectious diseases and six nurses were allowed to transfer to the Jewish Invalid Hospital. The Jewish Invalid Hospital was evacuated on 17 September. Less than two weeks later, on 29 September, the Jewish Council was dissolved and the few Jews remaining at large were rounded up. Deportation of Holland's Jews marked completion of the second phase of the Final Solution (Presser, *Ashes in the Wind*, pp. 211–13).
19. Ibid.
20. For accounts of women resisters, see Laska, *Women in the Resistance and in the Holocaust*. See also Joan Miriam Ringelheim's discussion of meanings of women's resistance in her article "Viewpoint: Women and the Holocaust."

CHAPTER 11

1. Prell, "The Double Frame of Life History in the Work of Barbara Myerhoff," p. 254. See also Rabinow, *Reflections on Fieldwork in Morocco*.

2. Geertz, *Works and Lives*, p. 9.

3. Ibid.

4. Ibid., pp. 9–10; parentheses in original, my emphasis.

5. Ibid., p. 2.

6. Rose, *The Tulips Are Red*, and life history conducted with Lani Silver, World Gathering of Jewish Holocaust Survivors, Jerusalem, Israel, June 1981.

7. See Geertz, "'From the Native's Point of View,'" pp. 55–70. Compare Geertz with Trinh T. Minh-ha, *Woman, Native, Other*, pp. 47–76.

8. Crapanzano, "The Life History in Anthropological Field Work," and *Tuhami*, p. 5.

9. Crapanzano, *Tuhami*, p. 5.

10. Myerhoff, "Re-membered Lives," p. 77.

11. Clifford, "On Ethnographic Authority," in *The Predicament of Culture*, p. 47.

12. Interview with Leesha Rose (n. 6 above), p. 23.

13. On polyphony, see James Clifford, "On Ethnographic Authority," which draws on the work of Russian critic Mikhail Bakhtin to survey modes of authority in texts. For Bakhtin, according to Clifford, speaking subjects in the polyphonic novel are represented directly, through multiple discourses. Novels in this genre—those of Dickens and Dostoyevsky, for instance—accommodate "discursive complexity, the dialogical interplay of voices" (p. 47), rather than imposing a single, controlled, objective, indirect voice.

14. Dorff and Rosett, *A Living Tree*, p. 193.

15. Rosaldo, "Grief and a Headhunter's Rage," p. 178; emphasis in original.

16. Popular Memory Group, "Popular Memory," p. 211.

17. Rosaldo, "Grief and a Headhunter's Rage," p. 183.

EPILOGUE

1. Haraway, "Situated Knowledges," pp. 592–93.

2. Ibid., p. 593.

3. On locating the Holocaust within Western "civilized" traditions, see Rubenstein, *The Cunning of History*; and Bauman, *Modernity and the Holocaust*.

4. For several decades, definitions of genocide have been debated and contested in the literature. See Chalk and Jonassohn, *The History and Sociology of Genocide*, pp. 8–40. These authors propose the following definition: "*Genocide* is a form of one-sided mass killing in which a state or other authority intends to destroy a group, as that group and membership in it are defined by the perpetrator" (p. 23, emphasis in original).

5. Statistics on genocide in the twentieth century are from ibid. On the USSR under Stalin, see p. 320; on the Final Solution of the Gypsies, see p. 366; on Indonesia, see p. 381; on Bangladesh, see pp. 395–96; on Kampuchea (Cambodia), see p. 402.

6. Ibid., pp. 27–28.

7. Ibid.

8. Bateson and Bateson, *Angels Fear*, p. 207.

9. Feig, *Hitler's Death Camps*, pp. 343–44. See also Spector, "Aktion 1005," in Gutman, ed., *Encyclopedia of the Holocaust*, p. 11.

10. Feig, *Hitler's Death Camps*, p. 344.

11. Meyerding, ed., *We Are All Part of One Another*. On interbeing, see Thich Nhat Hanh, *Interbeing*; and Badiner, ed., *Dharma Gaia*.

12. Griffin, *Woman and Nature*, pp. 185–86.

GLOSSARY

(Cz)	**Czech**	**(Hu)**	**Hungarian**
(D)	**Dutch**	**(P)**	**Polish**
(G)	**German**	**(Sp)**	**Spanish**
(H)	**Hebrew**	**(Y)**	**Yiddish**

aliyah (H) Literally, ascent; emigration to Israel.

Appell (G) Twice-daily roll call in the concentration camps when all inmates were forced to stand at attention.

Ashkenazim (H) German and Eastern European Jewry, from whom most American Jews are descended.

Auschwitz/Birkenau (G) "The symbol of all camps" (Feig, *Hitler's Death Camps*, p. 333). The Auschwitz/Birkenau complex, near Cracow, Poland, covered forty square kilometers and consisted of three camps: Auschwitz I, the base camp; Auschwitz II (Birkenau), the killing center; and Auschwitz III (Monowice/Buna), I. G. Farben's synthetic rubber plant. Auschwitz/Birkenau was the largest death camp. At least four million people died there.

ba'alat teshuvah (H) Woman who has "returned" to Orthodox Jewish observance.

bar mitzvah (H) Traditional coming of age ceremony in the Jewish community, occurring at a boy's thirteenth birthday. Reform and Conservative Judaism have instituted the bat mitzvah as an equivalent ceremony for girls.

bashert (Y) Inevitable, predestined.

Belzec (P) Death camp in Poland where 550,000 people were murdered.

Bergen–Belsen (G) Detention camp in Germany, which functioned as the official "reception and holding center."

B'nai Brith (H) Oldest and largest international Jewish service organization devoted to communal and philanthropic activities.

Buchenwald (G) One of the largest death camps in Germany, where 43,045 inmates were killed.

charoset (H) A ceremonial food served at Pesach (Passover) made of walnuts and apples. Charoset symbolizes the mortar used by Jewish slaves in Egypt to cement the bricks of the pyramids.

Chelmno (P) Death camp in Poland where 320,000 Jews were gassed.

concentration camps Generic term for detention, slave-labor, and death camps established throughout Europe by the Nazis. "At least eighteen million

---

[Jewish and gentile] Europeans passed through the [concentration-camp] system, . . . [and] at least eleven million died in it" (Feig, *Hitler's Death Camps*, p. 26).

Dachau (G) The first concentration camp, established by the Nazis in Germany in March 1933, where mainly political prisoners were interned.

davening (to daven) (Y) Praying, usually accompanied by swaying movement.

desaparecidos (Sp) People living in Latin America who have been abducted, held without due process, tortured and/or murdered by police, death squads, and paramilitary groups, and whose whereabouts and fate remain unknown.

Drancy Transit camp located outside Paris.

Einsatzgruppen (G) "Special-duty groups," "striking force" (Dawidowicz, *The War Against the Jews*, p. 114). Mobile units of the Nazi Security Police (SD) deployed during the years 1939–45, especially before the killing centers were established. The Einsatzgruppen operated principally in Poland and Russia, directly behind the occupying German troops. Along with other units of the SD, they murdered two million civilian Jews.

Eretz Yisroel (H, Y) Land of Israel, the Holy Land. Traditional focus of Jewish hopes for redemption.

Final Solution The plan to mass murder European Jewry that emerged at the Wannsee Conference held in January 1942.

First and Second Temples Located in Jerusalem, the Temple was the center of the nation of Israel's religious, political, and intellectual life. Ritual sacrifice was the dominant practice of the Temple priests. The First Temple was completed in 950 B.C.E., during King Solomon's reign, and destroyed by the armies of Nebuchadnezzar in 560 B.C.E. In 515 B.C.E. the Temple was rebuilt. Its destruction by the Romans in 70 C.E. marked the beginning of the Jewish diaspora.

galut (H) Diaspora; exile of the Jews from Eretz Yisroel, dating from destruction of the Second Temple in Jerusalem in 70 C.E.

Gestapo (Geheime Staatspolizei) (G) Secret state police in Nazi Germany that played a key role in murdering European Jewry. In April 1934 the Gestapo came under SS jurisdiction and assumed "a pseudo-military character with all the military titles and uniforms brought in by the new staff from the SD and SS" (Dawidowicz, *The War Against the Jews*, p. 80).

ghetto A medieval system revived by the Nazis that consisted of secluding an entire Jewish community inside a walled section of a city. Ghettos were usually located in the worst part of town with minimal sanitation facilities and overcrowded living conditions. Jews were prohibited from leaving under penalty of death, except with strict supervision. They were subject to constant surveillance by Nazi guards and Jewish police. Ghettos eventually became collection points for deporting Jews to the death camps. In Poland, the first ghetto was established in Lodz in 1939. Warsaw had one of the largest ghettos, established in 1940.

Haggadah (H) Collection of stories, prayers, psalms, and hymns read at the
  Passover seder, which retells the Jews' exodus from ancient Egypt.

Hanukkah (H) Festival of Dedication or the Feast of Lights, celebrated by
  lighting menorah candles on eight consecutive nights, 24 Kislev–1 Tevet.
  The Hanukkah story recounts the Maccabees' military victory over the
  Syrians in 164 B.C.E. and the miracle of their one-day supply of oil burning
  for eight days.

High Holidays Days of Awe: Rosh ha-Shanah, Jewish New Year (1–2 Tishri)
  Yom Kippur, Day of Atonement (10 Tishri); and the ten days in between
  them. This is the most solemn time during the Jewish liturgical year.

Hollandse Schouwburg (D) Jewish theater in Amsterdam used as a concentration center for Amsterdam Jewry.

Holocaust The destruction of European Jewry by the Nazi regime during World
  War II. *Holocaust* is the Greek rendering of the biblical term for a burnt
  offering dedicated to God. In English, *holocaust* means vast destruction
  by fire.

Jewish Council *See* **Judenrat**.

Joodse Raad (D) *See* **Judenrat**.

Judenrat (G) Council of Jewish Elders. Local "self-governments" imposed on
  the Jews by the Nazis that were responsible for administering the ghettos,
  carrying out anti-Jewish edicts, and, ultimately, selecting Jews for deportation.

Kanada Concentration-camp jargon for the warehouse area at Birkenau where
  all clothing and food confiscated from incoming inmates were sorted,
  repaired, and stored before being sold on the black market or shipped back
  to Germany for civilian use.

kapos (G) Camp inmates appointed by the SS to supervise *kommandos* (work
  gangs composed of other prisoners). Often, *kapos* were German criminals.
  They frequently mistreated the inmates they oversaw.

kifli (Hu) Sweet, crescent-shaped pastry filled with butter and walnuts, choco-
  late, or cheese.

knaidlach (Y) Matzoh balls made from matzoh meal and eggs, served in chicken
  soup.

kommando (G) Prisoners' work gang; also, a subcamp of a concentration camp.

korcsma (Hu) A small inn.

kosher (H, Y) Food permitted by and prepared according to Jewish dietary laws.

Kulmhof (G) *See* **Chelmno**.

landsmännin (G) Female compatriot.

Magen David (H) Star of David. Six-pointed star that is a symbol of Judaism.

maggid (H) Literally, "telling" of the Passover story.

Majdanek Labor/extermination camp near Lublin, Poland, where 360,000 Jews
  were killed.

matzoh (H, Y) Unleavened bread traditionally eaten by Jews during Pesach.
  Matzoh symbolizes the haste in which the ancient Israelites prepared their

bread during the exodus from Egypt.

Mauthausen Death camp in Upper Austria where more than 110,000 people were killed.

mazel tov (H, Y) Literally, good luck or good fortune. Colloquially used to offer congratulations.

Mengele, Dr. Josef Infamous Nazi physician and medical researcher posted at Auschwitz in May 1943. On the Auschwitz ramp where newly arriving inmates disembarked from deportation trains, Mengele selected who would live—at least for the short term—and who would die immediately. He also performed medical experiments on inmates, including Jewish and Gypsy twins, and killed inmates directly with phenol injections.

menorah (H) Candelabrum with nine branches used at Hanukkah. *See* **Hanukkah**.

mishpokheh (H, Y) (Extended) family.

muselmänner (Y) The walking dead. Concentration-camp jargon for prisoners on the verge of death who had lost the will to live. According to Marrus, the term is derived from an alleged Muslim belief in fatalism—"'people who were so deprived of affect, self-esteem, and every form of stimulation, so totally exhausted, both physically and emotionally, that they had given the environment total power over them'" (Michael R. Marrus, *The Holocaust in History*, p. 130, citing unidentified source).

nakhes (Y) Pleasure and pride, especially in one's children.

NIZ Netherlands Israelite Hospital, located in Amsterdam.

NSB (D) Nationaal Socialistische Beweging, the Dutch Nazi party.

Nuremberg Laws Two laws passed on September 15, 1935, depriving all Jews in Germany of their citizenship and their civil and political rights, and prohibiting intermarriage as well as extramarital sexual relations between Jews and Germans. The Nuremberg Laws also prohibited Jews from employing German female domestic help under the age of forty-five and from raising the Jewish flag.

onderduikers (D) Jews in Holland who went into hiding.

oneg shabbat (H) Literally, sabbath delight. Gathering on the eve or day of shabbat.

Oswiecim/Brzezinka (P) *See* **Auschwitz/Birkenau**.

passing on the Aryan side During the Nazi occupation of Europe, Jews were forbidden to live outside the ghettos on the Aryan side of cities. Yet through connections and/or money, some Jews managed to obtain false identification papers that allowed them to "pass" as Aryans. Still, even well-forged papers didn't always protect Jews from being informed on or caught by the Nazis.

Passover *See* **Pesach**.

peña (Sp) Traditional Chilean gathering for cultural events and celebrations.

persoonsbewijs (D) Identity card.

Pesach (H) Eight-day festival (15–22 Nisan) commemorating the deliverance of the Jews from slavery in Egypt. The first two evenings of Pesach are celebrated by reading the Haggadah at a ritual meal called a seder. *See* **seder** and **Haggadah**.

pogrom (Y) Spontaneous or incited riot against Jews.

Ravensbrück Largest and earliest major concentration camp for women, founded in May 1939 in Mecklenburg, Germany. In 1942 and 1943, notorious medical experiments were conducted in the camp on Polish inmates. Ravensbrück eventually included a separate men's camp and a children's camp. A killing installation for women operated there from January to April 1945.

Rosh ha-Shanah (H) First and second days of the month of Tishri that mark the Jewish new year.

schreibstube (G) Concentration-camp administration office.

schutzhaft (G) Legal term for taking Jews into "protective custody" and transporting them to concentration camps.

seder (H) Literally, "order." Ritual meal held on the first two evenings of Pesach at which symbolic foods are eaten, the story of the Exodus is retold, and songs are sung celebrating the Jews' liberation from slavery.

selection A regular action in the labor-extermination camps when inmates judged unfit for work by SS doctors were "selected" to die in the gas chambers.

shabbat (H) *See* **shabbos**.

shabbos (Y) The Jewish sabbath, lasting from sundown Friday evening until sundown Saturday evening.

Shavuot (H) Festival of the Giving of the Torah; Feast of the Weeks. Falling seven weeks after Pesach, Shavuot originally celebrated the grain harvest. It also marks the giving of the Torah at Sinai. Celebration of Shavuot in Jerusalem gave rise to the Christian holiday of Pentecost.

sho'ah (H) Holocaust; the destruction of European Jewry during World War II.

shtetl, pl. **shtetlach** (Y) Small Jewish communities in Eastern Europe, all of which had been destroyed by the end of World War II.

shul (Y) Synagogue, derived from the German word for school. The etymology of *shul* reflects Judaism's emphasis on Torah study as a central spiritual activity.

Sobibor (P) Death camp in Poland where 200,000 people were gassed.

Sonderkommando (G) Special Commando. (1) Detachments of Jewish inmates, mainly those who worked in the gas chambers and crematoria of the death camps. On 7 October 1945, the Jewish Sonderkommando in Birkenau revolted. During the uprising two crematoria were destroyed, several guards were killed, and a mass escape was attempted. (2) *Sonderkommando* also refers to the German unit that carried out the killing operation at Chelmno, and to other units responsible for obliterating the traces of mass murder by exhuming and burning corpses. (3) Inside Lodz ghetto, a Jewish Sonderkommando handled criminal offenses and functioned as part of the Jewish ghetto police (see Spector, "Sonderkomman-do," p. 1378).

SS (Schutzstaffel) (G) Literally, Defense Corps. "Elite" military organization formed in 1925 to protect Hitler, top Nazi party leaders, and party meetings. Eventually, the SS grew into the most powerful organization within the Nazi party and state. Its chief function was policing ghettos and concentration camps.

Terezin (Cz) Concentration camp near Prague, Czechoslovakia, which, for propaganda purposes, was officially labeled a ghetto (Feig, *Hitler's Death Camps*, p. 237). Terezin served as a concentration center for Protectorate Jews and privileged Jews from Germany, Austria, Holland, and Denmark. It was also a transit camp for Jews en route to death camps in the east, mainly Auschwitz. The Nazis used Terezin as a "model camp" to camouflage the Final Solution and impress visiting Red Cross commissions.

Theresienstadt (G) *See* **Terezin**.

Tisha b'Av (H) The ninth day of the month of Av, when destruction of the Temple is mourned.

Torah (H) The first five books of the Bible; the Pentateuch. Torah also refers to all Jewish law, written and oral.

trayf (H, Y) Nonkosher food.

Treblinka (P) Death camp in Poland, where 750,000 people were gassed.

tsimmes (Y) A holiday dish served at Pesach made with vegetables and fruit. Since *tsimmes* takes some trouble to prepare, the word has come to denote a fuss, an upset.

unterscharführer (G) Guard.

Vught Transit and labor camp in Holland for Jews.

Westerbork Transit camp in Holland from which the Dutch Jews were deported to death camps, mainly Auschwitz.

yellow star Cloth facsimile of a Magen David, which Jews in Nazi-occupied territories were required to wear on their outer clothing.

Yiddish The language of Eastern European Jewry.

Yiddishkeit (Y) Jewish culture of the Eastern European *shtetlach*.

Yom ha-Shoah (H) The twenty-seventh of the month of Nisan and the fifth day following the end of Pesach when the Holocaust is commemorated.

Yom Kippur (H) Day of Atonement (10 Tishri). *Yom Kippur* is the most solemn day of the Jewish liturgical calendar.

Zionism The political and ideological movement founded in the late nineteenth century by Theodor Herzl, a Viennese journalist, calling for world Jewry's return to Zion, the Land of Israel. Zionism is rooted in the biblical mission granted to Abraham and his descendants to inhabit the land which God gave them.

BIBLIOGRAPHY

Agar, Michael H. 1982. "Toward an Ethnographic Language." *American Anthropologist* 84:779–95.

American Sociological Association. 1989. "Code of Ethics." Typescript.

Antonelli, Judith S. 1988. "Holocaust Memorial Group Revamps." *Jewish Advocate*, 8 December, p. 3.

Arad, Yitzhak, Yisrael Gutman, and Abraham Margaliot, eds. 1981. *Documents on the Holocaust: Selected Sources on the Destruction of the Jews of Germany and Austria, Poland, and the Soviet Union.* Jerusalem: Yad Vashem.

Arendt, Hannah. [1963] 1977. *Eichmann in Jerusalem: A Report on the Banality of Evil.* New York: Penguin Books.

———. 1968. "Isak Dinesen: 1885–1962." Pp. 95–109 in *Men in Dark Times.* New York: Harcourt, Brace and World.

———, ed. 1969. "Introduction: Walter Benjamin: 1892–1940." Pp. 1–55 in *Illuminations*, by Walter Benjamin. Harry Zohn, trans. New York: Schocken Books.

Badiner, Allan Hunt, ed. 1990. *Dharma Gaia: A Harvest of Essays in Buddhism and Ecology.* Berkeley: Parallax Press.

Bateson, Gregory, and Mary Catherine Bateson. 1987. *Angels Fear: Towards an Epistemology of the Sacred.* New York: Macmillan.

Bateson, Mary Catherine. 1984. *With a Daughter's Eye: A Memoir of Margaret Mead and Gregory Bateson.* New York: William Morrow and Co.

Bauer, Yehuda. 1978. *The Holocaust in Historical Perspective.* Seattle: University of Washington Press.

———. 1979. "Forms of Jewish Resistance During the Holocaust." Pp. 26–40 in *The Jewish Emergence from Powerlessness.* Toronto: University of Toronto Press.

Bauman, Zygmunt. 1989. *Modernity and the Holocaust.* Ithaca, NY: Cornell University Press.

Beck, Evelyn Torton, ed. 1982. *Nice Jewish Girls: A Lesbian Anthology.* Watertown, Mass.: Persephone Press.

Behar, Ruth. 1992. *Translated Woman: Crossing the Border with Esperanza's Story.* Boston: Beacon Press, forthcoming.

Benjamin, Walter. 1969a. *Illuminations.* Hannah Arendt, ed., Harry Zohn, trans. New York: Schocken Books.

———. 1969b. "The Storyteller: Reflections on the Works of Nikolai Leskov." Pp. 83–109 in *Illuminations.* Hannah Arendt, ed., Harry Zohn, trans. New York: Schocken Books.

———. 1969c. "Unpacking My Library: A Talk about Book Collecting." Pp. 59–67 in *Illuminations.* Hannah Arendt, ed., Harry Zohn, trans. New York: Schocken Books.

———. 1982. *Das Passagen-Werk.* Rolf Tiedemann, ed. Vol. 5 of *Gesammelte Schriften,* Rolf Tiedemann and Hermann Schweppenhauser, with the collaboration of Theodor W. Adorno and Gershom Scholem, eds. Frankfurt am Main: Suhrkamp Verlag, 1972–.

Bennett, James. 1982. "Annotated Bibliography: Holocaust Resistance." *Shmate: A Journal of Progressive Jewish Thought* 1, no. 4, 25–28.

Bernstein, Burton. 1982. "Personal History (The Bernstein Family)." *New Yorker,* pt. 1, 22 March, pp. 53–127, and pt. 2, 29 March, pp. 58–121.

Bethel, Lorraine, and Barbara Smith, eds. 1979. *Conditions* 5, "The Black Women's Issue."

Blumer, Herbert. 1967. *Symbolic Interactionism: Perspective and Method.* Englewood Cliffs, N.J.: Prentice-Hall.

Brecht, Bertolt. 1967. "Wo ich gelernt habe" (Where I have learned). Pp. 502–7, in Suhrkamp Verlag Corp. with Elisabeth Haumptmann, eds., *Gesammelte Werke* 19 (edition Suhrkamp). Frankfurt am Main: Suhrkamp Verlag.

Brownstein, Ronald. 1980. "The *New York Times* on Nazism (1933–39)," *Midstream,* April, pp. 14–19.

Bruner, Edward M., and Stuart Plattner, eds. 1983. *Text, Play, and Story: The Construction and Reconstruction of Self and Society.* Washington, D.C.: American Ethnological Society.

Buck-Morss, Susan. 1989. *The Dialectics of Seeing: Walter Benjamin and the Arcades Project.* Cambridge, Mass.: MIT Press.

Buszko, Jozef. 1990. "Auschwitz." Pp. 107–19 in *Encyclopedia of the Holocaust,* Israel Gutman, ed. New York: Macmillan.

Caplan, Arthur. 1988. "'Legacy of the Holocaust': A 1989 Center Conference." *Center for Biomedical Ethics Newsletter,* July/August, p. 1.

Cesara, Manda. 1982. *Reflections of a Woman Anthropologist: No Hiding Place.* New York: Academic Press.

Chalk, Frank, and Kurt Jonassohn. 1990. *The History and Sociology of Genocide: Analyses and Case Studies.* New Haven: Yale University Press.

Charmaz, Kathy. 1983. "The Grounded Theory Method: An Explication and Interpretation." Pp. 109–26 in Robert M. Emerson, ed., *Contemporary Field Research: A Collection of Readings.* Boston: Little, Brown and Co.

Clifford, James. 1986. "Introduction: Partial Truths." Pp. 1–26 in *Writing Culture: The Poetics and Politics of Ethnography.* James Clifford and George E. Marcus, eds. Berkeley: University of California Press.

———. 1988. "On Ethnographic Authority." Pp. 21–54 in *The Predicament of Culture: Twentieth-Century Ethnography, Literature, and Art*. Cambridge, Mass.: Harvard University Press.

Clifford, James, and George E. Marcus, eds. 1986. *Writing Culture: The Poetics and Politics of Ethnography*. Berkeley: University of California Press.

Coffelt, Beth. 1983. "'The Holocaust' and the Art of War." *San Francisco Sunday Examiner and Chronicle, California Living Magazine*, 23 October, pp. 12–15.

Colbert (a.k.a. Sarahgold), Alison. 1980. "The 'All Women's Interests Are the Same' Line: A Trap for Non-Privileged Women?" Pp. 49–60 in *Top Ranking: A Collection of Articles on Racism and Classism in the Lesbian Community*. Joan Gibbs and Sara Bennett, comps. Brooklyn, N.Y.: February 3rd Press.

Collier, Peter, and David Horowitz. 1981. "Requiem for a Radical." *New West*, March, pp. 64–71 passim, 133–47 passim.

Combahee River Collective. 1979. "A Black Feminist Statement." Pp. 362–72 in Zillah R. Eisenstein, ed., *Capitalist Patriarchy and the Case for Socialist Feminism*. New York: Monthly Review Press.

"Commentary." 1981. *Contemporary Sociology* 10, March, pp. 167–71.

Crapanzano, Vincent. 1977. "The Life History in Anthropological Field Work." *Anthropology and Humanism Quarterly* 2:3–7.

———. 1980. *Tuhami: Portrait of a Moroccan*. Chicago: University of Chicago Press.

Dawidowicz, Lucy S. 1975. *The War Against the Jews: 1933–1945*. New York: Holt, Rinehart and Winston.

DeVault, Marjorie L. 1990. "What Counts as Feminist Ethnography?" Paper presented at "Exploring New Frontiers: Qualitative Research Conference." York University, Toronto, 13–16 May.

Dorff, Elliot, and Arthur Rosett. 1988. *A Living Tree: The Roots and Growth of Jewish Law*. Albany, N.Y.: State University of New York Press.

Dover, Debbie. 1989. "Women Plan a Convoy to U.S. and Central America." *Central America Reporter*, February, p. 2.

Durkheim, Emile. [1951] 1961. *The Elementary Forms of the Religious Life*. J. W. Swain, trans. New York: Collier Books.

Elnasdätter, Rūnda. 1976. "To Whom It May Concern." *Thornside* 1:1, pp. 5–7.

Epstein, Helen. 1979. *Children of the Holocaust*. New York: Bantam Books.

Feig, Konnilyn G. 1981. *Hitler's Death Camps: The Sanity of Madness*. New York: Holmes and Meier.

Fein, Helen. 1979. *Accounting for Genocide: National Responses and Jewish Victimization during the Holocaust*. New York: Free Press.

———. 1980. "The Holocaust and Auschwitz: Revising Stereotypes of Their Victims." Review of *Values and Violence in Auschwitz*. *Contemporary Sociology* 9 (July 1980): 495–98.

Fishman, William J. 1975. *East End Jewish Radicals, 1875–1914*. London: Duckworth in association with the Acton Society Trust.

Fleck, Ludwick. [1935] 1979. *Genesis and Development of a Scientific Fact*. Chicago: University of Chicago Press.

Frank, Gelya. 1985a. "Barbara, May She Rest in Peace, But Her Spirit Be with Us Always." Paper presented at the American Anthropological Association Annual Meeting, Washington, D.C., 4–8 December.

———. 1985b. "'Becoming the Other': Empathy and Biographical Interpretation." *Biography* 8:189–210.

Friedrich, Otto. 1981. "The Kingdom of Auschwitz." *Atlantic*, September, pp. 30–60.

Geertz, Clifford. 1983. "'From the Native's Point of View': On the Nature of Anthropological Understanding." Pp. 55–70 in Clifford Geertz, *Local Knowledge: Further Essays in Interpretive Anthropology*. New York: Basic Books.

———. 1988. *Works and Lives: The Anthropologist as Author*. Stanford, Calif.: Stanford University Press.

Glaser, Barney G. 1989. *Theoretical Sensitivity: Advances in the Methodology of Grounded Theory*. Mill Valley, Calif.: Sociology Press.

Glaser, Barney G., and Anselm L. Strauss. 1965. *Awareness of Dying*. Chicago: Aldine.

———. 1967. *The Discovery of Grounded Theory: Strategies for Qualitative Research*. Chicago: Aldine.

Gluck, Peggy Isaak. 1984a. "Controversy Shadows Dedication." *Northern California Jewish Bulletin*, 2 November, pp. 1, 16–17.

———. 1984b. "So We'll Never Forget." *Northern California Jewish Bulletin*, 9 November, p. 14.

Gouldner, Alvin W. 1970. *The Coming Crisis of Western Sociology*. New York: Basic Books.

"The Great Debate: Covering and Uncovering the Left." *Mediafile*, May 1981, pp. 5, 12.

Greer, Kirsten. 1977. "Journal Excerpt." Typescript.

Griffin, Susan. 1978. *Woman and Nature: The Roaring Inside Her*. New York: Harper and Row.

Gutman, Israel. 1990. "Roza Robota." Pp. 1286–87 in *Encyclopedia of the Holocaust*, Israel Gutman, ed. New York: Macmillan.

Haraway, Donna. 1988. "Situated Knowledges: The Science Question in Feminism and the Privilege of Partial Perspective." *Feminist Studies* 14:575–99.

Heilman, Samuel. 1984. *The Gate Behind the Wall: A Pilgrimage to Jerusalem*. New York: Penguin.

Herrigel, Eugen. 1953. *Zen in the Art of Archery*. New York: Pantheon.

Hilberg, Raul. 1985. *The Destruction of the European Jews*, def. rev. ed. 3 vols. New York: Holmes and Meier.

Horowitz, Irving Louis. 1980. "Bodies and Souls." Review of *Accounting for Genocide. Contemporary Sociology* 9 (July): 489–92.

Hughes, Everett C. 1964. "Good People and Dirty Work." Pp. 23–36 in Howard S. Becker, ed., *The Other Side*. New York: Free Press.

Inscriptions, nos. 3/4 (1988).

Jay, Martin. 1973. *The Dialectical Imagination: A History of the Frankfurt School and the Institute of Social Research, 1923–1950*. Boston: Little, Brown and Co.

Katz, Esther, and Joan Miriam Ringelheim, eds. 1983. *Women Surviving the Holocaust: Proceedings of the Conference*. New York: Institute for Research in History.

Kondo, Dorinne K. 1986. "Dissolution and Reconstruction of Self: Implications for Anthropological Epistemology." *Cultural Anthropology* 1 (February): 74–88.

———. 1990. *Crafting Selves: Power, Gender, and Discourses of Identity in a Japanese Workplace*. Chicago: University of Chicago Press.

Krall, Hanna. 1986. *Shielding the Flame: An Intimate Conversation with Dr. Marek Edelman, The Last Surviving Leader of the Warsaw Ghetto Uprising*. Joanna Stasinska and Lawrence Weschler, trans. New York: Henry Holt and Co., and Philadelphia: Jewish Publication Society.

Krieger, Susan. 1991. *Social Science and the Self: Personal Essays on an Art Form*. New Brunswick: Rutgers University Press.

Kwiet, Konrad. 1979. "Problems of Jewish Resistance Historiography." *Leo Baeck Institute Yearbook* 24:37–57.

Laqueur, Walter. 1979. *The First News of the Holocaust*. New York: Leo Baeck Institute.

Larrabee, John. 1987. "How to Remember: Controversy erupts over GI, Holocaust Memorial." *Tab*, 22 December, p. 32.

Laska, Vera. 1983. *Women in the Resistance and in the Holocaust: The Voices of Eyewitnesses*. Westport, Conn.: Greenwood Press.

———. 1985. *Nazism, Resistance, and the Holocaust in World War II: A Bibliography*. Metuchen, N.J.: Scarecrow Press.

"Letters to the editor in reply to 'Requiem for a Radical.'" *Mediafile*, July–August 1981, pp. 4–5.

Levine, Philip. 1976. *The Names of the Lost*. New York: Atheneum.

Lifton, Robert Jay. 1986. *The Nazi Doctors: Medical Killing and the Psychology of Genocide*. New York: Basic Books.

Linden, R. Ruth. 1983. "Tribute to Marion Hozenpud Berry: 18 June 1886–24 November 1983." Typescript.

———. 1988. "Speaking Gently of Genocide." *Awakening: An Interhelp Quarterly* 1, no. 1 (Spring): 11–12.

Linden, Robin Ruth, Darlene Pagano, Diana E. H. Russell, and Susan Leigh Star, eds. 1982. *Against Sadomasochism: A Radical Feminist Analysis*. East Palo Alto, Calif.: Frog in the Well.

Linden, Robin Ruth, and Susan Leigh Star. 1980. "Survived by Her Silence: For the Memory of Fay Abrahams Stender, 1932–1980." Typescript.

Lorde, Audre. 1984. *Sister Outsider*. Trumansburg, N.Y.: Crossing Press.

Lorde, Audre, with Susan Leigh Star. 1982. "Interview with Audre Lorde." Pp. 66–71 in Robin Ruth Linden et al., eds., *Against Sadomasochism: A Radical Feminist Analysis*. East Palo Alto, Calif.: Frog in the Well.

Lubetkin, Zivia. 1981. *In the Days of Destruction and Revolt*. Hakibbutz Hameuchad and Am Oved.

Lyons, Gracie. 1976. *Constructive Criticism: A Handbook*. Berkeley, Calif.: Issues in Radical Therapy Press.

Mannheim, Karl. 1936. *Ideology and Utopia: An Introduction to the Sociology of Knowledge*. Louis Wirth and Edward Shils, trans. New York: Harcourt, Brace and World.

Marcus, George E. 1980. "Rhetoric and the Ethnographic Genre in Anthropological Research." *Current Anthropology* 21 (August): 507–10.

Marcus, George E., and Michael M. J. Fischer. 1986. *Anthropology as Cultural Critique: An Experimental Moment in the Human Sciences*. Chicago: University of Chicago Press.

Marrus, Michael R. 1987a. "The History of the Holocaust: A Survey of Recent Literature." *Journal of Modern History* 59:114–60.

———. 1987b. *The Holocaust in History*. New York: New American Library.

Mascia-Lees, Frances E., Patricia Sharpe, and Colleen Ballerino Cohen. 1989. "The Postmodernist Turn in Anthropology: Cautions from a Feminist Perspective." *Signs* 15:7–33.

Mazur, Gail. 1986. *Pose of Happiness*. Boston: David Godine.

Mead, George Herbert. 1934. *Mind, Self, and Society from the Standpoint of a Social Behaviorist*. Vol. 1. Chicago: University of Chicago Press.

"Memorials 'Distort' Holocaust, Says Scholar." *Houston Post*, 30 October 1988, E4.

Meyerding, Jane, ed. 1984. *We Are All Part of One Another: A Barbara Deming Reader*. Philadelphia: New Society Publishers.

Mills, C. Wright. 1959. *The Sociological Imagination*. New York: Oxford University Press.

Mitscherlich, Alexander, and Fred Mielke. 1949. *Doctors of Infamy: The Story of the Nazi Medical Crimes*. New York: Henry Schuman.

Moore, Sally F., and Barbara G. Myerhoff. 1977. "Introduction: Secular Ritual: Forms and Meanings." Pp. 3–24 in Sally F. Moore and Barbara G. Myerhoff, eds., *Secular Ritual*. Amsterdam: Van Gorcum, Assen.

Moraga, Cherríe, and Gloria Anzaldúa, eds. 1981. *This Bridge Called My Back: Writings by Radical Women of Color*. New York: Kitchen Table Press.

Myerhoff, Barbara. 1978. *Number Our Days*. New York: E. P. Dutton.

———. 1980. "Re-membered Lives." *Parabola* 5:74–77.

———. 1986. "'Life Not Death in Venice': Its Second Life." Pp. 261–86 in Victor W. Turner and Edward M. Bruner, eds., *The Anthropology of Experience*. Urbana: University of Illinois Press.

———. 1988. "Surviving Stories: Reflections on *Number Our Days*." Pp. 265–94 in Jack Kugelmass, ed., *Between Two Worlds: Ethnographic Essays on American Jewry*. Ithaca, N.Y.: Cornell University Press.

Myerhoff, Barbara, and Deena Metzger. 1980. "The Journal as Activity and Genre: Or Listening to the Silent Laughter of Mozart." *Semiotica* 30:97–114.

Myerhoff, Barbara G., and Virginia Tufte. 1975. "Life History as Integration: An Essay on an Experiential Model." *The Gerontologist* 15 December: 541–43.

Oliver, H. 1983. *The International Anarchist Movement in Late Victorian London.* New York: St. Martin's Press.

Olsen, Tillie. [1971] 1979. "One Out of Twelve: Writers Who Are Women in Our Century." Pp. 22–46 in *Silences.* New York: Delta/Seymour Lawrence.

Pawelczynska, Anna. 1979. *Values and Violence in Auschwitz: A Sociological Analysis.* Trans. Catherine S. Leach. Berkeley: University of California Press. Translated from the Polish edition, *Wartosci A Przemoc. Zarys socjologicznej problematyki Oswiecimia.* Warsaw: Panstwowe Wydawnictwo Naukowe, 1973.

Piercy, Marge. 1988. "Black Mountain." *Tikkun* 3.

Pool, Robert. 1991. "Postmodern Ethnography?" *Critique of Anthropology* 11:309–31.

Popular Memory Group. 1982. "Popular Memory: Theory, Politics, Method." Pp. 205–52 in Richard Johnson et al., eds., *Making Histories: Studies in History-Writing and Politics.* Minneapolis: University of Minnesota Press.

Prell, Riv-Ellen. 1989. "The Double Frame of Life History in the Work of Barbara Myerhoff." Pp. 241–58 in Personal Narratives Group (ed.), *Interpreting Women's Lives: Feminist Theory and Personal Narratives.* Bloomington: Indiana University Press.

Presser, Jacob. 1968. *Ashes in the Wind: The Destruction of Dutch Jewry.* London: Souvenir Press.

Proctor, Robert. 1988. *Racial Hygiene: Medicine under the Nazis.* Cambridge, Mass.: Harvard University Press.

Rabinow, Paul. 1977. *Reflections on Fieldwork in Morocco.* Berkeley: University of California Press.

———. 1986. "Representations are Social Facts: Modernity and Post-Modernity in Anthropology." Pp. 234–61 in James Clifford and George E. Marcus, eds., *Writing Culture: The Poetics and Politics of Ethnography.* Berkeley: University of California Press.

Reinharz, Shulamit. 1979. *On Becoming a Social Scientist: From Survey Research and Participant Observation to Experiential Analysis.* San Francisco: Jossey-Bass.

Rich, Adrienne. 1983. *Sources.* Woodside, Calif.: Heyeck Press.

Richardson, Laurel. 1991. "Postmodern Social Theory: Representational Practices." *Sociological Theory* 9:173–79.

Ricoeur, Paul. 1973. "The Model of the Text: Meaningful Action Considered as a Text." *New Literary History* 5:91–117.

Ringelheim, Joan Miriam. 1985. "Viewpoint: Women and the Holocaust: A Reconsideration of Research." *Signs* 10:741–61.

Roiphe, Anne. 1981. *Generation Without Memory: A Jewish Journey in Christian America.* Boston: Beacon Press.

Rosaldo, Renato. 1984. "Grief and a Headhunter's Rage: On the Cultural Force of Emotions." Pp. 178–95 in Edward M. Bruner and Stuart Plattner, eds., *Text, Play, and Story: The Construction and Reconstruction of Self and Society.* Washington, D.C.: American Ethnological Society. Reprinted in Renato Rosaldo, *Culture and Truth: The Remaking of Social Analysis,* pp. 1–21. Boston: Beacon Press, 1989.

Rose, Leesha. 1978. *The Tulips Are Red*. New York: A. S. Barnes.

———. 1981. Life history conducted with Lani Silver at the World Gathering of Jewish Holocaust Survivors, Jerusalem, Israel. June. Files of the Holocaust Oral History Project.

Rubenstein, Richard. 1975. *The Cunning of History*. New York: Harper.

Ruby, Jay. 1980. "Exposing Yourself: Reflexivity, Anthropology, and Film." *Semiotica* 30:153–79.

Russell, Diana E. H. 1979. "Fay Stender and the Politics of Murder." *Chrysalis* 9 (Fall): 11–13.

Sabina, Jill. 1976. "The Myth of Student as Consumer: A Manifesto for Student Liberation." *Thornside* 1:1, pp. 2–5.

Scholem, Gershom. 1976. "Walter Benjamin." Pp. 172–97 in Gershom Scholem, *On Jews and Judaism in Crisis: Selected Essays*. Werner J. Dannhauser, ed. New York: Schocken Books.

Segal, Lore. 1988. "Memory: The Problems of Imagining the Past." Pp. 58–65 in Berel Lang, ed., *Writing and the Holocaust*. New York: Holmes and Meier.

Silver, Lani, and R. Ruth Linden. 1983. "Santa Rita Jail Diary." Typescript.

Smith, Reginald. 1983. "Panel Accepts Holocaust Sculpture: Supervisors to Vote Monday." *San Francisco Chronicle*, 15 December, p. 3.

Spector, Shmuel. 1990. "Aktion 1005." Pp. 11–14 in *Encyclopedia of the Holocaust*, Israel Gutman, ed. New York: Macmillan.

Stacey, Judith. 1988. "Can There Be a Feminist Ethnography?" *Women's Studies International Forum* 11:21–27.

———. 1990. *Brave New Families: Stories of Domestic Upheaval in Late Twentieth Century America*. New York: Basic Books.

Stanley, Julia Penelope, Mary Daly, Audre Lorde, Judith McDaniel, and Adrienne Rich. 1978. "The Transformation of Silence into Language and Action." *Sinister Wisdom* 6:4–26.

Starhawk. 1982. *Dreaming the Dark: Magic, Sex and Politics*. Boston: Beacon Press.

Stein, Gertrude. [1933] 1960. *The Autobiography of Alice B. Toklas*. New York: Vintage Books.

"Steve Ross Sparks Plans for Hub Holocaust Memorial." *Jewish Advocate*, 2 July 1987.

Stewart, Kathleen. 1988. "Nostalgia — A Polemic." *Cultural Anthropology* 3 (August) 227–41.

Strauss, Anselm L. 1969. *Mirrors and Masks: The Search for Identity*. Mill Valley, Calif.: Sociology Press.

———. 1987. *Qualitative Analysis for Social Scientists*. New York: Cambridge University Press.

"Student Union?" *Student Union News* 1, no. 1 (April 1976): 4.

Thich Nhat Hanh. 1987. *Interbeing: Commentaries on the Tiep Hien Precepts*. Berkeley: Parallax Press.

Thornside 1, no. 1 (30 January 1976).

Todorov, Tzvetan. 1988. "On Heroic Narrative." Typescript. Ms files of the author.

Traweek, Sharon. 1988. *Beamtimes and Lifetimes: The World of High Energy Physicists.* Cambridge, Mass.: Harvard University Press.

Trawick, Margaret. 1990. *Notes on Love in a Tamil Family.* Berkeley: University of California Press.

Trinh T. Minh-ha. 1989. *Women, Native, Other: Writing Postcoloniality and Feminism.* Bloomington: Indiana University Press.

Trunk, Isaiah. 1972. *Judenrat.* Briarcliff Manor, N.Y.: Stein and Day/Scarborough House.

Turner, Victor. 1977. "Variations on a Theme of Liminality." Pp. 36–52 in Sally F. Moore and Barbara G. Myerhoff, eds., *Secular Ritual.* Amsterdam: Van Gorcum, Assen.

———. 1978. "Foreword." Pp. ix–xiii in Barbara Myerhoff, *Number Our Days.* New York: E. P. Dutton.

Turner, Victor W., and Edward M. Bruner, eds. 1986. *The Anthropology of Experience.* Urbana: University of Illinois Press.

Tyler, Stephen A. 1986. "Post-Modern Ethnography: From Document of the Occult to Occult Document." Pp. 122–40 in James Clifford and George E. Marcus, eds., *Writing Culture: The Poetics and Politics of Ethnography.* Berkeley: University of California Press.

Tyrnauer, Gabrielle. 1982. "'Mastering the Past': Germans and Gypsies." Pp. 178–92 in Jack Nussan Porter, ed., *Genocide and Human Rights: A Global Anthology.* Washington, D.C.: University Press of America.

———. 1989. *Gypsies and the Holocaust: A Bibliography and Introductory Essay.* Montreal: Interuniversity Centre for European Studies and Montreal Institute for Genocide Studies.

———. 1990. "'Mastering the Past': Germans and Gypsies." Pp. 366–77 in Frank Chalk and Kurt Jonassohn, *The History and Sociology of Genocide.* New Haven: Yale University Press.

Van Maanen, John. 1988. *Tales of the Field: On Writing Ethnography.* Chicago: University of Chicago Press.

Vishniac, Roman. 1983. *A Vanished World.* New York: Farrar, Straus, and Giroux.

Wasserstein, Bernard. 1979. *Britain and the Jews of Europe.* New York: Oxford University Press.

White, Hayden. 1973. *Metahistory: The Historical Imagination in Nineteenth-Century Europe.* Baltimore: Johns Hopkins University Press.

Williams, Gareth. 1984. "The Genesis of Chronic Illness: Narrative Re-construction." *Sociology of Health and Illness* 6:175–200.

Wittig, Monique. [1971] 1985. *Les Guérillères.* David Le Vay, trans. Boston: Beacon Press.

Wyman, David S. 1984. *The Abandonment of the Jews: America and the Holocaust 1941–1945.* New York: Pantheon Books.

Young, James E. 1988. *Writing and Rewriting the Holocaust: Narrative and the Consequences of Interpretation.* Bloomington: Indiana University Press.

———. 1989. "The Biography of a Memorial Icon: Nathan Rapoport's Warsaw

Ghetto Monument." *Representations* 26 (Spring):69–106.

Zaris, Ruth. 1990. "Exchange: Jews and Germans." Pp. 457–59 in Israel Gutman, ed., *Encyclopedia of the Holocaust*. New York: Macmillan.

Zola, Irving Kenneth. 1979. "When Getting into the Field Means Getting into Oneself." *New England Sociologist* 1:21–30.

———. 1982. *Missing Pieces: A Chronicle of Living with a Disability*. Philadelphia: Temple University Press.

INDEX

9-20-94